The
CHARLESTON, SAVANNAH & COASTAL ISLANDS
Book

A Complete Guide

Wade Spees

THE CHARLESTON, SAVANNAH & COASTAL ISLANDS BOOK

A Complete Guide

CECILY McMILLAN

Berkshire House Publishers
Stockbridge, Massachusetts

On the cover and frontispiece: Photographs by Wade Spees. *Frontispiece:* The Lowcountry's historic urban districts are as much lived in as they are admired. *Front cover background:* Azaleas at Rice Mill Pond, Middleton Place. *Front cover insets:* Lowcountry home and flowers. Les Ballets de Monte Carlo, Spoleto Festival U.S.A. opening. Tidal creek at sunset. Hands of a sea grass basket weaver. *Back cover insets:* Hobiecat sailboats at a weekend regatta. Sunday brunch at the Palmetto Cafe in the Omni Hotel, Charleston. Carriage ride on the East Battery.

The Charleston, Savannah & Coastal Islands Book: A Complete Guide
© 1993 by Berkshire House Publishers
Photographs © 1993 by credited photographers

Library of Congress Cataloging-in-Publication Data

McMillan, Cecily, 1956-
    The Charleston, Savannah & Coastal Islands book : a complete guide / Cecily McMillan
        p.   cm. — (Great destinations series, ISSN 1056-7968)
    Includes bibliographical references (p.) and index.
    ISBN 0-936399-39-2 (pbk.) : $14.95
        1. Charleston (S.C.)—Guidebooks. 2. Savannah (Ga.)—Guidebooks. 3. Sea islands—Guidebooks. 4. Charleston Region (S.C.)—Guidebooks. 5. Savannah Region (Ga.)—Guidebooks.
I. Title. II. Title: Charleston, Savannah & Coastal Islands book. III. Series.
F279.C43M38 1993
917.57'9—dc20   93-3499
                                                                    CIP

ISBN: 0-936399-39-2
ISSN: 1056-7968 (series)

Editor: Philip Rich. Managing Editor: Sarah Novak. Original design for Great Destinations™ series: Janice Lindstrom. Original design for Great Destinations™cover: Jane McWhorter. Production services by Ripinsky & Company, Connecticut.

Berkshire House books are available at substantial discounts for bulk purchases by corporations and other organizations for promotions and premiums. Special personalized editions can also be produced in large quantities. For more information, contact:

Berkshire House Publishers
Box 297, Stockbridge MA 01262
800-321-8526

Manufactured in the United States of America
First printing 1993
10 9 8 7 6 5 4 3 2 1

No complimentary meals or lodgings were accepted by the author and reviewers in gathering information for this work.

The <u>GREAT DESTINATIONS</u> Series

The Great Destinations™ series features regions in the United States rich in natural beauty and culture. Each Great Destinations™ guidebook reviews an extensive selection of lodgings, restaurants, cultural events, historic sites, shops, and recreational opportunities, and outlines the region's natural and social history. Written by resident authors, the guides are a resource for visitor and resident alike. Maps, photographs, directions to and around the region, lists of helpful phone numbers and addresses, and indexes.

To the memory of George McMillan, who first brought me to the Lowcountry and turned my eyes to its subtleties, and to our son, Tom, with whom I continue to love it.

Contents

CHAPTER ONE
"No Fayrer or Fytter Place"
HISTORY
1

CHAPTER TWO
Getting Here, Getting Around
TRANSPORTATION
28

CHAPTER THREE
From the City to the Seashore
LODGING
51

CHAPTER FOUR
A Sense of Place
CULTURE
77

CHAPTER FIVE
Grits, Game, and Gumbo
RESTAURANTS & FOOD PURVEYORS
122

CHAPTER SIX
Having Fun On Land And Sea
RECREATION
155

CHAPTER SEVEN
The Old World and The New World
SHOPPING
185

CHAPTER EIGHT
Courts, Courses, Sails, and Sand
HILTON HEAD
211

CHAPTER NINE
Practical Matters
INFORMATION
252

Acknowledgments

A project as large as this one, which gathers together for readers both a sense of Lowcountry history and all the details that make for a successful visit, necessarily requires the efforts of friends and assistants. Fortunately, I've had both — luckier still, often in the same person. Though for all of us, this book is the reward, the kindness, patience and good-temper of the many who saw that it came to pass cannot go unappreciated.

In Charleston, Langhorne Howard put me up, ate with me, compared notes about a city she loves, and shared her insights, as she has for many years. The same may be said for Wade Spees, whose photographs for this book, like those that have graced other articles of mine, portray the Lowcountry as a place of serene beauty and rich humanity.

In Beaufort and on St. Helena Island, my home, help of all sorts was never far from hand. I could not have adequately covered the options for lodging and eating in Savannah, nor completed the Information chapter, without Dale Friedman, whose energy and organization saw that the job was done well. Susan Graber took time from her painting to bird-dog information. These and other friends like Gracie Reddicks, Connie and George Trask, Cheryl and Roger Steele, Toni and Jonathan King, Dorothy and Grant Dugdale, Mary Mack, and Lucille McTeer always extended themselves to my son Tom and me.

Beth Scott lent her skills in many ways: in restaurant reviewing, in researching the Transportation and Information sections, in suggestions for coverage, in encouraging me. As principal fact-checker, she was my backstop. Steve Wise, author, museum curator, and military historian, kindly critiqued my History chapter.

Vicki Mallon and especially Gwen Czura deserve special credit for the chapter on Hilton Head Island. If anybody knows that island — every golf course, every tennis program, every plantation resort — they do. Their research and writing are the backbone and ribs of the section.

Cherie Had, at the South Carolina Department of Parks, Recreation and Tourism, and Jenny Stacy, at the Savannah Area Convention and Visitors Bureau, went far beyond their job descriptions in getting information to me, as they have in the past. The staffs of the Chambers of Commerce in Beaufort, Hilton Head Island, and Charleston were thorough and prompt in answering my questions, as was Jim Wescott at the Lowcountry Tourism Commission. Special thanks to the Charleston Museum for the use of archival photos.

Sarah Novak, command central at Berkshire House, and Philip Rich, my editor, displayed commendable and consistent good humor and intelligence, even as they were operating under tight deadlines; Leslie Rich and Jean Provenzano of Editorial Alternatives provided helpful suggestions, editing, and proofreading. The level of commitment of these individuals to the project would satisfy any writer's expectations; their efforts made this a better, wiser, and clearer book.

In the end, of course, it is always the people closest to your daily life who must share your hopes and shore you up. Thanks to my family, especially Mav and Nick, to Tom, to Ann Neczypor, Anne Bushnell, Theresa Kitaeff, Liz Goodfellow Zagoroff, Joanne Cleary, and Liz Morgan for doing so, and also to Priscilla Johnson McMillan who has, in addition, constantly nurtured my Lowcountry life. To Jamie Richardson, I reserve special thanks for your generosity of spirit.

Introduction

There are some places about which we have such strong impressions that when we finally go there they seem familiar, as if we had known them forever. For many people, the Lowcountry is such a place. It seems to have lodged itself so securely in so many imaginations that I often find, when I am asked about it, that what I have to say matters less than the opportunity I may be giving someone to fine-tune the picture they already have.

Where these clustered impressions come from, whether learned in a history lesson on the Civil War, gathered from a friend, understood in a novel, or viewed on a movie screen, seems less important than the fact that they feel fully conceived. This isn't surprising, for in a sense the Lowcountry has earned our permanent attention. It is a compelling world. Like other places that have witnessed tremendous historic upheavals and whose residents have had to adjust to changed circumstances, it evokes a natural sympathy in us for its stories.

I first stepped foot in the Lowcountry late in the summer of 1979, and ever since I have been listening in on its history. I return again and again to places where I feel the presence of the past and its rituals: to the shores of St. Helena Sound, where I catch crabs on a string or dig for oysters much as Native Americans might have done; to Drayton Hall, where beds of lilies bloom as they did in Jefferson's Monticello garden; to Penn Center, where descendants of slaves honor their heritage and the strength of their forebears in song; to the squares of Savannah, laid out more than 250 years ago and still possessing a power of geometry that untangles nature and orders the pace of urban life.

The region's physical beauty is just as evocative. The landscape is soft, uninterrupted by hills on land, carpeted with marsh grass and flowing waters at its edges. The air itself seems to press down, weighted by all the humidity, wrapping the Lowcountry like a package. There are distinctive seasons here which bring their own changes in color and light, in bird migrations and blossoms. Every day the shoreline is redefined by the tides.

This book is intended to both introduce you to some of the long-standing pleasures and pastimes found in the Lowcountry and point you in directions where you might discover ones of your own. In individual chapter openings, and in the History chapter, it lays out a broad context into which you may place yourself, as a traveler looking to plan a day or as a reader adjusting the imaginary pictures you arrived with to those you observed first hand.

Sometimes, your efforts may be studious — admiring architecture, exploring sites of historic and cultural significance. At other times, you will be content to satisfy your senses: to feel the beach between your toes, smell the salt marsh, watch a pelican dive, taste fresh shrimp. Don't neglect to listen for old stories, either.

It may turn out that, having come to the Lowcountry for a vacation, you end up joining the ranks of those who return for good. The glossy residential resorts on the developed islands like Kiawah, Seabrook, and Hilton Head have drawn national attention to the area; Beaufort has appeared on so many "Best Small Town" lists and attracted so many new visitors that it is possible, as it was not even five years ago, to walk down its main street and see only unfamiliar faces. The Spoleto Festival has put Charleston on an international map. The yachting events scheduled for the 1996 Summer Olympics should do the same for Savannah.

Yet the inexorable need in many of us for community, for a sense of continuity that comes from bringing the past forward, keeps the Lowcountry alive, keeps it from resting solely on the life of its past for vitality. New restaurants, bookstores, jazz and blues clubs, clothing shops, galleries, and B&Bs are embedding themselves in the old Lowcountry places, in its old buildings, enlarging the remnant world as spats fasten on oyster banks and make them grow.

The success that has come to the Lowcountry as a tourist destination has not forced its hand. Not everything is obvious. The ever-willing, eager-to-please personality of the New South it could take on has been held in check by its conservative, deeply ingrained traits of pride and tradition. Achieving such a balance is perhaps the most significant sign that the Lowcountry has come of age.

Cecily McMillan
St. Helena Island, South Carolina

THE WAY THIS BOOK WORKS

This book is divided into nine chapters. Each one serves a purpose and stands alone. But, like a shelf of individual volumes, it encourages browsing: you may want to thumb through the opening sections of individual chapters, for example, to get a historic overview of the subject and why it is what it is in the Lowcountry. Or you may want to start with the History chapter and then pick and choose among the others as your visit unfolds and your needs become apparent.

If you're interested in finding a place to eat or sleep — and during the high season in spring you're encouraged to consider advance planning — look over the restaurant and lodging charts in the *Index* (organized by area and price); then turn to the pages listed in the general index and read the specific entries for the places that most interest you.

Entries within most of the chapters are arranged alphabetically under the following north-to-south geographical headings: "Charleston" or "Charleston

Area," "Beaufort" or "Beaufort Area," and "Savannah" or "Savannah Area." Hilton Head Island has its own chapter. Sometimes special attractions are noted in smaller places like Edisto Island and Bluffton, places in orbits of their own.

Some entries, most notably those in the Lodging and Restaurant chapters, include specific information (telephone, address, hours, etc.) organized for easy reference in blocks in the left-hand column. All such information has been checked for accuracy as close to the time of publication as possible, but details change, so it's best to call ahead.

PRICES

Prices change, too, and for that reason we've avoided listing specific prices in favor of noting their range. Lodging price codes are based on a per-room rate, double-occupancy in the high season months. Low season rates, which may apply in the summer (except at beach resorts) and in December and January, are usually about 20 percent less. In the high season, many places, small and large, require a minimum two-night stay and may also have specific rules regarding adequate notice and refunds in the event of cancellation. Check ahead.

You might also confirm information that we've provided about policies in effect concerning such things as handicapped access, off-street parking, and rules about smoking.

Restaurant prices indicate the cost of a meal including appetizer, entree, and dessert, but not bar beverages, tax or tip. *Prix-fixe* menus are noted. Here again, the season of your visit may bring on special conditions: when there are crowds, most restaurants extend their hours of operation, serving meals both earlier and later. In the winter, they may shut down for a day or two.

Price Codes

	Lodging	*Dining*
Inexpensive	Up to $50	Up to $10
Moderate	$50 to $110	$10 to $20
Expensive	$110 to $180	$20 to $30
Very Expensive	Over $180	Over $30

Credit cards are abbreviated as follows:

AE: American Express	DC: Diner's Club
CB: Carte Blanche	MC: Master Card
D: Discover Card	V: Visa

For year-round tourist information see the sources listed on tha last page of the Information chapter.

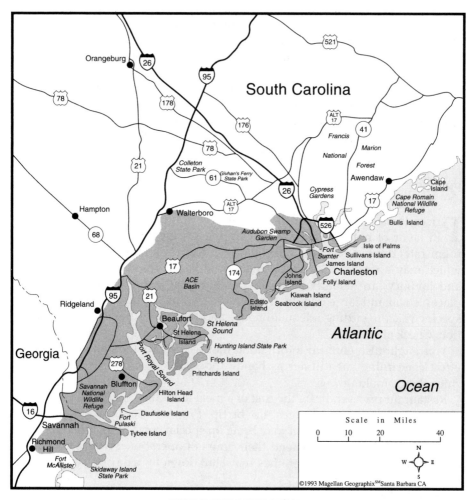

THE LOWCOUNTRY

The
CHARLESTON, SAVANNAH & COASTAL ISLANDS
Book

A Complete Guide

CHAPTER ONE
"No Fayrer or Fytter Place"
HISTORY

Toward the middle of the 16th century, European adventurers were spreading across the Atlantic Ocean in a wild burst of exploring, hoping to claim for their sovereigns and sponsors vast territories of land and the riches they believed to flourish there. Aboard what now seem to be preposterously small ships and guided by hopeless maps (few of these expeditions ever landed where they intended), they arrived, established forts, and set to their business. One of the places they landed — Spanish, French, and English in succession — was the region we now know as the Lowcountry of South Carolina and Georgia.

Wade Spees

The vastly rich, tidal world the explorer Ribaut praised: "No fayrer or fytter place."

The next 150 years was a period of settling and retreating, of establishing colonies and defending them — from one another, from the Native Americans who lived there, and from the twin scourges of disease and deprivation. Motivated by religious zeal and political unrest at home, as well as by the drive to acquire real estate, slaves, or converts to Christianity, the Europeans kept returning to build, to trade, to map, to start life over in new places on which they imposed an Old World order. In the end, it was the English who dominated the Lowcountry.

While the accounts of these years outdo one another in their use of superlatives to describe God and king, they contain even richer praise for the new country. Captain Jean Ribaut, a Frenchman who led a group of Huguenot colonists to the Lowcountry in 1562, claimed in a report (translated into English the following year) that there was "no fayrer or fytter place" than the area of Port Royal Sound, near present-day Beaufort, one of the "goodlyest, best and frutfullest countres that ever was sene"; where egrets were so plentiful the bushes "be all white covered with them"; where there were "so many sortes of fishes that ye may take them without net or angle." As impressed as he was with the Lowcountry, Ribaut left his colony, called Charlesfort, soon after he arrived and was never to return; nor was he able, upon reaching France — a France badly divided by religious warfare — to find new recruits for his colony.

To a modern traveler who chances upon a rookery in Hunting Island State Park, or to the youngster throwing a cast net and needing the strength of two to draw it in, perhaps nothing has changed. Today, as centuries ago, the natural resources of the Lowcountry are breathtakingly impressive wherever you go. There will be schools of dolphin by your boat off Hilton Head, dozens of crabs in the basket you hauled to Kiawah Island, hundreds of eggs in the loggerhead turtle's nest on Pritchard's Island, and thousands of terns, which — when they rise all at once off Egg Bank in St. Helena Sound — appear as a cloud of smoke on the horizon. And there will be late-afternoon light so intense and golden it makes the dun bark of the grayest sycamore shimmer with light.

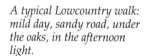

A typical Lowcountry walk: mild day, sandy road, under the oaks, in the afternoon light.

Wade Spees

And remember: when Ribaut called the Lowcountry a place "where nothing lacketh," Charleston, Beaufort, and Savannah had not even been invented.

By 1740, each of these towns had developed the intense self-consciousness — the spirit of place — that is apparent there today. You can find it in the watercolors of a native artist, in the concert of an African-American chorus, in the words of a docent, in the tales of a fisherman. Before the first roads were laid, the wharves constructed, the means of governance fully conceived, the continuity of culture that characterizes all the Lowcountry was begun. It is the rare American place to have evolved intact, with its monuments and houses and symbols of achievement still pointing to a documented and recognized past.

So overwhelming is the sense of place in the Lowcountry that I have often felt of people I know that, if they ever left the city limits of Charleston — or Beaufort or Savannah — they would vaporize.

There's no doubt, to read from their accounts, that visitors from the earliest days of settlement have shared the feeling that the Lowcountry is a special place, a dramatic place apart. Looking backwards, it is hard to pinpoint precisely when the term "Lowcountry" — or even, as it is sometimes spelled, "Low Country" — became widely used. It is certainly an apt geographical description for an area that is hill-less and hardly above sea level. But to accurately define the Lowcountry, to comprehend it at its broadest, you must consider that it is many things: a place of dozens of distinctive, interconnected natural communities and ecosystems; a site where historical forces have been converging, sometimes with disastrous consequences, for 400 years; a region whose tiny society influenced national culture; a self-conscious political subdivision of the United States.

Technically, the Lowcountry is divided from what is known as the South Carolina Upcountry by the fall line, that feature of geography that bisects the state from the Georgia border at Augusta, approximately 90 miles from the coast, to North Carolina. Upland of the fall line the soil is red clay, and it is hilly; downward the land quickly flattens out to flat, alluvial plains that soon meet the sea.

As to its other defining attributes, the Lowcountry that stretches from Charleston to Savannah and encompasses the Sea Islands in between seems to be characterized by a sense of pride that will never leave it. Old families, old houses, old customs, old loyalties remain, if not guiding principles, then ones whose legacy is passed on, as one might give a quilt or a dowry to the next generation. As the writers of the classic *WPA Guide to The Palmetto State* wrote in 1941, the Lowcountry inhabitant "may live in Charleston, a city that competes with the New Jerusalem in his dreams; or he may live in a drafty Georgian country house" but he "recalls his past glory with a pride that surpasses his ability to appreciate thoroughly the good things of the present."

Of course, the protection of this vital spirit has come at a price. Lowcountry residents were willing to pay it once, to take the drastic measure of firing on Fort Sumter, and they are continuing that commitment. Maintaining Historic Districts, scenic vistas, two-lane island roads, Gullah communities, marine sanctuaries comprising tens of thousands of acres — these are among the accomplishments of present-day preservationists who seek to insure the presence of the past in everyday life. Their victories are for you to savor, too.

NATURAL HISTORY

The coastline that defines the Lowcountry was, until about 245 million years ago, still more or less attached to the eastern rim of what became present-day Europe and Africa. The shifting of geologic plates that caused the movement of the landmass and created the southern Appalachians, among other mountain ranges, led to the formation of the Atlantic Ocean and the Lowcountry coastal plain.

Sand Hills

"I continued through this forest nearly in a direct line towards the sea coast, five or six miles, when the land became uneven, with ridges of sand hills, mixed with sea shells, and covered by almost impenetrable thickets, consisting of Live Oaks, Sweet-bay, Myrica, Ilex, . . . The dark labyrinth is succeeded by a great extent of salt plains, beyond which the boundless ocean is seen. Betwixt the dark forest and the salt plains, I crossed a rivulet of fresh water, where I sat down a while to rest myself, under the shadow of sweet Bays and Oaks.; the lively breezes were perfumed by the fragrant breath of the superb Crinum, called by the inhabitants, White Lily. This admirable beauty of the sea-coast islands dwells in the humid shady groves, where the soil is made fertile and mellow by the admixture of sea shells . . . and the texture and whiteness of its flowers at once charmed me."

— From *Travels of William Bartram*
(first published in 1791)

In the geologic history of the southeast region, the coastal plain is a rather new development. Long before the present-day coastline earned its shape, toward the end of the Miocene — third epoch of the Cenozoic Era — the upcountry regions already were well established. They were formed in an earlier era, the Mesozoic (220–70 million years ago, the time when the dinosaurs came and went), and their ancient mineral formations contrast sharply with those of the coast.

Over time, a cycle was begun. Eroded material from these highland ridges was carried by streams draining the Blue Ridge and Piedmont uplands and deposited, again and again, to the south and east. This cretaceous material extended the land mass. Periodic inundation by the sea followed, thus covering the sediment and creating distinctive geologic layers of clay, sand, and gravel. At least seven such terraces have been identified, ranging in elevation from 25 feet to 270 feet. Mining activity near Charleston has unearthed fossils of sharks' teeth and mammoth vertebrae.

In short, millions of years ago, much of the present-day Lowcountry was under water, while as recently as thousands of years ago, the Native

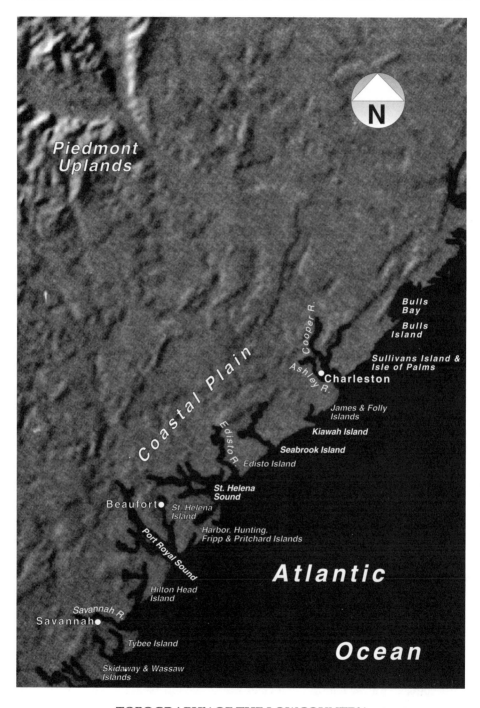

TOPOGRAPHY OF THE LOWCOUNTRY

Americans who lived here probably collected oysters and shellfish from beds that, were we to locate them today, would lie some 95 miles out to sea.

Today, well beneath the sandy soil, ranging in thickness from 1,000 to 3,000 feet, lie the sandstone, silt stones, shale, and limestone that were dumped there. They undergird the land and stretch well beyond it into the ocean to form the continental shelf and the upper slope. The oldest rocks of the coastal plain lie in scattered sections under these layers, and it is activity in their faults that can, and has, caused earthquakes, such as the one that damaged Charleston in 1886.

The geologic history of the Lowcountry has given its farmers, residents, and for a time its phosphate-mining industry, some unique advantages. Unlike northern coastal areas such as New England, the area is free of surface rocks. Preparing a field never required the building of a stone wall beside it. The nature of subterranean rock formations has provided some especially good soils for timber cultivation. More important, the deeper layers of rocks serve as aquifers to provide potable water for agriculture, industry, and homes — not an idle resource, given the near sea-level elevation of the Lowcountry.

Finally, if the Lowcountry were without the plentiful deposits of easily eroded rock that tumbled from the highlands over the years, the region would have no beaches. The sand you traverse, across miles of coastal and barrier beach, is their legacy.

The phenomenon of rocks-into-sand is just one piece of the Lowcountry's geologic history. The other is the transformation of one massive ocean into a landscape of sculptured sounds, estuaries, and marshes. Their evolution has defined the Lowcountry as the site of one of the nation's most productive fisheries, a home to dozens of species of native and migratory birds, and a habitat for mammals small and large. Even the trees and plants of the coast flourish in direct response to these various bodies of water.

THE MARINE ENVIRONMENT

The Lowcountry marine environment includes several distinctive parts: swamps, estuaries, marshes, maritime forests, dunes and interdune meadows, tidal creeks and sounds, alluvial and blackwater rivers. Their functions are interdependent; to all, tidal action — about six to eight feet throughout the region — is significant. Evidence of the complexity of the marine ecosystem is best seen at any number of points where the land meets the sea, for it is here that some of the most dynamic and subtle dramas of nature are played out. To witness them, a traveler need do no more than lean over a bridge at low tide, step out of car by a rural creek, or walk the beach.

Perhaps the most common sight of the Lowcountry is the field of smooth cordgrass (*Spartina alterniflora*) that makes up the salt marsh, and the muddy banks and flats that cut through it. Rimmed by wax myrtle and Carolina cher-

An oysterman digs on the banks where land meets sea.

Wade Spees

ry laurel on its banks, overshadowed by huge live oaks whose limbs are draped with Spanish moss (an air plant, member of the pineapple family), and dotted with resurrection fern, the salt marsh is probably nature's most productive nursery.

What you will see here is this: filter feeders such as snails, crab, oysters, shrimp, and mullet ingesting the detritus — a potent mixture of decomposed marsh grass, animal matter, algae, and fungi. Or something larger, a heron, say, or a bottle-nose dolphin (locally called porpoise), or a raccoon eating its smaller prey. The fiddler crabs with their lopsided claws will gather and disperse by the hundreds, a muddy cavalry. Look up and there are the shrimp boats, nets dragging at their sides. Behind them flock the gulls scavenging for cast-off fish. You will hear the marsh pop as it is submerged by an incoming tide.

A Pleasing Music

"A beautiful green frog inhabits the grassy, marshy shores of these large rivers. They are very numerous, and their noise exactly resembles the barking of little dogs, or the yelping of puppies: these likewise make a great clamour, but as their notes are fine, and uttered in chorus, by separate bands or communities, far and near, rising and falling with the gentle breezes, affords a pleasing kind of music."

— From *Travels of William Bartram*, 1791

The Lowcountry provides a habitat for the bald eagle and many other endangered species.

Wade Spees

In brackish marshes slightly farther inland, along tidal rivers, there will be more sediment, flushed from the upland, and greater plant diversity. In the shelter of the vegetation lie the nests of waterfowl; in the highest trees is, perhaps, the nest of a bald eagle. Three of the rivers, the Ashepoo, Combahee, and Edisto, form one of largest estuarine systems on the East Coast — the ACE Basin, located in and around U.S. Highway 17 south of Charleston. Protection of the basin is assured by a consortium of federal, state, and private interests. Farther south, the Savannah Wildlife Refuge offers another opportunity to see these natural forces at work.

THE WORLDS OF ISLANDS AND CITIES

The barrier islands offer another view of the marine ecosystem. Developed or not, they maintain a sense of isolation and fragility at "the edge of the

---

Voluptuous Charm

"Picket life was of course the place to feel the charm of the natural beauty on the Sea Islands. We had a world of profuse and tangled vegetation around us, such as would have been a dream of delight to me, but for the constant sense of responsibility and care which came between. Amid this preoccupation, Nature seemed but a mirage, and not the close and intimate associate I had before known. I pressed no flowers, collected no insects or birds' eggs, made no notes on natural objects, reversing in these respects all previous habits. Yet now, in the retrospect, there seems to have been infused into me through every pore the voluptuous charm of the season and the place; and the slightest corresponding sound or odor now calls back the memory of those delicious days."

— From *Army Life in a Black Regiment*
by Thomas Wentworth Higginson
(First published in 1869)

world." Even as they appear solid, they are in fact changing shape all the time, their dunes migrating, growing, eroding, their forests shaped by the unforgiving winds and salt spray. The lives of the birds and mammals that make their homes here are impacted daily by the elements. If the beach has suffered from erosion, oak-tree roots and upended palmettos will obstruct your path. As if to mock this rough beauty, dozens of sanderlings play at the water's edge, while overhead, the big brown pelicans impose an order of their own as they fly in unerring formation.

You may be lucky enough to participate in a late-night "turtle watch," when groups of residents observe the 300-pound loggerhead sea turtles drag themselves up the beach, dig holes, and lay eggs. On several barrier islands, teams of people are charged with marking the nests and moving the eggs to a secure hatchery, away from predators, poachers, and high tides. At the time of release, the hatchlings make their way to the ocean in groups of two and three, and then somehow, miraculously, paddle with their tiny fins to the open sea.

Precisely where these turtles go is not known. From Lowcountry marinas, it takes a big fishing boat several hours to reach the Gulf Stream, where, as every fisherman knows, the big fighting fish swim — creatures that might eat a turtle in a second. And there are other giants in this marine wildness — the right whales and the manatees.

Coastal refuges show life in abundance; but even in the cities, away from the water's edge, you will be surrounded by natural beauty. In downtown Savannah, the parkways are filled to bursting with azaleas and flowering dogwood in the spring. Honeysuckle, jessamine, wisteria, and trumpet vine tumble wildly over garden walls or race up the trunks of trees. And then there are the birds: the tiny Carolina wren, practically domesticated as it makes its nest in a flower box; mourning doves cooing on telephone wires; and the ever-present mockingbird.

The Mock-Bird

"This ancient sublime forest, frequently intersected with extensive avenues, vistas and green lawns, opening to extensive savannas and far distant Rice plantations, agreeably employs the imagination, and captivates the senses by scenes of magnificence and grandeur. The gay mock-bird, vocal and joyous, mounts aloft on silvered wings, rolls over and over, then gently descends, and presides in the choir of the tuneful tribes."

— From *Travels of William Bartram*, 1791

Mark Catesby, the naturalist who "discovered" the mockingbird in this region over 250 years ago, noted its fantastic ability to mimic. Today it is said that the bird can imitate 39 songs and 50 call notes, not to mention the cackling of hens, the creak of old gates, and the croaking of frogs. Given the diversity and abundance of Lowcountry life, the mockingbird has songs enough for a lifetime.

SOCIAL HISTORY

This sculpture, "Landing Brave" by Peter Toth, stands at Charles Towne Landing. It honors the Native Americans who lived off the area's natural bounty and taught the early settlers of Charles Town to do so.

Wade Spees

EARLY HUMAN INHABITANTS

The Native Americans who ranged along the coast from the earliest days — as far back as 10,000 B.C. — have left the merest impression of their lives in patterned pottery shards, woven reed baskets, huge shell middens and shell rings, cypress-log canoes, and the remains of burial or religious sites scattered throughout the region. They also left their names, now anglicized in common usage, to confirm their presence in a dozen Lowcountry places. Some of the most prominent archaeological remains have been found on coastal islands — Hilton Head, Callawassie — suggesting that these early inhabitants possessed both geographic agility and a sense of territorial significance. Their population is thought to have numbered 50,000 at its peak.

The Native Americans of the Lowcountry were divided into loose tribal confederations, each of which may have communicated in its own tongue. They spent the summers along the coast and on the coastal islands, farming and harvesting fish and shellfish; in winter they retreated inland, where they hunted deer and small game. An apparently abundant food supply and an absence of harshness in the climate or geography seem to have helped insure the stability of these native societies. Communal farming produced several crops a year of corn and bounteous harvests of beans, peas, pumpkin, and watermelon. The forests yielded wild fruits, nuts, berries and plants, roots and bark for medicinal drinks. Well-fortified towns, rimmed with circular stockades and enclosing an ever-burning ceremonial fire, established their home base.

The Indians' houses had the appearance of rude Quonset huts, long and domed. They were constructed of wooden frames over which mats, woven from palmetto fronds, could be draped, or, during hot weather, removed. Inside, the walls were lined with benches for sleeping. Some houses were grander than others, featuring rooms and pillared platforms usually reserved for a chief or tribe member believed to have unusual wisdom or healing powers.

A larger structure, perhaps 200 feet in diameter, served as a community center for religious and social activities. Early European observers noted devout attention to ritual celebrations in praise of harvest, accompanied by singing, dancing, and the playing of instruments — cane flutes, drums, and rattles made from shells and seed pods. Some Native American games included forms of bowling and lacrosse. They laid their dead to rest, wrapped like swaddled babies, atop high scaffoldings.

ENCOUNTERS WITH EUROPEANS

By the time of their first encounters with white men, the coastal Native Americans had sorted themselves into various confederacies. From Charleston to the Savannah River lived a group of tribes known collectively as the Cusabo, including the Combahee, Ashepoo, Edisto, Stono, Wando, Kiawah, and Etiwan.

Their responses to the incursion of Europeans were mixed: some were generous and open to trade, teaching the newcomers how to fish and make secure shelter, and in so doing probably saved their lives. Some Native Americans also shared farming techniques. One white settler told of his success in cultivating with the Indians such crops as grape vines, pomegranates, orange and fig trees, barley, onions, and garlic. Some tribes and their chiefs, known as *caciques*, helped the Frenchmen of Charlesfort build a ship, caulked with moss, for a return voyage to Europe. Some delivered to English explorers the prime high-bluff settings on which the newcomers laid the cities of Charles Town and Savannah. Some even boarded ships and went abroad, or to Barbados.

Other accounts, however, report canoe flotillas fleeing in shock, the villagers hiding for days in the woods. Fighting and massacres were not unknown. Among the Europeans, the toll was largely on French and Spanish settlers, who were the first to land.

If the settlers faced an uneasy alliance with the Cusabo, the Cusabo themselves knew an even stronger enemy in the Westo, a vigorous inland tribe.

Over time, the Westo dominated, until they in turn were swept out by stronger tribes and the English settlers of early Charles Town.

By the time of persistent English colonization, toward the end of the 17th century, another tribe, the Yemassee, had gained prominence in the region. Once friendly with the Spanish explorers to the south and educated in ways of their civilization, this group shifted its allegiance to the English as its members migrated north. They proved to be loyal supporters of Colonel "Tuscarora Jack" Barnwell, a flamboyant Irishman who had recently come to the Lowcountry, in a campaign to subdue hostile North Carolina tribes. Barnwell, who is buried in St. Helena's Episcopal Churchyard in Beaufort, proved to be a diplomat, as well: in 1719, he was called on by the settlers of Charles Town to represent their grievances to the Lords Proprietors, an action that resulted in the formal establishment of a royal colony.

The Yemassee carried on a healthy deerskin trade with the new Europeans, and there developed over time a far-ranging network of agents, outposts, and agreements. Yet, finally, the very success of the enterprise and the pressure of increased migration onto native lands, proved to be the colonists' undoing. Long-simmering resentment of unscrupulous traders, unfair taking of land, and abuse of their people led to a gathering of fifteen Native American nations, who directed an assault from the Yemassee town at Pocotaligo. They attacked on Easter Sunday, 1715, killing as many traders as they could and sending the residents of Beaufort to their ships. The bloody Yemassee War lasted two years. At times, hundreds of warriors were dangerously close to Charles Town, reminding its residents of their isolation and pitiful protection under the crown. Eventually, the Yemassee forces disbanded and moved out of the region for good. By the middle of the 18th century, the last remnant tribes near Savannah had left the area.

THE SETTLING OF CHARLES TOWN

Carolina was originally known to Europeans as "Carolana," and it was the dream of the kings of Spain and France to have it. Their struggle for domination, played out on lands far distant from their own, and among native inhabitants who had been there for centuries, marked the earliest days of settlement.

The Spanish arrived first, in 1521, under the leadership of Francisco Gordillo: he named the Sea Island area Santa Elena. Further colonization was planned for but never materialized. Five years later, another Spaniard, Vasquez de Ayllon, having heard marvelous stories of the rich, vast land of Santa Elena, gathered 500 settlers and established his party at a point farther north along the coast. Their hopes, too, were to be dashed — by illness, a revolt among the slaves they had brought, Indian attacks, and unusually harsh winter weather.

In 1562, Captain Jean Ribaut established Charlesfort, the first Protestant colony in North America, in the area he named Port Royal. Charlesfort, too, soon petered out, and by 1565, the area had been reclaimed by the Spanish, who commenced to build a string of forts along the coast. In 1629, Charles I of England announced his intentions of ownership. In the end, it was the English claim that stuck, although the early residents of Charles Town faced down Spanish, French, and Indian forces several times before they were secure.

Time passed, however, before the English pursued their claim by actually settling. It took a monarch pressed to return favors — and a group of men with means, entrepreneurial spirit, and a keen sense of the market — to reap the benefits imagined for so long by so many. The monarch was Charles II, king of England during the Restoration. The group of men was Carolina's Lords Proprietors: Sir John Colleton, the Duke of Albermarle (George Monk), Lord Craven, Lord Berkeley, Sir William Berkeley, Sir George Carteret, the Earl of Clarendon, and Lord Ashley (Anthony Ashley Cooper).

The familiar nursery rhyme that calls Old King Cole a "merry old soul" might aptly have applied to Charles II. By 1663, restored to the throne after the dispatch of Cromwell, Charles found himself short of cash and facing obligations to those who had helped him in the late civil war. As a token of his appreciation, he gave to his loyal friends the territory "described in the parts of America not yet cultivated or planted, and only inhabited by some barbarous people who have no knowledge of Almighty God." This was to be the Carolina Province. Its development, particularly along the lower coast, was to define a society that exists today.

Planning for colonization began immediately. Sir John Colleton, who had lived among the planters in Barbados, convinced his associates of the need for expansion of the society there (already nearly 40 years old) and of the profits to be made in overseeing its relocation. In the summer of 1663, Captain William Hilton sailed the ship *Adventure* into Port Royal Sound, and their project began in earnest.

Hilton's successful foray and contact with friendly natives led to another exploratory trip three years later under the leadership of Captain Robert Sandford. This time, the English left behind Henry Woodward, a surgeon whose interest in the culture, language, and habits of the Native Americans was to ease the way, several years hence, for the first settlement at Charles Town. That day finally came in 1670 with the arrival of the ship *Carolina*, the only one of three ships to complete the voyage from England via Barbados.

It was at first unclear precisely where to settle — whether in the vicinity of Port Royal Sound, which Hilton had explored, or farther north, along the North Edisto River, where Sandford had ventured. Finally, after further viewing of both sites under the piloting and careful guidance of the *cacique* of the Kiawah tribe, the colonists established a fort at Albermarle Point, in the lands of the Kiawah, at Old Towne Creek up the Ashley River from present-day Charleston.

The earliest years of this colony have been brought to life at Charles Towne

Early settlers building a fortification on an isolated bit of high ground.

Courtesy of The Charleston Museum, Charleston, SC

Landing, which today offers a true sense of the importance of siting — high on a bluff from which unfriendly Spanish ships might be seen — and evidence of agricultural successes and failures. Small-scale farming worked; large cash crops, upon which rested the hopes of the Barbadian planters, didn't as yet.

In 1671, another shipload of colonists arrived, including more from Barbados, accompanied by their slaves; and by the following year the colony consisted of 30 houses and 200 people.

The colonists prospered and gained confidence, such that by 1680 they had removed themselves from Albermarle Point to a site on the peninsula at the mouth of the harbor, where they laid out their city. From this time forward, the development of Charles Town — indeed of the entire Lowcountry of which it was the capital — proceeded rapidly.

EARLY GROWTH AND PROSPERITY

Between 1690 and 1720, according to the historian Carl Bridenbaugh, the population of Charles Town tripled. New immigrants included French Huguenots and Irish, who established themselves in business and govern- ment. Wharves, churches, protective sea walls, defensive bastions, and homes were built. Streets were named (Church, Broad, Meeting, Tradd, and Queen are among those you can see today), and some of them were even paved with oyster shells. Trade with the Indians was lively, and exports thrived: deerskins and fur were shipped to England; pork, corn, naval stores, and lumber went to Barbados and the southern islands. The vast natural networks of creeks and rivers opened up the countryside to planters, who raised beef and pork, culti- vated cotton, rice, and indigo, and harvested lumber. And of course the water- ways were crucial to transporting all these goods to Charles Town.

In governance, the influence of the Barbados colony continued to be felt in the key areas of law and representation by parish, and in the adoption of the slave code. The settlers from Barbados also imposed their architecture — the classic house design with its raised basement and upstairs piazzas — and their intent to develop plantations outside the city limits. The increasing importation of slaves followed, an absolute essential in making large-scale agriculture succeed.

Thus, from the very beginning, Charles Town was a society in which profitability and expansion — not to mention ease of living, even among the less grand — were inextricably tied to slaves and their management by law and custom. The historian Peter Wood estimates that by 1715 the slave population exceeded the European population.

Prosperity did not guarantee security, though. Charles Town faced threats from outsiders: there were skirmishes with Indians, Spanish soldiers, even pirates such as Blackbeard (Edward Teach) and Stede Bonnet. In 1718, 49 pirates were hanged.

Success in trade and a growing, more diverse population did, however, embolden the citizens to improve their lot. Prompted by resentment toward England (which refused to help pay for the defense of the city, attempted to enact trade restrictions, and raised the colonists' quitrents, among other heavy-handed actions), the citizens challenged the very form of proprietorship under which their colony had been established. In 1721, after much to-and-fro with England, the Carolina Province became a royal colony. By the 1730s, it was referred to by its new name, Charlestown. Only after the Revolution, when it was incorporated as the new state of South Carolina's first city, would it finally settle into its now-familiar spelling as Charleston.

EXPANSION IN THE COLONIAL LOWCOUNTRY

Once people were settled, once they were safe, once they had established their markets and their means of production in slaves, the Lowcountry around colonial Charlestown started its meteoric climb to achieve what it eventually became: person for person, the wealthiest region in the colonies.

It started with rice; then came indigo, and finally cotton. The fact that all these crops were suited to Lowcountry cultivation, that there was land to support them and slaves to work them, that there was desire abroad for their harvest (in some cases a bounty paid for it), and hefty profit to be made on it, left only a need for a class of men to seize the opportunity to grow rich. As was the case in other colonies, there were plenty of them, and they promptly did so.

The world they began to establish, the ways they embellished it, the physical order they imposed on it, and the choices they made to keep it alive defined Lowcountry culture right up to the Civil War. Even after that, even today, the echoes of those efforts resound in Lowcountry political, social, and economic life. In the deepest way, they form the basis of the stories people tell themselves about who they are.

As planters and their families spread out — and as new colonists continued

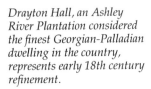
Drayton Hall, an Ashley
River Plantation considered
the finest Georgian-Palladian
dwelling in the country,
represents early 18th century
refinement.

Wade Spees

to arrive from Barbados — they ventured across the Ashley River to Magnolia and Drayton Hall and Middleton Plantation; they went to Goose Creek and points inland, to Beaufort, across the Sea Islands of Kiawah, Seabrook, Johns, Edisto, St. Helena, Lady's, and Hilton Head. In addition to their main house in the city, they might establish a "big house" on one plantation and then own several others that were far more rustic, run by overseers and a slave crew. Profits were turned to acquire new land and slaves. A merchant, having amassed a fortune in town, would follow a path similar to the one taken by this newly landed gentry. Planters were businessmen, and vice versa.

Thus emerged a small society that was at once far-flung across the Low-country but glued together by shared aspirations, tastes, assumptions about plantation life and the treatment of blacks, even by marriage.

The relation between city and country was intimate. Charlestown, already the throbbing commercial heart of this society, came to display all its wealth. There were theatrical performances, clubs of every variety, subscription concerts followed by elaborate balls, racetracks, even a "season" that included "Race Week" in February, which was marked by nonstop celebrations, balls, concerts, and festivities attended by city residents and by planters and their families who would travel in from the country. Thomas Elfe, a magnificent cabinetmaker whose work can be seen at the Heyward-Washington House, set a standard for stylistic elegance. Direct trade with England, estimated to have been six times what it was with the other colonies, delivered the latest in fashionable household goods. Children were sent abroad to be educated.

By 1740, a reliable monthly postal service allowed members of this class to connect with their counterparts throughout the colonies. The hierarchy was in place, as was a concomitant sense of "breeding" and the unique sense of power derived from owning much of the population (the slaves) and determining the lives of most everyone else belonging to the tiny, dependent mid-

A "single house" of the Georgian period, built of cypress and adorned, as the best houses might be, with a drawing-room mantel by Thomas Elfe.

Wade Spees

dle class. The vast tidal landscape and the people who inhabited it had been brought under control.

Carl Bridenbaugh has written of this period that the first families of Charlestown presented "the unusual spectacle of a class of culture and leisure living on the very edge of the wilderness a life of refinement." In fact, there was still a lot of wilderness. To the south, it was just being tamed. By 1742, when there were nearly 7,000 people living in Charlestown, Savannah's population numbered only in the hundreds.

THE FOUNDING OF SAVANNAH

By comparison with the settling of Charlestown, the founding of Savannah in 1733 was seen as a far less ambitious enterprise — and perhaps a morally loftier one. In the early years, slavery was outlawed; it was thought people wouldn't work as hard if they owned their laborers. Rum was forbidden, and trade with the Indians was strictly regulated.

The 114 or so settlers who arrived under the flag of King George were mostly of modest means, and their goal — as outlined by the English Trustees — was the development of exports, including wine and silk. They were also supposed to defend the colony from the Spanish, and thus provide a buffer for prosperous Charlestown.

They were led by General James Oglethorpe, a high-minded Englishman with a caretaker's concern for his flock. Many addressed him as "Father." Such was his sense of mission that when the ship *Ann* arrived in Charlestown Harbor for consultations with the royal governor, the passengers were required to remain aboard and fish for their supper, so as not to have their heads turned by the glamorous city ashore.

Continuing south, the *Ann* stopped at tiny Beaufort. Here, passengers *were* allowed to fraternize with residents, whose standard of living probably appeared to be more in line with what the newcomers, in the best of circumstances, might hope to accomplish. General Oglethorpe chose as his site for Savannah a place where "the river forms a half-moon, along the south side of which the banks are about 40 feet high, and on the top a flat, which they call a bluff." He was assisted by Colonel William Bull, a engineer from Charlestown with local surveying experience, and guided by Tomochichi, a friendly Yamacraw chief. The site was about 18 miles upriver from the river's mouth on the Atlantic, on water sufficiently deep for ships drawing up to 12 feet to navigate within 10 yards of shore.

Oglethorpe and Bull immediately set themselves to the task of planning the city, and it is the legacy of their inspired effort that distinguishes Savannah today. The city was, and is, a meticulously planned urban environment, stretching back from the river in a series of squares and boulevards which, then as now, are landscaped focal points. Space was designated for public buildings and market areas, as well as for secure retreats, in which settlers living outside the city limits could take cover in the event of Indian uprisings. The plan has been designated a National Historic Civil Engineering Landmark.

As things turned out, relations with the Indians remained friendly. Tomochichi supported the colonists' work throughout his life and was instrumental in winning the trust of Indians in the area. He was also willing to support Oglethorpe in battles with the Spanish, which were to occur sporadically over the next 10 years. The existence of a trading post nearby — run by John Musgrove from South Carolina and his wife, Mary, who was part Creek — also smoothed the way for natural contact.

Given such a propitious start, it was up to the settlers to dig in, to clear and build, hunt and farm, and establish the Trustees' garden. This they did, on the grants of 50 acres received by heads of families (five acres in the city, 45 outside it for farming). The settlers were also the beneficiaries of hundreds of head of livestock from their South Carolina neighbors, as well as rice and horses. For quite some time, even after Savannah got on its feet, South Carolina, and the port of Charlestown in particular, was to dominate the commercial life of the southern coast.

More settlers, including Irish, Scots, Swiss, Germans, and Italians, came very quickly. Jews and Protestant Salzburgers from the German-Austrian border area sought refuge from religious persecution. By 1741, there were 142 houses, a courthouse, jail, storehouse, market building, and a 10-acre, fenced public garden.

Soon enough, the settlers found that some of the original restrictions intended to guide development were hampering it. The settlers wanted free title to their land and the right to own slaves to exploit it. They were unable to compete with South Carolina in the export markets. In 1752, the Trustees abandoned their charter, and two years later, Savannah was established as a royal colony.

Thus in a sense released from Oglethorpe's idealism, the colonists proceeded to develop plantations as their neighbors had. However, it took until the close of the French and Indian War in 1763 (when Florida was ceded to England) for Savannah to begin to flourish as a colonial city and primary port serving the Georgia backcountry. By the time of the Revolution, the South Carolina and Georgia colonies had settled lingering border disputes, were engaging freely in trade, and were communicating through four Lowcountry newspapers. The region had pulled together, united by shared commercial and social goals, and a culture deeply affected by slavery.

THE AMERICAN REVOLUTION

Ten years before reports of the battles of Lexington and Concord reached the Lowcountry, its residents were taking independent action to defy British rule, especially its methods of colonial governance and taxation. By the time of the Stamp Act in 1765, they had become wealthy, self-confident, and better organized in their own military defense. Having built their cities from scratch, they were in no mood to be further subjugated, and their responses were violent. In Charleston, long-festering political disagreements between the colonists and the royal governor burst to the surface. They bitterly resented his order to move the Assembly and center of government to Beaufort, a day's journey by boat. In Savannah, where relations between colonists and

By the end of the 18th century, the owning and selling of slaves was an established custom in Savannah, despite early, idealistic efforts to forbid it.

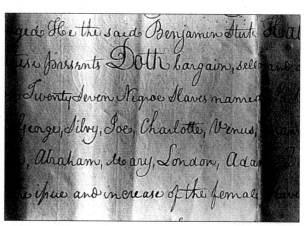

Wade Spees, from a document in the King-Tisdale House collection

governor had been more cordial, groups of Liberty Boys nevertheless were openly challenging loyalists and destroying British property.

By 1774, many colonists had become defiant. The merchants of Charlestown refused to buy tea that had been taxed, preferring to let it mold in the Exchange Building, which you can see today at the foot of Broad Street. British products were boycotted. Five delegates were sent to the First Continental Congress. In Savannah, leaders gathered at Tondee's Tavern to sign a petition denouncing the acts Parliament had passed in response to the Boston Tea Party (the Intolerable Acts) and insisting on the independent rights of the people.

At this point, war seemed inevitable, even though there were loyalists throughout the Lowcountry who urged negotiation and reconsideration of non-importation policies. In 1776, four South Carolinians and three Georgians signed the Declaration of Independence. Colonial rule was over, but the fighting had just begun.

In the first significant victory of the Revolution (June 28, 1776), General William Moultrie, outnumbered and outgunned, defeated an invading fleet of 50 British warships from his position on Sullivan's Island, in a fort built of palmetto logs. Visitors to the site today are impressed by the degree of risk and bravery that battle entailed.

But the Lowcountry was not yet secure. In December 1778, the British captured Savannah, and in May 1780, after a one-month siege, they finally subdued Charlestown. The British wreaked vengeance on the colonists by imprisoning and executing patriots. When they finally left the Lowcountry, in 1782, they were loaded down with war booty.

The American Revolution had a profound effect on the heretofore stable Lowcountry society. It was nothing less than a civil war dividing families and generations. According to Robert Rosen in *A Short History of Charleston*, William Bull was for the king; his nephews for the revolutionaries. Daniel Heyward was a Tory, but his son Thomas signed the Declaration of Independence. Similar clashes of ideals and politics occurred in other prominent Lowcountry families such as the Draytons, Pinckneys, Manigaults, Horrys, and Hugers.

The political questions raised by the conflict sensitized new classes of people to their own self-interest. The governments that came into place afterward reflected these diverse new motivations. No longer were mechanics and other artisans — "the little people" — satisfied with government dominated by the planter class, especially when planters' slaves soaked up most of the available work. As for the wealthy, they were forced to read the handwriting on the wall; fortunately, some of the Lowcountry's planters were themselves ardent patriots, and they adjusted to democratic government, though their influence remained out of proportion to their numbers.

The years following the Revolution saw a fantastic boom in population, in building, and in commerce. Many of the houses of the Lowcountry date from this Federal period, in which new fortunes were made and old ones even further enhanced. If the architecture of the Lowcountry can be read as a book, then this is its first great chapter.

Entrepreneurs, ship captains, military people, and merchants from New England came to the cities and the Sea Islands to build their plantations. While the bounty on indigo was a casualty of war and led to a decline in that crop, the invention in 1793 of the cotton gin, on a plantation near Savannah, meant that the process of removing seeds from cotton could occur with greater ease and speed. Slaves working in the ginhouses still plucked by hand seeds from the most highly prized strain then being grown: Sea Island cotton, whose long, silky fibers would be broken by the action of the gin. These seeds were saved, talked about, compared, and the best of them used for the following crop. Despite ups and downs in the cotton market and competition from the rest of the new American republic, for most of the next 60 years the Lowcountry flourished.

Fortunes earned in the post-Revolutionary boom were spent on homes characterized by lavish detail. These examples are at Charleston's Center for Historic Preservation.

Wade Spees

PLANTATION LIFE AND GULLAH CULTURE

The first African-American slave came to the Lowcountry to stay in 1670. Ever since then, slaves, freedmen, and their heirs have defined in the most essential way imaginable the politics, growth, lifestyle, culture, language, and habits of the Lowcountry. The complexity of relations between blacks and whites — who, in city or country, lived in close quarters and experienced daily contact but were governed by strict social codes enforced by penalties — has informed all Lowcountry history. Fear of black uprising, especially after the ill-fated Denmark Vesey rebellion in 1822, made for a regulation of life unknown outside the South.

For the best overview of slave life, visit The Charleston Museum. Or drive to Middleton Place, another site which, with its landscaped gardens and farm-yard, offers splendid evidence of the world the slaves built. Imagine the daily bustle of slaves around what is now Charleston's Market Area, or in Savannah's waterfront warehouses, now restored.

When you are out and about in the Lowcountry, probably the two most significant things to ponder, when thinking about its past, are the immense *enterprise* that characterized plantations (where now they may be silent and grand, they once were fantastically busy places with dozens of buildings) and the *isolation* the slaves endured there.

The world of the plantation was self-sufficient, marked by dozens of specific activities taking place according to the season: gathering marsh hay for fertilizer, harvesting, clearing and burning the fields, building and repairing, growing food crops, ginning cotton, packing it in the cotton house, taking it to the landing to be shipped on barges. Within that world of action, and responding to its often crushing demands, there arose a culture among slaves, now generally called the Gullah culture, which included elements of their African past. Scholars have identified these remnant "Africanisms" in religious and mythical beliefs, in patterns of speech and dress, in basketry, art, dance, and song. In its totality, Gullah is a way of life that informed — and still informs — the manner in which slaves and their descendants managed their relationship toward white people and kept intact some expression of their own identity.

From the earliest days, black slaves from certain rice-growing regions of the West African coast were prized for their knowledge of that crop's cultivation. Rice-growing is a tricky business. It requires periodic flooding of fields, the design, building, and maintenance of a dike-and-gate system, and hundreds of people, including children, to protect the rice plants from birds, gather it, separate the grain from the chaff by means of sea-grass "fanner baskets," and clean it with mortar and pestle. In all of these areas, black people were experienced, and they taught what they knew.

Indigo and cotton crops demanded another kind of hard labor, in preparing the fields with usually nothing more than a hoe and a plow-dragging ox, in building pits to soak the indigo or in chopping weeds to free the cotton plants, in extracting the dye or picking tufts from spiky bolls. Labor was apportioned

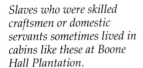

Slaves who were skilled craftsmen or domestic servants sometimes lived in cabins like these at Boone Hall Plantation.

Wade Spees

by "tasks" of land, a task being about a quarter of an acre, for which slaves were responsible. Plantation ledgers were organized around work completed according to this system. In addition, slaves were used as carpenters, black-smiths, cooks, loggers, boatbuilders, butchers, and house servants. While planters left at the onset of "the sickly season" to escape malaria, blacks were immune to this fever and worked through the miasmic heat of summer.

A caste system grew up within the population that served the needs of the plantation master: slaves associated with domestic life were at the top, and field hands were at the bottom. Becoming a black "driver" meant that a slave would work with an overseer to direct crews; it also meant meting out punishment and whippings to fellow slaves. With blacks outnumbering whites by vast majorities, keeping order through work and brutality was essential.

The treatment of slaves varied widely in the Lowcountry. It is important to remember that while the majority of white people in the city and the country owned slaves, only a very small portion of them owned more than a dozen. Some planters bought and sold families; some kept them together, some did not. Some allowed friendships or marriage to occur between plantations; some took skilled slaves to the city and hired them out. Some planters allowed slaves to hunt and fish, keep gardens, raise fowl, and sell eggs. Some gave them staples — molasses, cloth, tobacco, shoes — on a periodic basis.

Slaves lived in cabins or slave rows that shared a common wall and had dirt floors. On the plantations they worshipped at praise houses — usually small, clapboard buildings lined with benches — where services were marked by recitations of the gospel, praying, and the singing of spirituals in which an elder "deaconed out" a line and the worshipers responded in unison. They buried their dead in separate slave cemeteries, dozens of which are in still in use today.

Whatever the specific case, a slave's identity (and that of his family) was tied to one place, which he might never leave during his lifetime. If ever he did travel, it was under a strict pass or ticket system. His fortunes were often tied to one white family, and his heirs to its heirs. Education of slaves was either haphazard or strictly forbidden.

It is not possible to overestimate the way in which the Civil War disrupted the order imposed by the plantation world and the society it held in check. When recovery came to the Lowcountry, it would come to the countryside last.

THE CIVIL WAR AND THE YEARS OF POVERTY

If the Lowcountry is seen by visitors as a place rich in references to the Civil War, both physical and spiritual, perhaps it is because there was such a difference in the "before" and "after." The cataclysmic changes wrought by that great conflict are well known.

Perhaps less well know is the fact that even before the Civil War, the Lowcountry already had been undergoing a slow transformation. Historians

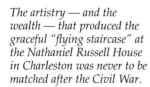

The artistry — and the wealth — that produced the graceful "flying staircase" at the Nathaniel Russell House in Charleston was never to be matched after the Civil War.

Wade Spees

point to a definite drift of the Lowcountry after the 1820s, from occupying a place at the center of colonial and post-Revolutionary commerce to becoming just one of many prosperous regions in the South.

The Lowcountry's golden age was, in fact, the now-distant time of relative innocence and optimism long before the antebellum era, a time of cosmopolitan outlook and quiet accommodation with the rest of the country that was lost during the overheated days immediately prior to the Civil War. (It has only been in the later years of the 20th century — some might say as recently as the great resort booms, the "second Yankee invasion" — that the Lowcountry has been able to consider itself as reentering the mainstream of American culture.) The nostalgia for long-lost days, which most every visitor to the Lowcountry feels, is probably for a time more nearly 200 years ago than 140.

By the 1850s, due to a number of factors, including the price and availability of cotton elsewhere, protective tariffs for new industries in the north, and the emergence of the abolitionist movement, the Lowcountry had lost its position of national preeminence. As a result, its outlook became more narrowly regional. Political positions hardened; tolerance for a national view of things receded. The institution of slavery was viewed less as a necessary evil — possibly temporary — and more as a positive benefit, one from which Southerners could not turn back. And there were many politicians, like John C. Calhoun, who made an eloquent case for this vision. As Mary Boykin Chesnut wrote in her diary at the time of secession: "South Carolina had been rampant for years. She was the torment of herself and everyone else. Nobody could live in this state unless he were a fire-eater."

Of course, life did go on, populations increased, profits were made. Charleston and Savannah grew, with the addition of magnificent mansions in the Greek Revival style — such as Charleston's Edmondston-Alston House — or the Regency style — such as the William Scarbrough House in Savannah. Small towns like Beaufort raised their own gentry. Nonetheless, planters' soci-

"Secession is the fashion here. Young ladies sing for it; old ladies pray for it; young men are dying to fight for it; old men are ready to demonstrate it."

— From a dispatch to the London *Times*, April 1861, sent from Charleston by English journalist William Howard Russell

eties that might, in the past, have discussed nothing more ominous than crop yields, seed types, and the accounting practices of their agents and cotton factors, now found their attentions turned to defensive matters concerning their slaves, their fortunes, and their state's rights.

In December 1860, led by Lowcountry secessionists, South Carolina separated itself from the Union. The following year, Georgia followed suit. Soon, the harbor forts that watched over both cities — Fort Sumter and Fort Pulaski — were battle sites. Both of the forts can be visited today, and the story of their defense is a dramatic one.

Additional glimpses of the Civil War period are poignantly on display at the Confederate Museum in Charleston, with its frayed uniforms and flags, and in the Green-Meldrim House in Savannah, headquarters of General Sherman, who, after completing his victorious March to the Sea in 1864, not only celebrated Christmas in Savannah but also offered the city itself as a gift to President Lincoln.

A less well known chapter of Civil War history, having Beaufort as its center, concerns the efforts on the part of Northern abolitionists to live among the newly freed slaves and prepare them for full "citizenship." The enterprise, which came to be known as the Port Royal Experiment, followed by several months the Union invasion of Port Royal in November 1861. Over the next several years, a hundred or so men and women took up residence in the abandoned plantation houses, managed the plantations for the government, which

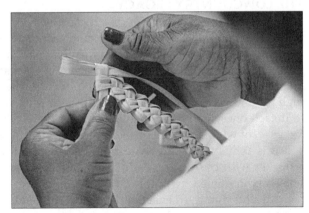

The traditional skills of basket-making are kept alive by women like Ruth Singleton Middleton.

Wade Spees

looked to cotton crops for revenue, and set up schools for slaves young and old in front parlors and cotton houses. One legacy of this period is Penn Center, on St. Helena Island, which has remained a center for teaching native islanders.

After the Civil War, the Lowcountry, now impoverished, turned in upon itself. It was as if people simply went home and stayed there, hoarding their gentility in their city homes as they might their last pennies, taking in sewing, teaching, and boarding guests. In the country they concentrated on making a living again as farmers, albeit far more modest ones. People were thrown back on their resources — their fishing and hunting and farming — and they made do. Only small numbers of freedmen actually received, and were able to hang on to, land they had been promised.

Although phosphate mining, timbering, and shipyards emerged as centers of postwar activity, the economy was slow to repair itself. An idea of just how poor conditions were, right up until World War II, can be glimpsed in the work of Walker Evans, Marion Post Wolcott, and other photographers sent by the Farm Security Administration in the 1930s to document Lowcountry life.

As it turns out, the legacy of poverty was just as crucial in preserving the built environment of the Lowcountry as prosperity had been, in the early years, for bringing it to life. As early as the 1920s, Charlestonians were organizing to save their old buildings. In 1931, the city passed the nation's first Historic District zoning; some 20 years later, the Historic Savannah Foundation was founded to oppose the demolition of the Isaiah Davenport House.

Ever since, these cities' Historic Districts and properties in the country nearby have been central attractions to generations of tourists. They have provided architects, landscape gardeners, historians — even novelists — with material for inspiration. It is a remarkable testament to the Lowcountry's enduring legacy and powers of regeneration that, despite all this intellectual trawling, the region doesn't seem fished out.

THE LOWCOUNTRY LEGACY

Through all its changes, the Lowcountry landscape has retained its immense allure for those who have lived and traveled here, from roving early settlers to today's nomads of the bus tour. Perhaps this is because a sense of history and a sense of place intersect at so many points in the Lowcountry. There is no high ground here. History itself provides the only vantage point, the only way to detach oneself from an insular sense of place that is always responding to forces — of wind and tide, of society and war — greater than itself.

It was and is a place to be desired. Whether your quest is satisfied by filling a bucket with oysters, or paddling a canoe in the marsh, or visiting an old home accompanied by nothing more than your imagination, the Lowcountry offers a rare chance to enact and to observe the subtle rituals of the past, and to take from them the pleasures they've delivered for so long to so many.

"To describe our growing up in the lowcountry of South Carolina, I would have to take you to the marsh on a spring day, flush the great blue heron from its silent occupation, scatter marsh hens as we sink to our knees in the mud, open you an oyster with a pocketknife and feed it to you from the shell and say, 'There. That taste. That's the taste of my childhood.' I would say, 'Breathe deeply,' and you would breathe and remember that smell for the rest of your life, the bold, fecund aroma of the tidal marsh, exquisite and sensual, the smell of the South in heat, a smell like new milk, semen, and spilled wine, all perfumed with seawater."

— From *The Prince of Tides* by Pat Conroy
(Boston: Houghton Mifflin Company)
© 1986 by Pat Conroy

CHAPTER TWO

Getting Here, Getting Around

TRANSPORTATION

The first and most important fact about the Lowcountry is that it is mostly water. Land is an illusion, an accident, nothing to count on. Perhaps this is why the old houses of the region's cities and towns — and the dense feeling of permanence they exude — are so wildly venerated, above and beyond their architectural and historic status. While they certainly represented the values of an elite planter class up until the Civil War, they also appear — now, as in the past — literally to triumph over their surroundings, as if daring wind, water, and the harsh storms of hurricane season to teach them the lessons of frailty.

Wade Spees

Visitors approaching Hunting Island State Park are reminded of what residents know from experience.

In September 1989, Hurricane Hugo did just that. Walls of water pushed 40-foot boats onto the downtown streets of Charleston. For weeks the drinking water tasted of turpentine, resinous and tannic, as fallen trees decomposed into rivers and leached into the water table, which in the best of times has never been more than a few feet away from the salty sea.

And that was just one storm. Day in and day out, water defines the Lowcountry, its aesthetics, its cuisine, its recreation, the siting of its houses, its economy, its history, its means of transportation. The way people get from place to place today still is determined by a force Lowcountry residents know they can never control, no matter how high bridges are built to accommodate the boat traffic beneath, nor how wide the causeway across the marsh. It takes but one glance at a boat stranded on a mud bar at low tide — as often happens — to realize how dependent the region is on the good graces of the tides.

The tides, which cast the riches of sea life toward shore and offered the first

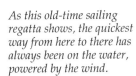

As this old-time sailing regatta shows, the quickest way from here to there has always been on the water, powered by the wind.

Courtesy of The Charleston Museum, Charleston, SC

planters the possibility of harnessed power, bestowed on the Lowcountry a natural abundance of marine and bird life and brought vast wealth in the cultivation of rice. The settlements that clustered around what we know today as peninsular Charleston, flanked by the Ashley and Cooper rivers, grew up there to take advantage of the tidal watercourses. Flat-bottomed plantation barges loaded with rice and, later on, bales of cotton, plied the rivers and creeks to the city harbor. Throughout the Lowcountry, eight-oared bateaux, made on the plantations and navigated by slaves, clove the marsh from one plantation to another, carrying news, goods, and passengers. In Savannah, the river offered both protection to an English colony in the Southern wilderness and a commercial means by which its first English citizens — many of them destitute or castaway — could start their new lives.

For nearly 200 years, water was the best highway in the Lowcountry. Quite often, what roads existed were hardly distinguishable from the water. In 1784, a traveler noted of a "common highway" that "as lonely and desolate as this part of the road is, without shade and with no dwellings in sight, it is by no means a tedious road. The number of shells washed up, sponges, corals, sea grasses and weeds, medusae, and many other ocean products which strew the beach, engage and excite the attention."

As time went on, people of the Lowcountry took nature one step further: they made roadbeds of oyster shell, fashioning a crown at the "center line" to facilitate drainage. These were the best roads around, and in some towns like Beaufort they were in use well into the 20th century. An unimproved road, such as you'd find — and still find today — on the Sea Islands, was plowed through fine sand, perhaps a foot deep, rutted and banked. More than one elderly Lowcountry resident can tell a tale of pushing a Model T Ford through this sand, or of watching the ice melt through the sawdust when the iceman got stuck.

Perhaps as a result of the reliance on water travel, as well as the sheer isola-

Swamps

"Nearly one-third of this vast plain is what the inhabitants call swamps, which are the sources of numerous small rivers and their branches: these they call salt rivers, because the tides flow near to their sources, and generally carry a good depth and breadth of water for small craft, twenty or thirty miles upwards from the sea, when they branch and spread abroad like an open hand, interlocking with each other,and forming a chain of swamps across the Carolinas and Georgia, several hundred miles parallel with the sea coast. These swamps are fed and replenished constantly by an infinite number of rivulets and rills, which spring out of the first bank or ascent."

— From *Travels of William Bartram*, 1791

tion of the plantations and their rural dependencies, a thickly veined series of land transportation routes never really developed in the Lowcountry. Instead of trains and roads and bridges with soaring arcs, there evolved a fleet of small packet steamers that made their way from island to island, picking up passengers, mail, produce, and cotton to deliver in Charleston and Savannah. And ox-drawn carts, or horses, or marsh "tackies" (diminutive horses, something like a Shetland pony) serviced them! When, in 1894, the historian Henry Adams visited St. Helena Island, he traveled first by train, then by carriage over a sand road, then on a shell road, then by foot to the ferry crossing, then over the river to board the steamer *Flora*, which carried him to his destination.

These days, your car will take you almost anywhere you want to go in the Lowcountry (which, for purposes of this book, comprises the coastal plain from Charleston to Savannah, from the Atlantic inland about 40 miles). Driving here is convenient, of course, but the seamless experience of transportation provided by the automobile has displaced an older, deeper feeling — that of reliance on the tides, the whimsy of weather, and navigators who

The men of Charleston's "Mosquito Fleet" rowed bateaux and collected oysters while running with the tide.

Courtesy of The Charleston Museum, Charleston, SC

measured the desire to move against what was possible. It might be said that the rhythm of life in the Lowcountry, dubbed the "Slowcountry" by some, was nurtured in those enforced waiting moments; sometimes it seemed wiser to stay put.

Fortunately, the growth of travel services has produced options to help a modern visitor reclaim this feeling of "down-time," during which you can, in a most modern way, observe your surroundings closely and well. The choices are outlined in this chapter. These days, the boat that takes you in the creek may be a Boston Whaler with a powerful outboard engine, but once you get out on the water, eye-level with the fiddler crabs scudding along the bank, you may as well be riding in an old Lowcountry bateau.

Finally, if you're coming to the Lowcountry from a city, or from someplace where water only runs from the tap, and if you're coming in by plane, take all the time you can to look out the window as the pilot descends. If the plane is circling low, as it often does, notice the watery necklace of islands and savannahs, linked by tidal creeks, that make up the Lowcountry. As an abstraction at 10,000 feet, they seem mere daubs of color, surrounded and embraced by water. The truth is, that's the way they really are at ground level, too.

GETTING TO THE LOWCOUNTRY

BY CAR

Unless your visit to the Lowcountry is limited strictly to Charleston or Savannah or to a self-contained Hilton Head resort — and many delightfully complete visits are — you might consider this trip to be one where having your own car really pays off. The Lowcountry is decentralized; a lot of space separates those "points of interest." What's more, appreciating that very space by finding yourself in it lies at the heart of the Lowcountry experience. That's where you'll find some of the region's subtle treasures: the view of a marsh at sunset, the sight of feeding pelicans as they hit the water, the faded impression of an abandoned oyster-shell road strewn with wildflowers. It is in these very open spaces, in their linked geography, that the sense of times passed and lives abundantly lived will catch up with you and shape your awareness of what the Lowcountry is all about.

From Washington and points north: Travelers from the north can reach the Lowcountry by approaching it on I-95, which roughly parallels the coast. From there, well-marked exits direct you to downtown Charleston (via I-26), to Beaufort (via Highway 21), to Hilton Head (via Hwy. 46, then 278), and Savannah (via I-16). The coastal destinations beyond the big cities, such as Kiawah Island, Edisto Island, Beaufort, and Hilton Head, lie approximately an hour east of I-95. Distance from Washington to Charleston: 512 miles; to Savannah: 616 miles.

From Jacksonville and points south: Like visitors from the north, drivers from the south approach on I-95 and then turn east to the coast. Distance from Jacksonville to Charleston: 241 miles; to Savannah: 139 miles.

From Asheville and points northwest: Take I-40 to I-26, then follow I-26 toward Spartanburg and Columbia. About an hour out of Columbia, you meet I-95. At that point, either continue east to Charleston or turn south. Distance from Asheville to Charleston: 265 miles; to Savannah: 297 miles.

From Charlotte: Take I-77 south to I-20 at Columbia; follow I-20 for a few exits to link up with I-26 east. Distance to Charleston: 200 miles; to Savannah: 240 miles.

From Atlanta: Take I-75 to I-16. When it crosses I-95, go north for Charleston, or continue directly to Savannah. Distance to Charleston: 286 miles; to Savannah: 259 miles.

Once you're in the Lowcountry, you will discover **U.S. Highway 17**, one of the region's oldest roads and still perhaps the most direct, a two-lane ribbon of blacktop that threads its way from above Charleston to Savannah (and beyond) through marshes, old rice fields, and bottomland forests. It's worth cutting off I-95 to get there, or to use it exclusively as your north-south highway. Turnoffs that access the Sea Islands to the east (Kiawah, Seabrook, Edisto, Port Royal, St. Helena, Hilton Head) and the Ashley River plantations to the west (along Hwy. 61) are well marked, as are historic sites, parks, and picnic grounds.

Savannah's newest bridge spans the river between Georgia and South Carolina.

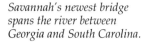

Wade Spees

BY BUS

Greyhound serves Charleston, Beaufort, and Savannah and maintains stations in those cities. It also serves points in between, but here the stops are less formal — perhaps as simple as a crossroads store. As a result, if you're planning to do a substantial amount of traveling by bus, you should consult both a detailed map and the bus schedule. Don't expect to find a taxi or rental-car stand — or even a working pay telephone — at every stop.

The service and price to Charleston and to Savannah from various points are roughly equal; in many cases the same bus goes to both cities. Sample listings of prices and frequency of service (both subject to change) from several cities follow.

To the *Savannah Greyhound Station*, 610 W. Oglethorpe Ave. (912-233-7723):

From New York (22 hours): *Greyhound* (212-971-6363) runs five buses daily from the Port Authority at 625 8th Ave. Only one is direct. The 1992 one-way fare was $125, round-trip $230.

From Washington D.C. (16 hours): *Greyhound* (202-289-5154) has seven buses departing daily from the terminal at 1005 First St. N.E. Only one is direct. The 1992 one-way fare was $95, round-trip $190.

From Jacksonville (3 hours): *Greyhound* (904-356-1841) departs four times daily from the station at 10 N. Pearl St. The 1992 one-way fare was $25, round-trip $45.

From Columbia (4 hours): *Greyhound* (803-256-6465) has four buses departing daily from the station at 2015 Gervais St. The 1992 one-way fare was $34, round-trip $68.

From Charlotte (6 hours): Four *Greyhound* buses (704-375-9536) depart from the station at 601 W. Trade St. daily. The 1992 one-way fare was $46, round-trip $92.

From Atlanta (6 hours): Five *Greyhound-Georgia Trailways* buses (404-522-6300) depart from the terminal at 81 International Boulevard daily. The 1992 one-way fare was $45, round-trip $90.

Travelers interested in the Atlanta-Savannah route might consider the *Nancy Hanks Luxury Bus Line* (1-800-964-1818 in Atlanta, 912-351-6043 in Savannah). The bus departs Atlanta daily at 6:00 p.m., except Tuesday, from Days Hotel at Lenox (3377 Peachtree Rd. NE, adjacent to Lenox Square), and it arrives in Savannah at the Holiday Inn Midtown, 7100 Abercorn St. (912-352-

7100) at 10:15 p.m. The return bus leaves Savannah at 8:00 a.m. and arrives at Lenox Square in Atlanta at 12:15 p.m. The round-trip costs $99, with a 10% discount awarded to riders 55 years of age and older. The round-trip for children with parent or guardian costs $10 for ages 2–4, $49 for ages 4–12. There are free movies, newspapers, snacks, and wide seats.

BY TRAIN

Amtrak travels the north-south corridor, making daily stops at North Charleston (about 25 minutes from downtown), Yemassee (about 30 miles west of Beaufort), and Savannah. On the long hauls from major cities like New York, Washington, and Miami, there are generally two trains a day, departing morning and evening and arriving either late the same day or early the following morning. Traveling by night is a nice option for these 8- to 13-hour trips: when you awaken, you're there.

The rates for sleeping accommodations (economy or first-class, which includes meals) are usually tacked on to the lowest coach fare — and that fare varies, depending on how far in advance you make your reservations. Call Amtrak (1-800-872-7245) or your travel agent for specific rates and schedules. Special packages with airlines might be available, as well as discounts if you can restrict your travel to certain days.

If you're staying near Beaufort, Yemassee is your station stop. Make prior arrangements to be picked up; it's a country station with minimum through traffic. The *Beaufort Cab Company* (803-524-4940) or *Yellow Cab Company of Beaufort* (803-522-1121) can carry you to town. The 1992 fare was $30.

Some 1992 Amtrak fares from selected cities follow.

From Washington: Trains depart Union Station twice daily for North Charleston, a trip that lasts about 8.5 hours. Coach fares run between $111 and $156 round-trip. With sleeping accommodations the round-trip fares are between $211 and $237. Round-trip coach fares to Savannah range from $122 to $173, and from $222 to $270 including sleeping accommodations.

From New York: Trains depart Penn Station for North Charleston in the morning and evening for the 13-hour ride. Coach fares range from $135 to $192 round-trip; with sleeping accommodations, from $235 to $321. To Savannah, the round-trip coach fares are $138 to $213; from $249 to $361 including sleeping accommodations.

From Chicago: One train runs daily to North Charleston, a 36-hour ride. Coach fares range from $138 to $169 round-trip, $393 for sleeping accommodations. To Savannah, a 30-hour ride, coach fares range from $169 to $269 round-trip, $459 with sleeping accommodations.

From Jacksonville: Trains depart once a day to North Charleston, twice a day to Savannah. A round-trip coach fare to North Charleston costs $112; to Savannah it's $68.

From Miami: The morning trains to Charleston and Savannah are direct; later ones may include a layover. The round-trip fare to either city is between $100 and $127.

BY COMMERCIAL AIRLINE

Travelers bound for the Lowcountry can arrive and depart from *Charleston International Airport* or *Savannah International Airport.* Or they can use *Hilton Head Airport,* which is smaller and handles private and commuter shuttle service.

Numerous domestic and international carriers serve the Lowcountry cities, either with nonstop flights or connecting service through the regional hubs of Charlotte, N.C., Raleigh/Durham, or Atlanta. The recent rebuilding of Charleston International into a good-looking and easy-to-navigate airport, and the expansion of Savannah International (to be completed by mid-1994) suggest enhanced traveling convenience.

Once you're at the airport, you may want to pick up a rental car (best reserved in advance). For complete information, see the section on rental cars under "Getting Around the Lowcountry."

BY PRIVATE PLANE

If you're flying on your own, you'll have the option of touching down at one of the following airports:

Charleston Executive Airport (Charleston Aviation Authority, 803-767-1100): on John's Island, close to the resort islands of Kiawah and Seabrook.

Beaufort County Airport (803-525-7647): on Lady's Island, midway between Charleston and Savannah.

Hilton Head Airport (803-681-6386).

Savannah International Airport (Signature Flight Support, 912-964-1557).

BY BOAT

The *Intracoastal Waterway* winds through creek and river, ocean and sound, from one end of the Lowcountry to the other, making for some of the finest and most sublime cruising on the East Coast. The region's history of reliance on water travel, plus the recent development of marinas affiliated with the new resorts, have conspired to produce facilities of top quality and

There are historic neighbor-
hoods — and there are
marina neighborhoods.

Wade Spees

convenient location. If you're planning a water-based trip, it's best to judge the local options according to your particular needs — the size of your boat, availability of on-site repair services, proximity to sightseeing or restaurants or shopping, length of your stay, your price range, etc.

Here are some options. You should also consider word-of-mouth recommendations along the way. For marinas on Hilton Head, see Chapter Eight. If you simply want to make use of the recreational services based at marinas, see Chapter Six, *Recreation*, for some ideas.

Charleston Area
Ashley Marina	803-722-1996
Bohicket Marina Village	803-768-1280
Dolphin Cove Marina	803-744-2562
Edisto Marina	803-869-3504
Mariner's Cay Marina, Inc.	803-588-2091 or
	1-800-446-6194

Beaufort Area
Lady's Island Marina	803-522-0430
Downtown Marina	803-524-4422
Dataw Island Marina	803-838-8410
Fripp Island Marina	803-838-5661
Port Royal Landing Marina	803-525-6664

Savannah Area
Delegal Creek Marina & Landings Harbor	912-598-1901 or
	912-598-0023
Thunderbolt Marina, Inc.	912-352-4931
Chimney Creek Fishing Camp	912-786-9857

LOWCOUNTRY ACCESS

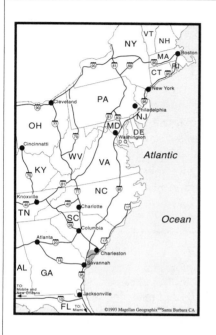

The approximate distances and driving times to Charleston from select-ed cities are given on the charts below. The distance between Charleston and Savannah is 114 miles, so depending on the direction from which you come, you should adjust accordingly. If you're touring within the Lowcountry, however, stopping along the way between Charleston and Savannah in places like Beaufort, Hilton Head, Bluffton, Edisto, or Walterboro, this trip easily may take a day. In general, traveling to specific Sea Island destinations located to the east of the major cities can add up to an hour to your trip.

To Charleston from:

CITY	MILES	HOURS
Atlanta	286	5
Boston	1012	17
Charlotte	219	4
Chicago	938	15.5
Knoxville	395	7
Miami	628	10.5
New Orleans	784	13
New York	775	13
Washington, D.C.	512	8.5

Isle of Hope Marina, Inc.   912-354-8187
Hogan's Marina   912-897-3474

GETTING AROUND THE LOWCOUNTRY

This section will help you to decide how you want to travel within the Lowcountry, for as you plan your trip, the kind of vacation you desire will really depend on how mobile you wish to be. For example, driving a rental car in the Lowcountry can be fun: the landscape is dead flat, and what hazards there are — ground fog that hangs about headlight-height, wild and brief summer showers — are local phenomena so site-specific that you may come upon them and then pass through them wondering all the time why it's not raining "over there."

The Shell Road

"The only thoroughfare by land between Beaufort and Charleston is the 'Shell Road,' a beautiful avenue, which, about nine miles from Beaufort, strikes a ferry across the Coosaw River. War abolished the ferry, and made the river the permanent barrier between the opposing picket lines. For ten miles, right and left, these lines extended, marked by well-worn footpaths, following the endless windings of the stream; and they never varied until nearly the end of the war. Upon their maintenance depended our whole foothold on the Sea Islands; and upon that again finally depended the whole campaign of Sherman."

— From *Army Life in a Black Regiment*, 1869
by Thomas Wentworth Higginson

On the other hand, if your destination is Charleston or Beaufort or Savannah, their **Historic Districts** are best savored on foot or bicycle, or by joining any one of the dozens of tours offered by city-licensed operators. While these guides offer their commentary on cultural, historic, military, and architectural sites, you can be riding in a horse-drawn carriage, a tour boat, a minivan, a motorized trolley, a bus — even a surrey with fringe on the top. Knowing the breadth and variety of these services should help you make your transportation choices. These touring options available within Charleston, Beaufort, and Savannah follow at the end of this chapter.

BY BUS

Greyhound is your carrier between Savannah and the North Charleston station at 3610 Dorchester Rd. (803-722-7721), with stops in Beaufort (803-524-4646) at 1307 Boundary St. Buses run twice daily and the trip takes about two hours and 45 minutes. In 1992, the one-way fare between Savannah and Charleston was $25.50, round-trip $51. The fare to Beaufort was $10 one-way, $20 round-trip. From Beaufort to Charleston costs $18.50 one-way, $37 round trip. There is no service to Hilton Head. For service within Hilton Head, see Chapter Eight.

In **Charleston**, the attractive trolleylike **Downtown Area Shuttle (D.A.S.H.)** makes continuous loops through the Historic District. Its home base is the Visitor Center at 375 Meeting St., where you are encouraged to park your car. Pick up D.A.S.H. maps and schedules here. All-day shuttle passes cost $1; single rides are $0.50., exact change required.

In **Savannah**, there's **C.A.T. — Chatham Area Transit** (912-236-0335). Fares are $0.75; service is throughout downtown. C.A.T. also provides specialized door-to-door service for disabled passengers, but you should call before your visit to arrange the specifics.

BY TRAIN

Amtrak runs two trains daily — one in the morning, one in the evening — between Charleston and Savannah, a trip of about 90 minutes. 1992 coach fares were $24 one-way, between $31 and $40 round-trip.

BY PLANE

The quickest way between points in the Lowcountry is by plane; and if you charter one, you can treat yourself to grand sightseeing as well. The following companies offer a variety of charter, touring, aircraft rental, and emergency services, some of which operate 24 hours a day:

Charleston
Million Air Charleston Executive
    at St. John's Island   803-559-2401
Million Air Charleston International   803-744-2581

Beaufort
Master Aviation, Inc.   803-525-1801

Savannah
Air Savannah   912-964-5655
Diamond Aviation   1-800-476-9181
Executive Business Charter   1-800-666-2359

In 1992, the average round-trip cost between Charleston and Savannah for a twin-engine plane (pilot plus five passengers) was $950, based on an hourly rate. You may be able to make arrangements for a single-engine plane, a jet, and even for one-way service, depending on your needs. The rates for sight-seeing tours start at $25 an hour per person, but they vary widely according to in-air time and Lowcountry location.

BY HELICOPTER

Helicopter service is available for short runs and tours with advance notice, and prices are fixed according to the needs of customers. In *Charleston*, call *Helicopters of Charleston* (803-559-1046); in *Savannah*, call *Omniflight Helicopter, Inc.* (912-964-8307) or *Lighthouse Lift Co.* (912-232-3410).

BY TAXI OR LIMOUSINE

In the heat of the summer, the ice-cold interior of a plush limousine will deliver heavenly relief; or, if modesty suits you better, you may want simply to hire a car and driver for a day. Whether you're touring by the hour or desire longer service, here are some options:

Charleston
Charlestowne Limousine, Inc.   803-554-0414
Low Country Limousine Service   803-767-7117 or
                                 1-800-222-4771

Carey of Charleston, Parker
    Limousine Service, Inc.   803-723-7601 or
                                 803-723-2383

Beaufort/Hilton Head
Jopala Limousine Service   803-838-5888
Allen Limousine Service   803-846-4242
Lowcountry Adventures Ltd.   803-681-8212

Savannah
McCall's   912-966-5364
Regal Limousine   912-232-4189

In addition, there are taxi, van, and limousine services at both the Charleston and Savannah airport terminals; you can use these if transportation is not provided by your hotel or resort area. If you're staying in a B&B, the proprietor may be able to make an arrangement for you or suggest a service. The 1992 one-way taxi fare from Charleston International to the city was $9; to the resort islands, $23. From the Savannah Airport to downtown costs between $15 and $20. The rates are based on one passenger traveling; group rates are available. If your destination is somewhat farther afield, say from Savannah to

Beaufort (a 60-minute ride), expect to pay between $45 and $60. Within the cities, taxis should be called in advance; street pickup is limited.

BY RENTED CAR

Arriving by air and then renting a car during your stay is your best option if you plan to explore the Lowcountry. However, if you are planning to stay in one city or resort, a car might not be necessary. In any event, it is imperative, if you are traveling in the spring — high season throughout the Lowcountry — that you make reservations early.

Get a map to anticipate your turns (the kind the rental agency gives is fine); it's not that there are so many, it's just that there may be but one sign — miss it and you'll find yourself 10 miles out of your way.

Most of the major car rental companies have cars available at the airport terminals as well as in Charleston, Savannah, Beaufort, and Hilton Head. They include:

Agency: 1-800-321-1972 (Charleston, 803-554-8275; Savannah, 912-352-9200)

Alamo: 1-800-327-9633 (Charleston International, 803-767-4417; Savannah International, 912-964-7364)

Avis: 1-800-331-1212 (Charleston, 803-722-2977; Savannah International, 912-964-1781; Hilton Head, 803-681-4216)

Budget: 1-800-527-0700 (Charleston International, 803-763-3300; Savannah International, 912-234-7368; Hilton Head, 803-785-8383)

Dollar: 1-800-800-4000 (Charleston International, 803-760-1112; Savannah International, 912-964-6080; Hilton Head, 803-681-6081)

National: 1-800-227-7368 (Charleston, 803-723-8266; Beaufort, 803-524-9140)

Thrifty: 1-800-367-2277 (Charleston, 803-552-7531; Beaufort, 803-522-9996; Savannah, 912-233-1699)

From Charleston International Airport: Follow the airport access road to I-26 into Charleston. Any downtown exit will take you to the peninsula. If you're traveling north of the city, to Sullivan's Island or Isle of Palms, exit at the terminus of I-26 to Hwy. 17 north. If you're heading to the resort islands, to Edisto, or to Beaufort, take I-26 from the airport to I-526. When it intersects with Hwy. 17, go south. Turns for individual Sea Islands are marked.

Miles: 15 to downtown Charleston; 30 to Sullivan's Island and Isle of Palms; 30 to Kiawah and Seabrook; 40 to Edisto; 70 to Beaufort.

Time: 25 minutes to downtown; 40 to Sullivan's Island; 60 to Edisto, 80–90 to Beaufort.

From Savannah International Airport: Follow the access road to Hwy. 307, then to I-16 downtown. For Hilton Head, follow Hwy. 307 to Hwy. 17, and pass through the Savannah Wildlife refuge to Hwy. 170. Turn right on Hwy. 278, the main road of Hilton Head Island. For Beaufort, take Hwy. 307 to Hwy. 21. At I-95 turn north. Take Exit 8 to Beaufort along State Rd. 88. At the intersection of Hwy. 278 turn left, and then take the next right. Follow this road, Hwy. 170, directly into Beaufort.

Miles: 11 to Savannah's Historic District; 35 to Hilton Head; 40 to Beaufort.
Time: 25 minutes to Savannah, 50 to Beaufort and Hilton Head.

From Hilton Head Airport: Exit the airport and travel south on William Hilton Parkway, Hwy. 278. Exits for individual plantations are clearly marked.

TOURING WITHIN THE HISTORIC DISTRICTS

BY BICYCLE OR ON FOOT

The Historic Districts of Charleston, Beaufort, and Savannah are absolutely manageable under your own steam, and discovering their nooks and crannies independently reproduces in a nearly magical way the scale and rhythm of the past. Furthermore, even though their homes, churches, and ballast-stone streets have been preserved impeccably, they are still neighborhoods, not museums. Getting out from under the windshield or behind the tinted glass

You can cover a lot of ground if you tour by bicycle; and there's no parking problem.

Wade Spees

will help you to understand the real, living context of these places, in which so much has occurred over time. Besides, it's probably dangerous to smell the jasmine and make a left turn at the same time.

In 1992, the rate for renting a bicycle by the hour was $4. Additional services by arrangement might include a two-hour personalized tour with a picnic.

Charleston

Charleston Bicycle Rentals	803-722-7433
East Bay Exchange	803-853-6300
Classic Carriage Tours	803-853-3747

Beaufort

Lowcountry Bicycles	803-524-9585

Savannah

Hyatt-Regency	912-238-1234

Walking tours have come of age in the Lowcountry. Extolling the virtues of one's city in lacy prose is what most old-time residents do naturally, and at the drop of a hat. There are many stories to tell, and an abundance of people to tell them. As guiding has evolved, so have tours tailored to specific interests: architecture, gardening, Civil War history, African-American culture, historic preservation. Some private guides will also craft a tour specifically for your group, with advance notice. In Charleston, a 16-page guidebook of walking tours is available for sale at the Visitor Center and several downtown shops; in Savannah, a guide-yourself Tour on Tape is available for rent at the Visitor Center and in shops downtown.

Here are some ideas. Walking tours generally last up to two hours and are scheduled in both morning and afternoon. Reservations are recommended. In 1992, the price per person ranged from $5 to $15, with children under 12 free or at a reduced cost. An asterisk in the list below indicates that arrangements in advance of your visit might be necessary.

Since some tours may be run out of private homes, you may encounter answering machines, not always with the name of the tour identified. If you leave a message, your call will most likely be returned; or, you can try another tour.

Charleston

Historic Charleston Walking Tours	803-722-6460
Charleston Tea Party Walking Tour	803-722-1779 or
	803-577-5896
Architectural Walking Tours	803-722-2345
Civil War Walking Tour	803-722-7033
Ethnic Charleston — Past and Present	803-556-0664

*Gullah Tours   803-556-7243 (after 5 p.m.)
*Charleston Guide Service   803-722-8240 or 803-723-4402
*Tours of Historic Charleston   803-722-0026 or 803-722-1238

Beaufort
Walking Tours of Beaufort   803-525-9202

Savannah
Tours by BJ   912-233-2335
Gray Line Walking Tour   912-234-8687
*Square Routes   912-232-6866
*Tales of the South   912-234-5884
*Convention Consultants   912-234-4088

BY CARRIAGE

Board a refurbished, horse- or mule-drawn carriage and find yourself imagining the past at a leisurely pace while your guide tells colorful tales. The companies listed below are some among several. Tours generally last one hour and are scheduled throughout the day and evening. In 1992, the price per person ranged between $9.50 and $12; children ride free or for reduced rates. Call for reservations and meeting sites.

Charleston
Olde Towne Carriage Co.   803-722-1315
Charleston Carriage Co.   803-577-0042
Old South Carriage Tours   803-723-9712
Palmetto Carriage Works   803-723-8145

In a Sulky

"I ride right through the morning, from nine till four, without suffering from the heat so much as in one trip to town and back one of our warm, still days at home. I have my white umbrella, there is usually some breeze, often a very cool one; the motion of the sulky puts me to sleep, but the heat of the sun has not been oppressive more than once or twice on this island. If I had attempted to follow all the directions I received before leaving, concerning my health, I should have been by this time a lunatic."

— Charles Ware to his family in Massachusetts, from St. Helena Island, July 30, 1862

From Letters from Port Royal, 1862-1868, _Elizabeth Ware Pearson, Editor — letters from the Northern abolitionists who went to the Beaufort area in early 1862 to teach the newly freed slaves._

The carriages haven't changed much, and neither have the mules.

Wade Spees

Beaufort
Carriage Tours of Beaufort   803-524-3163

Savannah
Carriage Tours of Savannah   912-236-6756

BY TROLLEY

Forget that there are no trolley tracks in sight. The Lowcountry trolleys simply look good. Open-air or enclosed, they offer comfort and an intimate view of the surroundings. In 1992, the price per person ranged from $8.50 to $12, with reduced rates for children.

Charleston
Colonial Coach and Trolley   803-795-3000

Savannah
Colonial Historic Tours   912-233-0083
Old Town Trolley Tours   912-234-8687

BY VAN OR SMALL BUS

Maybe, in the end, in the South, it all comes down to air conditioning: maybe that's the explanation for the "New South." There's no doubt that the comfort and cool of a van or bus tour — in which the guide is like your favorite classroom teacher and the atmosphere as fresh as a fine hotel room — has its virtues. These tours also travel to sites out of the city limits, such as historic forts and plantations. But remember that comfort comes at a sacrifice — larger vehicles may not be able to navigate the old, sometimes alley-width streets of Historic Districts, and the pace is swiftly modern. Here are some choices for the traveler who likes to go deluxe. Tours range from one to 2.5 hours. In 1992, the price per person ranged from $10 to $16, with reduced rates for children.

Charleston	
Livin' In The Past	803-723-0933
	803-871-0791
Gray Line	803-722-4444
Adventure Sightseeing	803-762-0088
Colonial City Tours	803-871-2828
Doin' The Charleston	803-763-1233
Savannah	
Gray Line	912-234-8687
Adventure Savannah	912-233-7770
Old Savannah Tours	912-354-7913
Helen Salter's Savannah Tours	912-355-5245
Negro Heritage Tour	912-234-8000
Savannah Historical Tour	912-355-1970

BY BOAT

Keep in mind that the Lowcountry is mostly water. If you can tear yourself away from the authentic seductions of what has come to be called by planners and preservationists "the built environment," you will be rewarded by views of marshes and marine life that exist in only a few places in the United States. Even better, you may be overcome by a feeling of wondrous detachment as you see the skylines — and, at dusk, the twinkling lights — of the Historic Districts fade from view. Some options for harbor and tour-boat cruises, and rides aboard sailboats and pontoon boats, follow. (Other options appear under "Boating" in Chapter Six, *Recreation*.) The trips generally last two hours, but longer excursions can be arranged. The 1992 per-person fares ranged from $8 to $21.

Charleston
Gray Line Water Tours   803-722-1112
Fort Sumter Tours   803-722-1691
Pelican Caye Cruises (Pontoon Boat)   803-588-6103
Bohicket Charters/Rentals   803-768-7294
Southern Windjammer (84-foot schooner)   803-795-1180

Beaufort
Windborne Cruises (sailboat)   803-524-3163
The Beaufort Belle   803-524-6519
Blackstone's Barge (Pontoon Boats)   803-524-4330
Lady Athena (Pontoon charters)   803-525-6664

Savannah
First Lady of Savannah   912-236-0407
River Street Riverboat Co   912-232-6404

You can still take in the view from a schooner, as passengers did 350 years ago.

Wade Spees

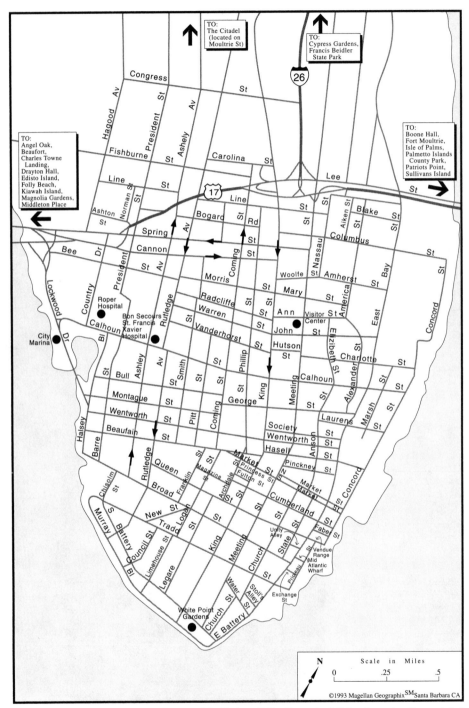

Courtesy of The Charleston Trident Convention & Visitors Bureau (used by permission)

CHARLESTON

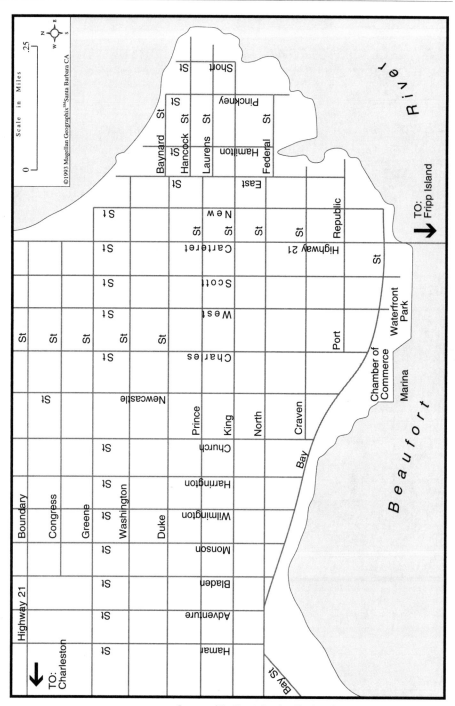

Courtesy of The Greater Beaufort Chamber of Commerce (used by permission)

BEAUFORT

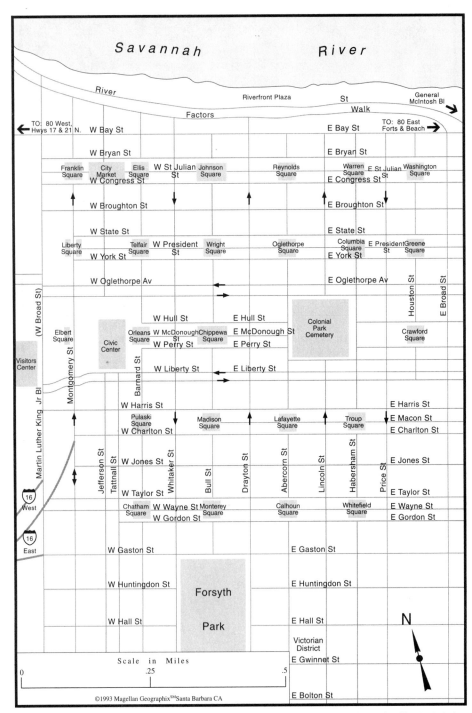

Courtesy of The Savannah Area Convention & Visitors Bureau (used by permission)

SAVANNAH

CHAPTER THREE

From the City to the Seashore
LODGING

When President George Washington toured the states of the new nation in 1791, he was determined to observe life as it was lived on all levels of society. In the Lowcountry, he accepted the hospitality and enthusiastic graciousness of the planters — he was rowed in their barges by slaves dressed in finery, and took meals in their mansions — but he preferred to spend the night in the "public houses" that existed along the main highways, in the simple places frequented by messengers and mail-carriers, small farmers and merchants. He even paid his own way, when he was permitted.

The public houses of Washington's day are long gone, of course, but the modest style of overnight lodging they offered, of clean rooms, shared bath-rooms, and perhaps com-

Wade Spees

George Washington didn't sleep here, but he came to visit.

munal meals, existed well into the 20th century. It was a custom, like most, that had its roots in necessity: during the years of hardship and poverty following the Civil War, taking in guests provided a means of income for families or Confederate widows, who still lived in the commodious old houses. Visitors seemed to like it, too: although Charleston and Savannah had a couple of big hotels, many people preferred the low price and splendid settings of city mansions. Soon "tourist homes" and "guest houses" sprang up to cater to Northern visitors, who were flocking to the area in spring to view the Low-country's celebrated gardens and to experience its faded charm.

Today, the only faded thing you'll find in the Lowcountry is a shirt that's been left out in the sun too long. As the region has brushed itself up, as the old houses have been renovated and the cityscapes renewed, dozens of splendid inns have emerged. Many beaches have been claimed by dazzling resorts. If you stay in rooms in an old house — and they are among the most romantic lodging options — you are likely to hang your clothes in an antique armoire, or view from your window walled gardens that are rimmed with flower beds and dense with camellias and azaleas.

This chapter surveys lodgings in four areas: downtown Charleston, Charleston's environs, the Beaufort area, and the Savannah area. Hilton Head accommodations are covered in Chapter Eight.

Within Charleston and Savannah, offerings are arranged by category: **Hotels, Luxury Inns,** and **Bed-and-Breakfast** style accommodations, which include individual rooms in old homes or their "outbuildings" such as kitchen houses and carriage houses. In addition, sections on **Resorts** and **Rentals** are included for Charleston's environs and Savannah.

Offerings in the Beaufort area are grouped alphabetically, both those in town and those on the islands.

This roster is by no means complete — new places are springing up all the time — but it suggests the range of what is available. For the Charleston and Savannah areas, there are additional listings of **rental agents** who might help you locate a house or villa in a quiet beach neighborhood, or in a private beach resort.

Each lodging option carries with it some unique possibilities for you to consider as you plan your trip. For example, distances between cities in the Low-country are not great, but if you intend to spend most of your time in Charleston or Savannah, to shop and eat out and take part in cultural life, you may not want to travel some distance to the beach for a night's sleep. Alternatively, if your vacation is centered around golf, tennis, boating, and being on the ocean, or if you're traveling with children, it might be wise to make a resort or rental home your base, traveling to the cities by day. Of course, for trips lasting several days, many combinations of lodging are possible.

Given the highly evolved level of tourist hospitality, some generalizations can be made. The large hotels are as well outfitted and provide as much service — valet and room service, bellhops and valet parking, cots and cribs added to the room — as any hostelries in the country. The luxury inns, for their part, seem to be outdoing one another in their touches of detail: decanters of sherry and fruit baskets in your room; evening turn-down service, complete with chocolates on the pillows; daily newspapers delivered with your breakfast; afternoon tea or refreshments served gratis in gardens, parlors, or courtyards. Even the bed-and-breakfast units, where a home's owner is your host, may offer helpful extras such as jogger's maps, a selection of restaurant menus, and tips on great places to walk or sights to see.

If you're traveling with children, some hotels and inns can recommend on-site babysitting services. You should inquire and make specific arrangements in advance. Some places discourage guests traveling with children, but the rules are not always hard and fast and can depend on a child's age, the number in your party, or the season. You will usually be charged for an extra person in the room; additional bedding can be provided. At the resorts, well-staffed activity programs occupy the younger set. If you have other special needs, you should ask to see if they can be accommodated. Pets, for example, are sometimes allowed, but few places really like to advertise the fact; many have regulations regarding smoking, both for the comfort of other guests and to conform with fire-safety laws. Off-street parking is usually provided by the hotel, or other arrangements are included in your tariff, but you should confirm the arrangement.

LOWCOUNTRY LODGING NOTES

RATES

A s the Lowcountry has come of age, the dates of its tourist season have become blurred. Generally, high-season rates prevail except between Thanksgiving and mid-February. The high season is the time for special and highly popular events like Charleston's Spoleto Festival in late May and early June, and house and garden tours in the spring and fall. July and August are sometimes considered to be low season in the cities, and rates may reflect that, although that assumption does not hold true for beach accommodations. The seasonal differences in price run about $10 to $20, depending on the overall cost of your room. Even in the less popular off-season months, the mild weather that characterizes this region brings comfortable days, perhaps even hot ones. There is no definable "rainy season," nor are there many instances of sustained freezing temperatures. Special off-season packages offer good values and, sometimes, a relaxing of minimum-stay requirements.

Inexpensive	Up to $50
Moderate	$50 to $110
Expensive	$110 to $180
Very Expensive	$180 and up

These rates do not include room taxes or special service charges that might apply during your stay.

CREDIT CARDS

> AE — American Express
> CB — Carte Blanche
> D — Discover Card
> DC — Diner's Club
> MC — MasterCard
> V — Visa

MINIMUM STAY

Many of the luxury inns and B&Bs require a minimum stay of two or more nights during the high season. It's best to check when you make your reservation.

DEPOSIT/CANCELLATION

It is necessary, generally, to reserve a room with a credit card, or well in advance by personal check for the amount of one night's stay. Rental agencies that handle individual properties may require more in the way of a deposit. Cancellation policies vary but can be strict, and you could find yourself paying for more than one night's stay if you're lax. Usually at least 72 hours' notice is required, but check with the individual establishment when you book your rooms.

HANDICAPPED ACCESS

The very nature of lodgings in the Lowcountry — houses raised on high foundations, inns in old converted buildings — presents a challenge to easy handicapped access. Many places have made adjustments, by means of ramps and specially outfitted bathrooms. Others are doing so to conform with federal law, although in the Historic Districts ordinances designed to preserve the architectural integrity of the old buildings often conflict with the new access laws. Accommodations having handicapped access are noted; the use of the term "Limited" is meant to suggest that there may be only one or two rooms designed for handicapped access, that adjustments can be made on-site at the time of your visit, or that while access to a room might be available, getting to other rooms such as parlors or dining areas might not be so easy.

OTHER OPTIONS

Chapter Six, *Recreation*, suggests other ways to stay in the Lowcountry. In the "Camping" section, you'll find listings of campgrounds in state parks and national forests, at private campgrounds and RV parks. Reservations are necessary here, too, when they are taken; sometimes, it's first-come, first-served.

LODGING — DOWNTOWN CHARLESTON

For many, a stay in the heart of Charleston remains an indispensable choice for a Lowcountry vacation. Here are some lodging options, arranged by category:

HOTELS AND LARGER INNS

KING CHARLES INN
A Best Western Property.
803-723-7451/1-800-528-1234.
237 Meeting St.,
Charleston, SC 29401.
Price: Moderate.
Credit Cards: AE, CB, D, DC, MC, V.

A clean, convenient place to stay in downtown Charleston for visitors on a budget. There are 91 rooms, including some for non-smokers and some with French doors that open onto small balconies. There's cable television with Home Box Office movies and a pool. It may be modest, but the service is attentive, and the location unbeatable at the price.

LODGE ALLEY INN
Manager: Norma Armstrong.
803-722-1611/1-800-845-1004.
195 East Bay St.,
Charleston, SC 29401.
Price: Expensive to Very Expensive.
Credit Cards: AE, MC, V.
Handicap Access: Limited.

Lodge Alley, one of the first top-notch inns to emerge when the old warehouses on East Bay Street were renovated, remains today a place of supreme comfort, high polish, and well-designed spaces, including a big courtyard. The original, massive beams and brick walls have been left exposed in many rooms. The solid feeling is augmented by heavy doors, thick bedspreads, armoires, ample club chairs, and, in some rooms, big sofas. There are 93 rooms, which run the gamut from modest in size (mostly in the main inn building) to big, plush, and private, adorned with fireplaces and refrigerators. One- and two-bedroom suites offer completely furnished kitchens and can be rented by the night or, in the winter and summer, by the month. A one-night deposit is required to secure reservations. The French Quarter Restaurant serves meals (dinner for two about $30 without wine).

THE MILLS HOUSE
A Holiday Inn Hotel.
803-577-2400/1-800-874-9600.
115 Meeting St.,
Charleston 29401

This is a big, bustling hotel with marble floors and glittering chandeliers, where you can relax and people-watch from one of the dining rooms, the cozy bar, or sitting on a banquette in the lobby. There are 214 plush rooms, tastefully outfitted with

Mail: P.O. Box 1013, Charleston, SC 29402.
Price: Expensive to Very Expensive.
Credit Cards: AE, CB, D, DC, MC, V.
Handicap Access: Limited.

reproduction furniture, and 19 suites that have spacious areas for relaxing or meeting friends. After a day of walking, you may want to take a few laps in the pool or stretch out on the deck with the newspaper. Children and pets are permitted.

OMNI HOTEL AT CHARLESTON PLACE
803-722-4900/1-800-843-6664.
130 Market St., Charleston, SC 29401.
Price: Expensive to Very Expensive.
Credit Cards: AE, CB, D, DC, MC, V.

The building of the Omni and the elegant shopping complex around it signaled a change in the look and feel of downtown Charleston: it's as if the city had finally hit the commercial big time. Fortunately, the presence of this huge (443 rooms), glossy hotel has not overshadowed the small, intimate scale of the rest of the city. It has, instead, delivered luxury services and attracted tourists and convention guests who make it hum year-round.

There are two restaurants and an elegant, popular bar on the premises, as well as a complete fitness center. For all its size and dramatic appointments — a grand staircase, a huge chandelier, massive pots of flowers, shiny marble floors, and rooms of polished furniture — it still has a friendly feel, like a village within a city. Special rate packages, which include tickets to Spoleto performances, are worth looking into.

The grand tradition of Charleston architecture, New World style, at the Omni.

Wade Spees

SMALLER LUXURY INNS

THE ANCHORAGE INN
Innkeeper: Liz Tucker.
803-723-8300/1-800-421-2952.

Just two years old, this inn has distinguished itself by taking on an Old-English theme: stucco-finished walls, tapestries, painted furniture, muslin curtains, beams exposed as they would have been

26 Vendue Range,
Charleston, SC 29401.
Price: Expensive to Very
Expensive.
Credit Cards: AE, MC, V.
Handicap Access: Limited.

in a cottage of Shakespeare's time. There are 19 rooms and suites, some with Jacuzzi tubs and big sofas, or handy card tables for writing all the postcards you promised to send. The breakfast is a splendid buffet, including hot entrees, fruits, yogurts, and breads; afternoon tea seems, well, more English here. The waterfront park is just down the street.

ANSONBOROUGH INN
Innkeeper: Allen B. Johnson.
803-723-1655/1-800-522-2073.
21 Hasell St., Charleston, SC 29401.
Price: Moderate to Expensive.
Credit Cards: AE, MC, V.

This inn is an excellent example of how tasteful renovation, this time of a circa-1900 stationer's warehouse near the Market, can bring new life to old buildings and invest them with modern amenities for guests. It's hard to believe that the airy lobby you see today — crisscrossed by massive exposed beams, dramatically lit, adorned with wildlife prints — and the spacious rooms above it were at one time probably no more than dark cubbyholes, accessed by drafty passageways. Each of the 37 suites has a kitchen facility for light meals or snacks — you can request basic cookware — and varieties of bed sizes so that your suite can accommodate comfortably everyone in your party. Non-smoking suites are available, and Continental breakfast comes to your door.

BARKSDALE HOUSE INN
Innkeepers: George and Peggy Sloan.
803-577-4800.
27 George St., Charleston, SC 29401.
Price: Moderate to Expensive.
Credit Cards: MC, V.

This 10-room inn is set on a side street in the center of Charleston's shopping district, just blocks from the Market and the Gaillard Auditorium. You can leave your car here and make several forays in a day, returning between expeditions to freshen up in the air conditioning, or in a whirlpool tub (five rooms have them), or by the mellow light of a gas-log fire. Formal decorating touches, such as patterned valances and drapes, Scalamandre borders, and tall armoires that hide the television, add to the sense of settled-down privacy. There's a courtyard for Continental breakfast, and a back porch where you can review the day's doings over a glass of lemonade.

BATTERY CARRIAGE HOUSE INN
Innkeepers: Katharine and Drayton Hastie.
803-727-3100/1-800-775-5575.

The main house at Number 20 South Battery was built in 1843, and today visitors stay in rooms beneath and behind it, in the old carriage house. South Battery defines the edge of the historic residential district known as "South of Broad." This is the neighborhood that comes to

20 South Battery,
   Charleston SC 29401.
Price: Expensive.
Credit Cards: AE, MC, V.
Handicap Access: Some
   street-level rooms.

mind when most people think of Charleston, a place of iron gates entwined with jasmine, columned houses set on high foundations, and narrow streets. There are 11 small rooms, all recently renovated to convey a sense of elegant minimalism. Rush rugs offset pencil-post beds; hanging pots of fragrant flowers soften the classic lines of the balcony; and modern conveniences like fax machines, computer hookups, and steam baths are designed to be unobtrusive within a very romantic setting. Continental breakfast and the newspaper arrive at your door, or you can start your day under the rose arbor.

ELLIOTT HOUSE INN
Manager: Al Boerman.
803-723-1855.
78 Queen St., Charleston,
   SC 29401.
Price: Moderate to Expensive.
Credit Cards: AE, MC, V.

This inn is right in the middle of things — between King and Meeting streets, just a block from Broad Street — but when you duck inside, you'll be surprised at how intimate it feels. There are 26 rooms, each one recalling the glory days of Charleston's antebellum period but never shirking today's luxuries. A heated Jacuzzi beckons in the courtyard. If you indulge in the rich breakfast of croissants, you may need to borrow one of the inn's bicycles and work it off!

**JOHN RUTLEDGE
   HOUSE INN**
Manager: Linda Bishop.
803-723-7999/1-800-476-9741.
116 Broad St., Charleston
   SC 29401.
Price: Expensive to Very
   Expensive.
Credit Cards: AE, MC, V.
Handicap Access: Some
   rooms.

Tradition has it that John Rutledge, who later signed the U.S. Constitution, built this imposing house in the heart of Charleston around 1763 for his bride, Elizabeth Grimke. The antique furnishings, parquet floors, high ceilings, carved mantlepieces, and rich fabrics that characterize the house today suggest its original opulence, such as might have impressed George Washington. Nineteen rooms, some designated non-smoking, are offered to guests, either in the main house or in two carriage houses, and each one includes color television and a mini-refrigerator. Suites are even more deluxe: additional sitting room, Jacuzzi tub, fireplaces. Continental breakfast is included, and full breakfast is available. The huge upstairs sitting room, where you will find scrapbooks on the house's history and a collection of antique firearms, is a wonderful place to take tea or sherry. A first-night's deposit is required seven days in advance, with a 24-hour cancellation policy.

MAISON DU PRE
Innkeepers: Lucille and
   Bob Mulholland.

Three restored "single houses" and two carriage houses make up the inn, which is a short walk from the Gaillard Auditorium. There are 15 guest

Tea in the courtyard at Maison DuPre, taken at most any season.

Wade Spees

803-723-8691/1-800-844-4667.
317 East Bay St.,
Charleston, SC 29401.
Price: Moderate to Very Expensive.
Credit Cards: AE, MC, V.

rooms spread throughout, some with private balconies that overlook the garden and courtyard, which are, themselves, among the inn's best features. Here you may imagine yourself sitting at a table as the light fades and the crepe myrtle blossoms float to the ground, sipping a glass of French wine, indulging yourself in a good novel or book on Charleston's history. Mrs. Mulholland is a painter, and her work, as well as that of other artists, graces the walls. The feeling is at once European and elegant but very cozy. Continental breakfast is complimentary, as is a wonderful afternoon tea party.

PLANTER'S INN
Manager: Charles Patty.
803-722-2345/1-800-845-7082.
112 N. Market St.,
Charleston, SC 29401.
Price: Moderate to Expensive.
Credit Cards: AE, CB, DC, MC, V.
Handicap Access: Some rooms.

A location at the intersection of North Market and Meeting streets makes this 41-room inn superbly convenient to nightlife, shopping, the Gibbes Art Gallery, and the historic residential areas. You can walk in any direction and find something going on. On weekend evenings, especially, the sidewalks will be crowded — the closest Charleston comes to having a "big city" feel. The rooms are cozy and plush, with big bathrooms, and many have gas fireplaces and four-poster beds. Non-smoking rooms are available. Continental breakfast is included.

QUEEN VICTORIA INN
Manager: Larry Spelts.
803-720-2944/1-800-933-5464; FAX 803-720-2930.

This Romanesque-style house, completed in 1889, has 16 recently renovated guest rooms and the feel of a lush Victorian setting. There's lots of light and space, and handy, well-stocked refrig-

208 King St., Charleston,
   SC 29401.
Price: Expensive.
Credit Cards: MC, V.
Handicap Access: Some
   rooms.

erators, in even the more modest rooms; the petite suites have whirlpool baths and fireplaces. Continental breakfast comes to your room. The garden and lobby are convivial places where you can meet other guests or just collapse with a refreshment at the end of the day.

Rooms in the shadows of an oak tree, piazzas to catch the breeze at Two Meeting Street Inn.

Wade Spees

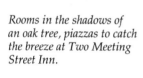

**TWO MEETING STREET
   INN**
Innkeepers: The Spell
   Family.
803-723-7322.
2 Meeting St., Charleston,
   SC 29401.
Price: Moderate to Expensive.
Credit Cards: None.
Handicap Access: Limited.

This Queen Anne mansion, with its wraparound porches and rocking chairs, Tiffany stained-glass windows, and carved oak paneling, just turned 100 years old; but it probably has never looked better. Its public sitting rooms and guest rooms are filled with Oriental rugs and period accessories, and are highlighted by fabrics and wall-coverings in rich, deep colors. There are nine rooms on three floors, all with private baths, most with ceiling fans, some with private balcony access. Honeymooners and couples celebrating a special anniversary often book rooms here a year in advance — especially those rooms with canopied four-poster beds so big that a special set of stairs is needed to climb into them. Continental breakfast is served in the dining room or on the patio. There is no smoking. Reservations are accepted with one night's tariff as a deposit; on weekends, a two-day reservation is required.

**VENDUE INN AND
   VENDUE WEST**
Innkeepers: Evelyn and
   Morton Needle.
803-577-7970/1-800-845-
   7900.

The inn and adjacent West building are located immediately behind Charleston's waterfront park — a great place for a walk — and the inn's rooftop deck and informal bar have a grand view of the harbor. The old complex of buildings offers a

19 Vendue Range, Charleston, SC 29401. Moderate to Very Expensive.
Credit Cards: AE, MC, V.
Handicap Access: Available on first-floor rooms.

range of accommodations, 34 in all, from small rooms off narrow hallways to sumptuous suites that feature fireplaces, marble tubs with Jacuzzis, well-stocked wet bars, even bathroom telephones. If you're traveling with another couple or with family, or if you intend to entertain during your visit, such a suite arrangement might be a good idea. You'll find period furnishings throughout — Evelyn Needle also runs a fine antiques store nearby, Vendue House — and other gracious touches, such as a player piano with several hundred piano rolls, shelves of books you are free to read, and informal chamber music performances in the courtyard. Continental breakfast is included, and dinners (approximately $30 per person without wine) are also offered at the inn's elegant Library restaurant.

BED-AND-BREAKFAST LODGINGS IN PRIVATE HOMES

Two central reservation services provide listings of rooms with private baths in the Historic District, in old homes or in larger, self-contained buildings like carriage houses. There are some bargains, but most rates fall into the Moderate to Very Expensive range. Such accommodations give you the chance to feel like a local, to get behind the garden walls, to have privacy. Some are well suited to larger parties, families, or couples traveling together, and they also may have their own kitchen facilities and gardens. Most have telephones and televisions, but if it's important, you should confirm. Rules regarding deposit and cancellation policies apply. As these services hope to find a "good match" between provider and customer, speak up if you have a fantasy lodging in mind: you may just get it.

Charleston Society Bed and Breakfast (803-723-4948; 84 Murray Blvd., Charleston, SC 29401) No credit cards.

A private entrance to your B&B takes you behind the garden walls.

Wade Spees

Historic Charleston Bed and Breakfast (803-722-6606; 43 Legare St., Charleston, SC 29401) AE, MC, V.

In addition, many homeowners have taken it upon themselves to open their properties to guests. Contact them directly for rates (credit cards noted), availability, and directions.

1837 TEAROOM AND BED AND BREAKFAST (803-723-7166; 126 Wentworth St., Charleston, SC 29401) Five guestrooms in the main house and three in a carriage house, verandas with rockers, full breakfast. Moderate. AE, MC, V.

36 MEETING STREET BED AND BREAKFAST (803-722-1034; 36 Meeting St., Charleston, SC 29401) Two guest suites with private bath in an 18th-century "single house"; kitchenette with breakfast goodies. Moderate. MC, V.

BRASINGTON HOUSE (803-722-1274/1-800-722-1274; 328 East Bay St., Charleston, SC 29401) Four rooms furnished with antiques, in an antebellum house approximately 200 years old; king-sized beds; cable television. Wine/liqueurs served in the afternoon. Breakfast included. Moderate. MC, V.

CAPERS MOTTE HOUSE (803-722-2263; 69 Church St., Charleston, SC 29401) Four guestrooms with private baths in a circa-1730 house listed on the National Register of Historic Places. Breakfast, access to pool, tennis. Moderate. MC, V.

THE COACH HOUSE (803-722-8145; 39 East Battery, Charleston, SC 29401) Overlooks the harbor and a formal garden. Two floors, one bedroom with queen-sized bed, one with twins. Small kitchen and breakfast goodies in refrigerator. Moderate. No credit cards.

THE KITCHEN HOUSE (803-577-6362; 126 Tradd St., Charleston, SC 29401) Two guestrooms with private baths located in a charming restored outbuilding (circa 1731) next to a Colonial herb garden. Moderate to Expensive. MC, V.

LODGING — CHARLESTON ENVIRONS

If you prefer to stay outside Charleston, near a plantation or on one of the Sea Islands, you'll find plenty to choose from. Here are some possibilities, arranged by locale, with separate sections on resort and rental accommodations and beach rental agents.

Outside Charleston

MIDDLETON INN
Manager: Brenda Burns.
803-556-0500/1-800-543-4774.
Ashley River Rd.,
 Charleston SC 29407.
Price: Expensive.
Credit Cards: AE, MC, V.
Handicap Access: Some
 rooms.

The Middleton Inn is located on a bluff adjacent to the beautiful gardens at Middleton Place, about 25 minutes from downtown Charleston. If you want to enjoy utter serenity and privacy, or to take long walks along the Ashley River or at the Middleton Place Gardens (admission waived for inn guests), this is for you. The inn was designed by W.G. Clark, completed in 1985, and it's handsomely modern on the outside, splendidly understated on the inside. There are working log fireplaces, custom-made furniture, soft colors, and large bathrooms. Floor-to-ceiling windows with louvered shutters filter the light and air. There are 55 rooms in the four-building complex, each with a refrigerator. Continental breakfast is included. The restaurant at Middleton Place serves lunch daily, and dinner on Friday and Saturday.

Edisto Island

CASSINA POINT PLAN-TATION BED AND BREAKFAST
Innkeepers: Bruce and
 Tecla Earnshaw.
803-869-2535.
P.O. Box 535, Edisto
 Island, SC 29438.
Price: Moderate.
Credit Cards: None.

The old house at Cassina Point was built around 1847 as a wedding gift for a member of a prominent Sea Island family. During the Civil War, it was occupied by Federal troops. Four years ago, it was renovated to accommodate four guest rooms on the second floor, overlooking the marsh. It's a quiet, lovely place for getting away from the city bustle. Continental breakfast is served in the dining room or on the screened porch. It could get pretty quiet out here — and that's why people come.

Settle in a porch rocker and unwind: that's what Edisto Island planters did here at the end of a day.

Wade Spees

Folly Beach

HOLLIDAY INN OF FOLLY BEACH (803-588-2191; 114-116 W. Ashley Ave.) A small, modest motel, one block from the beach. Nothing fancy. Inexpensive to Moderate. MC, V.

HOLIDAY INN (803-588-6464/1-800-465-4329; 1 Center St.) A big, basic, oceanfront hotel with game room, pool, restaurant, and bar. Handicap access, non-smoking rooms, pets allowed. Moderate to Expensive. All major credit cards accepted.

Isle of Palms

SEA CABINS (803-886-8144/1-800-745-0400; 1300 Ocean Front Blvd.) There are 138 units here, clean and spare. Two-night minimum stay. Moderate to Expensive. MC, V.

RESORTS AND RENTALS — CHARLESTON AREA SEA ISLANDS

The Sea Island resort areas around Charleston are approximately 25 minutes to an hour away from downtown. They are, by themselves, fully self-contained destinations, from which you can travel to the city by day to sightsee and shop, and to which you can return for recreation, dining, and relaxation. In the summer, the islands provide unsurpassed beach access, ample opportunities for tennis and golf, and organized activities for children and adults. For specifics, see Chapter Six, *Recreation*.

What follows here is a list of the *resorts* and an outline of their lodgings. If you are interested in longer stays of a week or more, you also may want to contact some of the *rental agents*, listed in the next section, who specialize in rental of private beach properties, including villas or houses located both within the resorts and outside of them.

Rental accommodations are usually fully furnished, including washer and dryer, but you should check to see if you need to bring anything, if there are special features like handicap access, or if a fee for cleaning after your departure is included. Deposits are necessary, and if you need to cancel, you often must do so up to three weeks in advance in order to have your deposit returned. During summer months, minimum stays of three days (in a villa) to a week (in a house) are often required.

The 1992 summer rental prices for a two-bedroom, oceanfront house ranged from $975 to $1500 per week. Of course, the farther you are from the beach — by a lagoon, say, or the marsh — the less expensive the rate. Prices are generally lower in the winter months, when many resorts offer discounted accommodations packages.

FAIRFIELD OCEAN RIDGE
803-869-2561/1-800-845-8500.
1 King Cotton Rd., Edisto Island SC 29438.
Price: Expensive.
Credit Cards: AE, DC, MC, V.

This 300-acre resort with villa accommodations lies at the south end of Edisto Beach, long a popular summer getaway for South Carolinians. It fits right in with the down-home, neighborly feel of the area, which caters to families and prides itself on its informality. The main attraction outside the resort is Edisto Beach and the summer life spilling out along its shoreline: people picnicking, fishing, bird-watching, shelling, waiting for the shrimp boats to come in. You could also spend a day simply exploring the rest of Edisto Island, with its old houses and churches, and feel you had done enough.

KIAWAH ISLAND INN AND VILLAS
803-768-2121/1-800-654-2924.
P.O. Box 12357, Charleston, SC 29422-2357.
Price: Expensive to Very Expensive.
Credit Cards: AE, CB, DC, MC, V.

This inn is a big, rambling building with wooden decks and breezeways, ceiling fans, and plenty of places to sit in the shade. Children have fun exploring its nooks, and adults appreciate its sense of privacy and quiet corners. Villa accommodations with kitchens (300 units) come in many sizes and are located throughout the resort. The beach is private and 10 miles long; there's an oceanfront pool, several smaller recreation areas, six restaurants, and some nice resort shops. Guests of Kiawah are entitled to advance tee times and court times. One of the best ways to get around is by bicycle, along the 16 miles of paved trails. Non-smoking rooms are available.

SEABROOK ISLAND RESORT
803-768-1000/1-800-845-2475.
1002 Landfall Way, Seabrook Island, SC 29455.
Price: Expensive to Very Expensive.
Credit Cards: AE, D, V.

Guests at Seabrook, a 2,200-acre private country club community, are accommodated in one-, two-, and three-bedroom villas with kitchens. It's very low-key here: you can be left alone to wander the beach, swim, lie in the sun, or catch crabs off a dock.

WILD DUNES RESORT
803-886-6000/1-800-845-8880.
P.O. Box 503, Isle of Palms, SC 29451.
Price: Expensive to Very Expensive.
Credit Cards: AE, MC, V.

Wild Dunes is just 15 miles north of Charleston, a convenient place to stay if you want to savor both beach and resort life and the nighttime excitement of the city. There are 250 units of varying sizes, with kitchens, and at your doorstep all the golf, tennis, and water sports you could want. Nearly three miles of beach lie within the resort; outside it, Isle of Palms has a commercial strip with restaurants and shops.

BEACH RENTAL AGENTS

The following agents may be helpful in locating just the right accommodations for your needs.

Beachwalker Rentals (803-768-1777/1-800-334-6308; 3690 Bohicket Rd., Johns Island, SC 29455) Accommodations on Kiawah Island.

Benchmark Rentals, Inc. (803-768-9800/1-800-992-9666; P.O. Box 773, Johns Island, SC 29457) Kiawah homes and villas.

Carroll Realty (803-886-9600/1-800-845-7718; 103 Palm Blvd., Isle of Palms, SC 29451) Homes and villas by the week, month, or year on Isle of Palms, Wild Dunes, and Sullivan's Island.

Edisto Sales and Rentals Realty (803-869-2527/1-800-868-5398; 1405 Palmetto Blvd., Edisto Beach, SC 29438) Beach cottages and golf villas at Edisto Beach.

Pam Harrington Exclusives, Inc. (803-768-0273/1-800-845-6966; 3690 Bohicket Rd., Suite 2-C, Johns Island, SC 29455) Homes and villas on Kiawah.

Island Realty (803-886-8144/1-800-476-0400; P.O. Box 157, Isle of Palms, SC 29451. Rentals on Sullivan's Island, Isle of Palms, and Wild Dunes.

The Lyons Co. (803-869-2516; 101 Jungle Rd., Edisto Beach, SC 29438) Rentals at Edisto Beach and Fairfield Ocean Ridge resort.

Ravenel Associates Rentals at Kiawah (1-800-845-3911); Seabrook (1-800-845-2233); Wild Dunes, Isle of Palms, Sullivan's Island (1-800-346-0606). Address: Two Beachwalker Drive, Kiawah Island, SC 29455.

LODGING — BEAUFORT AREA

The Beaufort area offers a range of accommodations. Here are some of them — first in the city, then on the neighboring islands.

Beaufort

BAY STREET INN
Innkeepers: Jeffrey and
Leslee Peth.

The Louis Reeve Sams House, built in 1852 and most recently the filming location for scenes in *The Prince of Tides* (it's where Lila lived with Reese

803-522-0050; 803-524-7720.
601 Bay St., Beaufort, SC 29902.
Price: Moderate to Expensive.
Credit Cards: MC, V.

Newbury), is the site of the inn. The three-story building with double porches overlooks the Beaufort River. From each of its six guest rooms, you can watch the boats cruise the Intracoastal Waterway or line up and wait for Beaufort's old swing-span bridge to let them pass. There are fireplaces in every room, window air-conditioning units, private baths, and loads of light. A library filled with books, on the first floor, is a great place for settling down. Full breakfast is included, served in a formal dining room; extras include bikes, fruit baskets, and sherry.

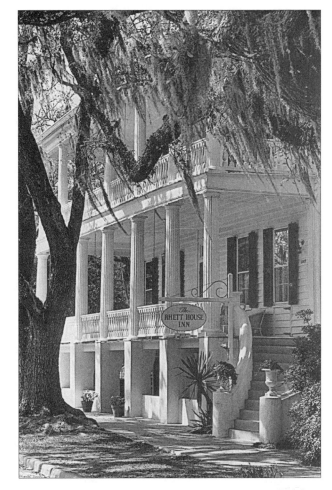

Beaufort's 19th-century prosperity is revived in its grand old homes now open for guests.

Wade Spees

OLD POINT INN
Innkeepers: Joe and Joan
  Carpentiere.
803-524-3177.
212 New St., Beaufort, SC
  29902.
Price: Moderate.
Credit Cards: AE, MC, V.

Four guest rooms are tucked away in this little turn-of-the-century Victorian inn, and the coziest of them are up under the eaves, lit by dormers and skylights. If you sit on the upstairs porch, you will feel embowered, lofted in the treetops, and very much a resident of Beaufort's "Point," one of its Historic District neighborhoods. There's also a nice back patio. Each room has a private bath. Continental breakfast is included.

RHETT HOUSE INN
Innkeepers: Steve and
  Marianne Harrison.
803-524-9030.
1009 Craven St., Beaufort,
  SC 29902.
Price: Moderate to Expensive.
Credit Cards: MC, V.
Handicap Access: Two
  rooms.

The Harrisons left their careers in New York's fashion business for good when they came to Beaufort, but they didn't leave behind their sophisticated taste or their meticulous attention to detail. Indeed, they've lavished these on their 10-room inn. It's a beautiful old place, circa 1820, full of sunlight and breezes (only steps from the waterfront), furnished with antiques and comfortable chairs, prints, and vases of fresh flowers, flanked in the back by a garden and on the side by a courtyard fountain. Many of the rooms have fireplaces or Jacuzzi tubs; all have private baths and color televisions with cable service. The porches, upstairs and downstairs, are dreamy places to have afternoon cookies and tea, or read and rest — there's even a hammock. Full breakfast, including homemade breads and muffins, is included, and if you ask, they will prepare a picnic basket to go. A four-course dinner is served several nights each week in a small, elegant dining room ($35 per person without wine).

TWOSUNS INN
Innkeepers: Carrol and
  Ron Kay.
803-522-1122/1-800-532-
  4244.
1705 Bay St., Beaufort, SC
  29902.
Price: Moderate.
Credit Cards: AE, MC, V.
Handicap Access: Yes.

This five-room inn faces the Beaufort River at one of its prettiest points, just as it turns the bend and heads away from town, making for exceptional views from the Bay Street bluff or its own front porch. If you sit a while, you'll see a steady stream of bicyclists, walkers, and joggers going by, just as they might have in 1917 when the house was built. If you would like to be among them, you can borrow a bicycle, ask for a picnic, and go exploring. On your return you may find Carrol Kay working at her loom in the front room, or guests enjoying the "Tea and Toddy Hour." The rooms, individually decorated to reflect Victorian, Oriental, and country themes, are enlivened by cozy, personal touches. Rates include a full breakfast.

SEA ISLAND INN
(Best Western)
803-522-2090/1-800-528-1234.
1015 Bay St, Beaufort, SC 29901.
Price: Moderate.
Credit Cards: AE, CB, D, DC, MC, V.

Conveniently located downtown, on Beaufort's main street, the locally owned and operated 43-unit motel has freshly decorated rooms with new reproduction furnishings, a pool, and shaded outdoor patio tables. Fax service is available, as is a wonderful map of Beaufort with suggested walking tours. An excellent budget choice.

Beaufort Area Islands

DATAW ISLAND (803-838-3838/1-800-848-3838; One Club Rd., Dataw Island, SC 29920) Dataw is a beautifully planned and maintained private 870-acre residential community, located about 20 minutes from Beaufort on the way to the beaches. It has limited accommodations, but if you are interested in viewing sales property (homesites or homes), you may call to make arrangements for an overnight or weekend stay.

FRIPP ISLAND RESORT (803-838-3535/1-800-845-4100; One Tarpon Blvd. Fripp Island SC 29920) This private, 3,000-acre island, bordered by an ocean beach, is about 35 minutes from Beaufort. It's a family-oriented residential community with golf, tennis, biking, resort shops, a pool, beach club, and marina. You can stay in homes accommodating up to 20, or in one-bedroom villas — more than 160 listings. In 1992, cost of a weekly home rental (sleeps six) started at $750.

HARBORSIDE RENTALS (803-838-4800/1-800-553-0251; 1675-B Sea Island Parkway, Harbor Island, SC 29920) Fully furnished villas and homes for rent on Harbor Island, a small private community with pool, tennis courts, and beach. Closer to Beaufort than Fripp, a good budget choice.

ROYAL FROGMORE INN (803-838-5400; Hwy. 21, St. Helena Island) A modest motel located midway between Beaufort and the beach.

LODGING — SAVANNAH AREA

Savannah and its environs offer a pleasing range of accommodations. Here are some options for in town — arranged by type of lodgings — followed by some resort and rental possibilities outside the city.

HOTELS AND LARGE INNS

DE SOTO HILTON
912-232-9000/1-800-426-8483.

This is a wonderful location in the heart of Savannah's Historic District, a short walk to the riverfront. Some of the 250 rooms have private

15 E. Liberty St., Savannah, GA 31412.
Price: Moderate to Expensive.
Credit Cards: AE, DC, MC, V.
Handicap Access: Yes.

balconies, many are non-smoking, many have great views of Savannah's splendid squares. There is a pool and health club.

A glossy new hotel shines in the midst of old Savannah.

Wade Spees

HYATT REGENCY SAVANNAH
912-238-1234/1-800-233-1234.
2 W. Bay St., Savannah, GA 31412.
Price: Expensive to Very Expensive.
Credit Cards: AE, DC, MC, V.
Handicap Access: Yes.

This big, glossy hotel, with the trademark Hyatt atrium lobby, towers over the riverfront with an unparalleled view of the ship and tugboat traffic. It is thoroughly modern, but not a tower of concrete and glass. There's an indoor pool and shopping arcade, and you're steps away from all the nightlife and daytime shopping on River Street, the main avenue of restored warehouses and commercial marine buildings.

THE MULBERRY
(Holiday Inn)
912-238-1200/1-800-465-4329.
601 E. Bay St., Savannah, GA 31401.
Price: Moderate to Expensive.
Credit Cards: AE, MC, V.
Handicap Access: Yes.

Right across the street from the commercial riverfront, this 120-room inn blends the close attention found in smaller inns with the services of a hotel. Informal piano concerts set the tone for afternoon tea, and complimentary hors d'oeuvres are served. Before you venture out to dinner, you can relax in the heated, rooftop Jacuzzi. There's an outdoor pool, too.

RADISSON PLAZA
912-233-7722/1-800-333-3333.
100 General McIntosh Blvd., Savannah, GA 31401.
Price: Moderate to Expensive.
Credit Cards: AE, D, DC, MC, V.
Handicap Access: Yes.

This is Savannah's huge, new waterfront hotel, and it probably will accommodate a lot of the activity associated with the 1996 Olympics — the water-related competitions will take place nearby. It's luxurious, with large lounges and a soaring atrium, an outdoor pool, and exercise facilities. What you may give up in intimacy and convenience, you'll reap in the service and fresh decor of a brand new place.

Teatime in the parlor at The Ballastone Inn renews the Southern custom of visiting.

Wade Spees

LUXURY INNS

BALLASTONE INN
Innkeeper: Dick Carlson.
912-236-1484/1-800-822-4553.
14 E. Oglethorpe Ave., Savannah, GA 31401.
Price: Moderate to Expensive.
Credit Cards: AE, MC, V.
Handicap Access: Limited.

At Christmas, the Ballastone Inn looks like a scene straight out of Dickens — holly, magnolia leaves, native mistletoe, and garlands of smilax carry its grand front parlor back in time to the townhouse's mid-19th century beginnings, when trade with England and English style held such sway in the city. The English influence is still felt here today, expressed in antiques, chintzes, patterned wallpapers, and porcelain. There are 20 rooms, including three deluxe suites — many of them with Jacuzzis and fireplaces. A handsome full-service bar on the first floor is a unique and wonderful amenity, as are the plush robes provided for guests. Continental breakfast is included. Cancellation of a reservation must take place 96 hours before scheduled arrival, or you will be charged the total cost of the stay.

EAST BAY INN
Innkeeper: Terry Nickells.
912-238-1225/1-800-553-6533.
225 E. Bay St., Savannah, GA 31401.
Price: Moderate.
Credit Cards: AE, CB, D, DC, MC, V.
Handicap Access: Yes.

This inn — a clean, modestly appointed, moderately priced establishment — is at a great location, across the street from the busy retail and nightlife hub of River Street. There are 28 guest rooms in this circa-1853 cotton warehouse, each furnished with queen-sized four-poster beds, reproduction antiques — even coffee-makers. Continental breakfast is included, and children under 12 stay free.

ELIZA THOMPSON HOUSE
Innkeeper: Lee Smith.
912-236-3620/1-800-348-9378.
5 W. Jones St., Savannah, GA 31401.
Price: Moderate to Expensive.
Credit Cards: AE, MC, V.
Handicap Access: Limited.

If you're interested in antiquing, you'll find the conversations here, as well as the accommodations, to your liking. The 25-room inn is owned by the family that runs Arthur Smith Antiques, an old Savannah establishment located next door, and there's a distinctive sense of family warmth (enhanced by a friendly chocolate-colored lab named Duke) amidst beautiful old objects. This was one of Savannah's first luxury bed-and-breakfast inns, and for years it was the benchmark by which others were measured; its Federal-style, English-gentleman's-club feel, its spacious courtyard and fountain, its wonderful location (on a brick-paved street embowered by oaks and lined with iron-balconied townhouses) all fulfill the expectations of visitors who come in search of the cities of the "Old South."

FOLEY HOUSE INN
Manager: Susan Steinhauser.
912-232-6622/1-800-647-3708.
14 W. Hull St., Savannah, GA 31401.
Price: Moderate to Expensive.
Credit cards: AE, MC, V.

The four-story townhouse faces Chippewa Square, one of Savannah's loveliest landscaped urban settings. A sense of the country in the city prevails inside the inn, where prints depicting the English countryside and vases of fresh flowers offset textured walls of "Savannah Gray" brick, the city's classic trademark building and paving material. There are 20 rooms with private baths (five of them have oversized whirlpool baths); most rooms have gas fireplaces and VCRs (to play any of the 300 tapes in the video library), and one is maintained for non-smokers. Breakfast comes on a silver service to your room, or you may have it in the courtyard. The rear patio features a hot tub. Guests often gather in the antique-filled parlor for tea and early-evening refreshments. Children are allowed.

FORSYTH PARK INN
Owners: Hal and Virginia Sullivan.
912-233-6800.
102 W. Hall St., Savannah, GA 31401.

This is a modest, quiet inn with 10 rooms, including a courtyard cottage that can accommodate up to four, but might best be used for a romantic weekend getaway for a busy couple. The main house is a Victorian-era mansion, furnished in

Price: Moderate to Expensive.
Credit Cards: AE, D, MC, V.

the same style with reproductions and four-poster beds. The baby grand piano in the entrance hall seems right in scale with the tall ceilings and long windows. Continental breakfast is included; there's no smoking. During special seasonal events, such as the St. Patrick's Day celebration and the annual tours of homes, a minimum stay may be required.

Modern luxuries like spacious Jacuzzi tubs are nestled within historic beauty at Savannah's inns: here, The Gastonian.

Wade Spees

THE GASTONIAN
Innkeepers: Hugh and
  Roberta Lineberger.
912-232-2869 / 1-800-322-
  6603.
220 E. Gaston St., Savannah, GA 31401.
Price: Moderate to Very
  Expensive.
Credit Cards: AE, MC, V.
Handicap Access: One room.

It had to happen to someone: the innkeepers, who were from Los Angeles, came once to play golf and they never wanted to leave. Within weeks, they owned a property on which they would spend time and money. Their efforts have not been in vain. The antiques and Persian rugs are top-notch, the colors of the interiors soft and muted. They do all the cooking, including two seatings of a full "Southern Breakfast" served in the formal, Georgian-style dining room. Each of the 13 guest rooms has a gas fireplace. All are non-smoking rooms. Many have four-poster beds, and some have Jacuzzi tubs. There's a sun deck with a hot tub, too. Local people are frequent guests, often reserving space months in advance for special occasions. Cancellations must be made five days in advance.

MAGNOLIA PLACE INN
Innkeeper: Ron J. Strahan.
912-236-7674 / 1-800-238-
  7674.
503 Whitaker St., Savannah, GA 31401.
Price: Moderate to Very
  Expensive.
Credit Cards: AE, MC, V.

This late-19th century inn of 13 rooms faces Forsyth Park, next door to the Georgia Historical Society. It has one of the nicest-looking interiors of all the Savannah inns, partly because a good eye selected the fabrics, rugs, and furniture, and partly because the rooms themselves have retained, even through renovation, the sense of scale and period detailing that originally distinguished them. Some

The inn stairs beckon visitors to the gracious world of the Old South.

Wade Spees

people praise the inn because it is so luxurious (more than half the rooms have their own Jacuzzi or soak tub in the bathroom, most have gas fireplaces, and there's a hot tub in the garden). But we liked it because it provides a total sense of privacy. It's comfortable without being folksy, sophisticated without being stiff. There's a lot of repeat business and word-of-mouth referral. Continental breakfast is included; children are welcome, pets are not. Reserve with a credit card, cancel within 72 hours. Ask to see the butterfly collection.

PLANTERS INN
Manager: Deborah Wade.
912-232-5678/1-800-554-1187.
29 Abercorn St., Savannah, GA 31401.
Price: Moderate to very Expensive.
Credit Cards: AE, CB, DC, MC, V.
Handicap Access: Yes.

This was the old John Wesley Hotel near the Pink House restaurant, and if you remember those landmarks, you know Savannah from the old days. Even though it's been updated and refurbished, the framework of the old hotel and its old-fashioned touches — beautiful heavy moldings and an expansive, cheerful lobby with lots of comfortable seating areas — give it a substantial feeling. There are 56 rooms, most of them outfitted with queen-sized beds, and several larger suites which have two private baths apiece. Non-smoking rooms are available. There is an elevator. Room service (lunch and dinner) is provided by the Pink House; Continental breakfast is included.

PRESIDENT'S QUARTER
Manager/owner: Muril Broy.
912-233-1600/1-800-233-1776.
225 E. President St., Savannah, GA 31401.
Price: Moderate to Expensive.

The theme here is United States Presidents — yes, there's a "Richard Nixon Room" for guests — and authentic memorabilia are everywhere. There are 16 rooms in all, nine double and seven suites, and you will find fruit and wine in them when you arrive. Breakfast features several kinds of homemade bread and includes a menu for "the

Credit Cards: AE, MC, V, D, DB.
Handicap Access: First floor; tub chairs available.

fitness oriented." If you are not among them, scan the eighty-plus titles in the video library, set one up on your VCR, and wait until the terrific teatime spread. The first night's tariff is required with your reservation; 48 hours' notice is required for refund. Four non-smoking rooms available. Children are okay, under 10 free, and cribs are available. No pets.

BED AND BREAKFAST ACCOMMODATIONS IN HOMES

Savannah, like Charleston, has two central listing services for accommodations in private homes in the Historic District. Just let them know what you have in mind, and they'll be able to find appropriate lodgings. Credit cards are accepted for some — but not all — lodgings; deposits are required, usually seven working days in advance, with penalties or charges for cancellation. Handicap access is available; some hosts allow pets. Rates are Moderate to Expensive.

R.S.V.P. Savannah (912-232-7787/1-800-729-7787; 417 E. Charlton St., Savannah, GA 31401) Call weekdays 9:30 to 5:30; leave a message at other times. Possible additional $5 charge for reservations of one night only. Offerings include rooms with private baths; private suites, such as carriage houses or first floors of townhouses with garden access; or villas at the beach. Some lodgings with kitchenettes. Bookings at small historic inns also offered.

Savannah Historic Inns and Guest Houses (912-233-7666/1-800-262-4667; 147 Bull St., Savannah, GA 31401) Accommodations in a dozen or so homes and small inns.

RESORTS AND RENTALS — TYBEE ISLAND

Savannah's main beach is *Tybee Island*, a place of great character and supreme informality, with shops, bars, and a down-home feeling. You may find yourself in the midst of what seems like one huge beach party. Condo complexes and inexpensive motels are the order of the day. Be prepared to have fun — concentrate on your tan.

BEST WESTERN DUNES INN
912-786-4591.
1409 Butler Ave., Tybee Island, GA 31328.
Price: Moderate.
Credit Cards: AE, Amoco, D, DC, MC, V.
Handicap Access: Yes.

Tybee's newest motel in a slightly revised version of the chain motel. Some rooms have kitchenettes, some king-sized beds and Jacuzzis. It's simple and clean and close to the beach. It also has a swimming pool.

HUNTER HOUSE BED AND BREAKFAST
Owner: John Hunter.
912-786-7515.
1701 Butler Ave., Tybee Island, GA 31328.
Price: Moderate.
Credit Cards: AE, MC, V.
Handicap access: No.

Four rooms in a circa-1910 house at the beach — sounds like an old-fashioned beach vacation. It's one block away from the water, just 20 minutes from downtown Savannah. Each room has queen-sized beds and a private bath. The atmosphere is very informal and charming.

TYBRISA BEACH RESORT
912-786-4080/1-800-868-4080.
One 15th St., Tybee Island, GA 31328.
Price: Moderate to Expensive.
Credit Cards: AE, MC, V.
Handicap access: Yes.

Condos and villas rent by the night, week, or month here. There are 48 in all, and they're very comfortable and basic. There are tennis courts on the premises.

RENTAL AGENTS AT TYBEE ISLAND

These agents will help you find the perfect beach or vacation spot for your stay:

Tybee Beach Rentals (912-786-8805/1-800-673-9364; 701 Hwy. 80, Tybee Island, GA 31328) Weekly and monthly rentals of properties at Lighthouse Point, Savannah Beach and Racquet Club, and private homes.

Tybee Realty Co. (912-786-7070; Hwy. 80, Tybee Island, GA 31328).

AN ALTERNATIVE

For lodgings that are neither in-town nor at Tybee, you might try the *Sheraton Savannah Resort and Country Club* (912-897-1612, 1-800-533-6706; 612 Wilmington Island Rd., Savannah GA 31410). It's a 200-plus acre resort located on *Wilmington Island* (not the ocean) about 25 minutes from downtown Savannah. Tennis, golf, swimming, boating, bicycling on paths, activities for children (who stay free) are available. Lodgings are in suites and villas furnished with period reproductions, but the overall feeling is not at all stiff or formal. Pets are allowed. The price is Expensive to Very Expensive, major credit cards are accepted, and there's handicap access.

CHAPTER FOUR
A Sense of Place
CULTURE

"A place that ever was lived in is like a fire that never goes out. It flares up, it smolders for a time, it is fanned or smothered by circumstance, but its being is intact, forever fluttering within it, the result of some original ignition. Sometimes it gives out glory, sometimes its little light must be sought out to be seen, small and tender as a candle flame, but as certain."

— Eudora Welty, 1944

From the earliest days of English settlement, the rhythm of life in the coastal Lowcountry, and the culture that supported it, have come forward through time intact and of a piece — a presence with roots in the land, in the activities of those who worked it and dominated it, and in cities where its rich expression was manifested in homes, public buildings, and artistic endeavors.

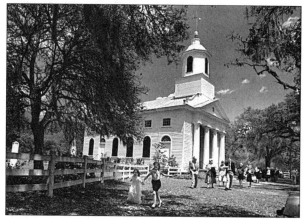

Wade Spees

Old churches still draw generations of worshipers.

Today this cultural legacy informs the smallest turn of phrase and the largest civic hopes of Lowcountry people. All that can be seen and felt in the region — much that has been, and is being, written about it by novelists — is lit from the hot forge of the past: from relationships between blacks and whites; from the symbolic icons of home, flag, and family; from the residue of feeling that the Lowcountry was for so long considered, both by those who lived there and by visitors, to be a place apart, with values so closely held that residents would, and did, die for them.

Compounding this sense of intense intimacy with the past is the indisputable fact of the physical expression of that past in the built and natural landscape, from the narrow alleys of Charleston and the squares of Savannah to the marshes and fields of the Sea Islands. While it is one thing to tell a story of the olden days, it is quite another to be able to locate and read that narrative in rural and urban settings that still exist and reverberate with meaning. In the broadest sense, this is the life of culture in the Lowcountry. It is not confined to objects or artifacts — although there are plenty of them — but rather exists because people still believe that a sense of history and place distinguishes their lives.

The Lowcountry has stayed small — some might say defiantly so — in a way different from any other region in the United States. After its heyday as the center of Southern culture, during the 18th and early 19th centuries, it did not feel compelled to reinvent itself over time. The traditional cultural pleasures — dress balls, small concerts, the cultivation of gardens, card playing, church picnics, and literary societies — continued for generations, through the antebellum years and even after the Civil War into the 20th century. The life of the plantation, in which families would be absent from the city except in seasonal bursts, permanently heightened the importance of domestic culture. It has been said that without the plantations, set at some distance from each other, the tradition of Southern hospitality and the domestic art of "visiting," so important to this day, would never have been developed.

Most obviously, the Lowcountry stayed the same for so long because it liked what it was, preferred its provincial insularity, the shadow of former greatness, to the vulgarity it perceived elsewhere. Especially in the early years of this century, the Lowcountry was too worn down to do much but carry on in the old ways, its people habituated to the familiar social roles they had inherited long after the society that had assigned those roles had been wiped out. They couldn't step out of their skin, and, for the most part, didn't want to. If they were "too poor to paint, too proud to whitewash," then so be it.

After World War II, at a time when Charleston began to feel the influence of social and economic changes elsewhere in the nation, and integration was federally mandated, Lowcountry residents with the means and interest to do so were faced with reconciling their historic cultural identity, on which they relied so deeply, with a post-war world that placed increasing emphasis on money, mobility, and a celebration of things modern and new. The time had come to set the activities associated with historic preservation, neighborhood renovation, and tourist attraction on a larger and more public stage. This the Lowcountry residents did, and in the process they became what might be called curators of their own collection.

The success of their efforts, which by themselves pretty nearly defined cultural activity for 25 years, meant that the authentic past was not only brought forward for all to see, but also "mainstreamed." Cities like Charleston, Savannah, and Beaufort and their adjacent rural areas seem to have escaped the trend that architectural critic Ada Louise Huxtable called the "theming of America," in which "authentic reproductions" of the past are constructed from scratch, squeaky clean. Lowcountry culture has no need to be replaced by a neater version of itself in order to be understood. The fact that the region has a plentiful supply of the resources that link individuals to themselves and

Charleston's stately icons may deserve veneration, but they're fun to hop on, too.

Wade Spees

their past has made for a strong culture — one that allows ample room both for preservation and for prudent modification and adaptation.

As a result, cultural activities today combine a continuous brushing up and reinvestigating of the old with a cultivation of the new. For every historic house in the Lowcountry, there seems to be an art gallery; for every garden tour, a lecture on slave life. Overall, the pitch is higher, the variety greater; the traditions of hospitality and graciousness have been transformed into visitor service. In that sense, the Lowcountry really has really come of age.

Where blossoming gardens were once celebrated informally, now programs and walks guide a visitor's appreciation. In Charleston, the annual Southeastern Wildlife Exposition gathers together such diverse enthusiasts of the outdoors as decoy carvers, watercolorists, hunters, and conservationists. For several weeks in May and June, the Spoleto Festival, not yet 20 years old, transforms the city with its dozens of operatic, theatric, dance, and musical performances of international stature. Modest sailing regattas have become Water Festivals; annual tours of private historic homes draw thousands; the spirituals of the praise houses and the blues of the cotton fields are performed on grand stages; harvest days on the Sea Islands are established annual celebrations of pride.

While it is true that the experience of culture in the Lowcountry relies deeply on the region's presence as a place in memory and the imagination, its people now seem willing — perhaps for the first time in their long history — to accommodate the unremembered, the future, without the feeling that the past is being given up.

Here is an alphabetical roster of the main cultural attractions. For a month-by-month listing of seasonal cultural and recreational events, see the end of this chapter; for additional events special to Hilton Head, see Chapter Eight.

St. Michael's Church steeple dominates Charleston's main intersection, Meeting at Broad.

Wade Spees

ARCHITECTURE

Appreciating architecture in the Lowcountry is a little like the experience of being a parent: you can read about it, you can hear it described fully and well, you can understand why people do it, and give it a rational and historic context. But you haven't begun to feel its power until you face it for yourself, four-square, on a lazy walk in the city, or glimpsed from your car on a day trip through the countryside.

In Charleston or Savannah, there's no reason — as there often is in other cities — to hit the ground running when you arrive. Whether or not you visit every historic house and church, or mentally catalogue their interior detailing, is not that important. You can buy an exquisite book for that (see Chapter Nine, *Information,* for suggestions, or visit a bookstore listed in Chapter Seven, *Shopping*). What's special about this region is that you can experience architecture in drifts, in vistas, as a harmonious whole that came into being as a response to the natural conditions of climate and the studied ones of prevailing fashions.

Further, the very settings of these built gems instill appreciation for their scale and for the surviving scale of the environment around them. This you can experience only by being there. There is absolutely no substitute for walking in the Historic Districts of Charleston, Savannah, and Beaufort. In the Lowcountry, in which so much life still occurs amidst the old buildings and inside them, visitors are given the privilege to feel as residents do: nothing is frozen in amber here, and life moves in and around these icons — people going to work, to school, home to lunch, to the market.

If you have the time and the means of transportation to get off the beaten track, visits to historic towns between Charleston and Savannah will give you a feeling for the continuity of Lowcountry life as it ebbed and flowed around

Fitness trends may come and go, but Beaufort's old houses remain.

Wade Spees

the big market cities. What you will see are old houses and churches in modest, neighborhood settings — places that often were first established as summer colonies. What they have to offer is not necessarily pulled together for tourists in the sense of organized daily tours, although notable buildings are designated by historic plaques, and maps are available at local chambers of commerce. While their assets may not be as self-evident or concentrated as those in the larger cities, these are the towns that give Lowcountry residents their deep sense of pride, their commitment to local history, their love for the "home place." They include Summerville and Mt. Pleasant (in the Charleston area), Edisto Island, Bluffton (near Hilton Head), and the inland towns of Hampton and Walterboro. Two excellent books to guide you in the backcountry are *Brown's I-95 Guide* and *Historic Resources of the Lowcountry*, both available in area bookstores. You can also request touring information from local sources (see Chapter Nine, *Information*).

If you have more than a passing interest in architecture, you might well approach the riches of the Lowcountry with a game plan and spend your time playing it out. Do you particularly like the small rooms and thickly carved mantels of the Colonial Period? Or perhaps the fine lightness of touch and classical decoration introduced by the Adam brothers? Or Regency rooms, with their free-hand imposition of Greek motifs? Do open-air living spaces afforded by piazzas and walled gardens appeal to you? Ironwork? Brick or clapboard? Small country churches or city steeples? Interiors or exteriors? Grand plantations or modest row houses? Rooms adorned with 18th-century furniture or ones that remain bare, objects in and of themselves? For suggestions on buildings that express these aesthetic considerations, see the "Historic Homes" listings later in this chapter.

If you're a generalist, it may be enough to visit one or two house museums, take a walking tour (for suggestions, see Chapter Two, *Transportation*), and touch base at the *Visitor Centers* in *Charleston* (375 Meeting St.) or *Savannah* (303 Martin Luther King, Jr. Blvd.). The growth of the preservation movement, as well as the arrival of new generations of visitors who possess academic or hands-on experience with old buildings and the decorative-art tradition, has invested these modern exhibit halls with intelligence and authority. Good audio-visual presentations, colorful display cases, and racks of brochures offer a useful historical overview. You can park your car: carriage tours, city shuttle buses, and mini-van tours with guides collect and discharge passengers here.

Charleston, because it is the area's oldest city, has a deep inventory of houses — from its famous "single houses," (one room wide standing endways to the street) to mansions with double piazzas that dominate harborside sites. Savannah's buildings echo the geometry of its squares and the influence of William Jay, the Regency-period architect. They seem more formal and restrained in design, colored from a muted palette of grays, greens, and tans. Beaufort is compact, village-sized: many of its antebellum homes were planter's summer residences. Beaufort could be your midday stop, after you've spent time in Charleston and have another day for Savannah.

When you're out and about, you will find that local people appreciate your interest and are happy to chat; but since most of the historic homes are privately owned, it is helpful to remember that while photographing is fine, entering gardens or taking your car up the driveway are not. For such closer looks, visit the area's many house museums, where knowledgeable docents are pleased to answer your questions. In addition, there are annual tours of private homes and gardens, sponsored by local preservation organizations or churches. The chambers of commerce in each locale will have the dates. They usually take place in March and October, last all day, and range in price from $15 to $25.

DANCE

Dance performances take place through most of the year, especially during the springtime Spoleto Festival in Charleston and during the spring and fall seasons elsewhere. Call ahead for schedules and ticket information.

Charleston

Charleston Ballet Theatre (803-723-7334; 281 Meeting St.).
Robert Ivey Ballet (803-556-1343; 1910 Savannah Hwy.).

The Charleston Ballet Theatre enhances the city's reputation for performing arts. This picture promoted "Broadway and Balanchine."

Wade Spees

Beaufort

Byrne Miller Dance Theatre (803-524-9148; 2400 Wilson Dr.).

Savannah

Ballet South (912-354-3899; 201 Varn Dr.).
Savannah Ballet Theatre (912-236-2894; P.O. Box 23604, Savannah GA 31403).

FILM

First-run movie houses tend to be located in malls away from downtown, and they account for most of the region's audiences. In the urban centers, only one or two movie theaters remain — *Stage One Cinema* in <u>Charleston</u> is a gem, with extra-special beverages and snacks — but from time to time, especially in Charleston during Spoleto, special film series are scheduled in college auditoriums or libraries. Check local newspaper listings — Charleston's *Omnibus* and Savannah's *Georgia Guardian* are best — or look for handbills posted around town.

In Charleston, one movie that plays year-round, several times daily, is *"Dear Charleston."* Make a point of seeing it (it's fine for kids, too). It runs about an hour. You'll enjoy its whimsy, its evocation of days gone by, and its irreverent portrait of a wildly self-confident society that can laugh at itself. The film is at the *Preservation Society* (803-723-4381; 147 King St. Admission: Adults $3.50; children $2).

Charleston Area

Ashley Landing Cinema I II and III (803-571-2380; Ashley Landing Mall).
Aviation Avenue Cinemas (803-747-4800; 2390 Aviation Ave., North Charleston).
Citadel Mall Cinema I-VI (803-763-7052; Citadel Mall).
James Island Cinema Theatre (803-795-9499; 1743 Central Park Rd.).
Mount Pleasant Cinema 1 2 & 3 (803-884-3614; 1001 Johnnie Dodds Blvd.).
Northwoods Mall Cinema (803-569-6794; Northwoods Mall).
South Windermere Cinema 1 & 2 (803-571-0230; South Windermere Shopping Center).
Stage One Cinema (803-722-1900; 30 Cumberland St., downtown).
Ultravision 1 & 2 Theatres (803-556-4200; 1812 Sam Rittenberg Blvd.).

Beaufort

Plaza 8 Theatres (803-524-9468; Beaufort Plaza, Hwy. 170).
Plaza 21 Drive-In Theatre (803-846-4500; Hwy. 21).

Savannah

Abercorn Cinema (912-925-2383; 12056 Abercorn St.).
Eisenhower Cinemas (912-352-3533; 1100 Eisenhower Dr.).
Tara Cinemas (912-925-2135; Largo Dr.).
Victory Square Cinemas (912-355-0110; 1909 E. Victory Dr.)

GALLERIES

Many of the galleries featuring the best work of Lowcountry artists are listed in Chapter Seven, *Shopping*. A visit to any of those listed below will enhance your appreciation of the region; the works on exhibit may or may not be for sale.

The presence of the Savannah College of Art and Design has led to many new galleries and frequently changing exhibitions of work, both in college buildings and throughout that city. When in Savannah, check local newspapers for up-to-the-minute information on exhibits.

Charleston

Elizabeth O'Neill Verner Studio and Museum (803-722-4246; 38 Tradd St.)
The artist, who was in her 90s when she died in 1979, produced etchings,

pastels, and pencil drawings of a Charleston life that seems long past. Visiting her studio is like a step back in time. It is also home of the Tradd Street Press, which publishes the work of Mrs. Verner, her daughter, Elizabeth Verner Hamilton, and other books of Lowcountry poetry, stories, and local history.

Gibbes Museum of Art (803-722-2706; 135 Meeting St.) The permanent collection includes views of Charleston from the 18th century to the present. Not to be missed are the exquisite miniatures by Charles Fraser of the most prominent citizens of the city's early days, and the watercolors of 20th-century plantation and rural life by Alice Ravenel Huger Smith. There is also a fine museum shop. Open Tues.–Sat. 10–5, Sun.–Mon. 1–5. Admission: Adults $2; children $0.50.

Savannah

Exhibit A Gallery (912-238-2480; 342 Bull St.) The gallery of the Savannah College of Art and Design, featuring work by students, faculty, and occasional guests.

Telfair Academy of Arts and Sciences (912-232-1177; 121 Barnard St.) Savannah's main art gallery, housed in a Regency-style mansion, with a permanent collection of American and European Impressionist paintings and frequent exhibits of modern art. Open Tues.–Sat. 10–5, Sun. 2–5. Admission: Adults $2.50; children $0.50.

Telfair Academy, Savannah's art museum for more than 100 years, has educated generations of viewers with classic and contemporary art.

Wade Spees

HISTORIC HOMES, GARDENS & RELIGIOUS SITES

Whether or not you visit a historic site and how much time you spend there will, of course, depend on your interest and schedule, whether you're traveling with children, and whether you have your own car. It may be preferable, for example, to do just one *big* thing in a single day (a boat ride to Fort Sumter, a visit to a plantation garden), plus two *smaller* ones (see a house museum or church, take a walking tour, picnic in a park).

The distances within cities are not great; traveling to gardens, lighthouses, or island sites from cities takes about 30 minutes. From Charleston to Savannah is about a two-hour trip by car.

The sites in the following list are open all year, unless otherwise noted. Admission fees and hours are as of 1992. Keep in mind that the last tours of the day start approximately 30 minutes before closing time. Visitors generally are welcome to enter religious sites, but are asked to observe the worship schedule and related courtesies of visitation, as few of the sites offer regular tour services.

Charleston Area

AIKEN-RHETT HOUSE
803-723-1159.
48 Elizabeth St.
Mon.–Sat. 10–5, Sun. 1–5.
Admission: Adults $5;
　children $3; discounted
　admission with combi-
　nation tickets to other
　Charleston Museum
　properties.

Built in 1817, representing high-style Greek Revival and Rococo interiors, the Aiken-Rhett House is preserved in a somewhat less formal way than other houses. It's full of atmosphere, a little worn at the edges, and still undergoing restoration. During the fiercest shelling of Charleston in the Civil War, it was the headquarters of Confederate General P.G.T. Beauregard, a purpose for which it was well suited by virtue of its scale, design, and location off the Battery.

AUDUBON SWAMP GARDEN
See "Nature Preserves" in Chapter Six, *Recreation*.

BOONE HALL PLANTA-
　TION
803-884-4371.
Hwy. 17, 8 miles N of
　Charleston.
April 1–Labor Day:
　Mon.–Sat. 8:30–6:30,
　Sun. 1–5; in low season:
　Mon.–Sat. 9–5, Sun. 1–4.
Admission: Adults $6;
　children $2.

Of particular interest at this plantation are the mid-18th century slave cabins (these housed house slaves and skilled craftsmen, not the field hands) and the magnificent avenue of oaks, which runs three-quarters of a mile. Boone Hall has been the setting for many scenes in the television mini-series based on John Jakes's novel, *North and South*.

CALHOUN MANSION
803-722-8205.
16 Meeting St.
Wed.–Sun. 10–4.
Admission: Adults $10;
   children $5.

Victoriana in all its glory — ornate plaster and woodwork, etched glass, a ballroom — Calhoun Hall is a rarity in Charleston, for it was built at a time (1876) when few people had the means to build 25-room mansions.

CONGREGATION BETH ELOHIM
803-723-1090.
90 Hasell St.
Mon.–Fri. 10–12.

The country's oldest synagogue in continuous use, built in 1840 to replace one that burned, this is a superb example of Greek Revival architecture.

CYPRESS GARDENS
See "Nature Preserves" in Chapter Six, *Recreation.*

DRAYTON HALL
803-766-0188.
Hwy. 61, 9 miles NW of
   Charleston.
Open daily: March–Oct.
   10–4; other months 10–3.
Admission: Adults $6;
   children $3; free to
   members of the National
   Trust for Historic
   Preservation.

It's a measure of the stunning greatness of this 18th-century Georgian-Palladian dwelling that it exists in an architectural class by itself — interior and exterior — even as it remains unfurnished, unrestored, largely unchanged (just stabilized), bare, and magnificent. Built in 1738 and set on a lovely Ashley River site, it is often called one of the most architecturally significant dwellings in America. It is jointly owned by the National Trust for Historic Preservation and the state of South Carolina. Tours are on the hour; written tours in French, German, and English are available. The tour guides are superior — not to be missed even in the pouring rain.

EDMONDSTON-ALSTON HOUSE
803-722-7171.
21 East Battery.
Mon.–Sat. 10–5, Sun.
   1:30–5. Last tour at 4:40.
Admission: Adults $5; $8
   with combination ticket
   to the Nathaniel Russell
   House.

First built in 1828 by one wealthy man, later enlarged by another, it reveals — in architecture, lavish decoration, documents, family furnishings, silver, and china — the best of what money could buy. You get a sense that, when the Civil War came, this is the life that was lost, and its loss regretted. An incomparable harbor view.

Closing the shutters to protect the silk curtains: housekeeping as it was in the mid-19th century.

0Wade Spees

**EXCHANGE BUILD-
ING/PROVOST
DUNGEON**
803-792-5020
122 East Bay St.
Daily 9:30–5.
Admission: Adults $3;
children $1.50.

Even before 1771, when this building was completed, the site on which it stands was used for a variety of public purposes in the young colony. Its commanding location, at the foot of Broad Street, defined both an end boundary for the city and also, from the water, its point of arrival. In terms of sheer geography, it looms large. It's the kind of outsized place that was, and still is, used for huge receptions. During the Revolution, the British held political and military prisoners in the basement.

**FRENCH PROTESTANT
(HUGUENOT) CHURCH**
803-722-4385.
136 Church St.

French Huguenots fleeing religious persecution worshiped in Charleston as early as 1687. This church, built on the site of earlier ones, dates from 1845.

Charleston's French Huguenot Church, first established in 1687, still offers a French liturgy service every spring.

Wade Spees

Fear of fire in homes relegated cooking to nearby "kitchen houses" like this one behind the Heyward-Washington House.

Wade Spees

**HEYWARD-
WASHINGTON
HOUSE**
803-722-0354.
87 Church St.
Mon.–Sat. 10–5, Sun. 1–5.
Admission: Adults $5;
children $3; discounted
admission with combi-
nation ticket to other
Charleston Museum
properties.

Built in 1772 by a rice planter whose son, Thomas Heyward, Jr., signed the Declaration of Independence, this house was also the head-quarters of George Washington during his visit to the Lowcountry in 1791. Its collection of furniture, including several 18th-century Charleston-made pieces and the magnificent Holmes bookcase, is unmatched. The back courtyard still features its dependencies, open to view, and a small garden.

**JOSEPH MANIGAULT
HOUSE**
803-723-2926.
350 Meeting St.
Mon.–Sat. 10–5, Sun. 1–5.
Admission: Adults $5;
children $3; discounted
admission with combi-
nation ticket to other
Charleston Museum
properties.

The outside of this structure is three stories of brick; the inside is something like shaped light. Designed by native son Gabriel Manigault for his brother and completed in 1803, this house, exuding both formality of plan and spontaneity in gesture, shows the nature of beauty and taste favored by elite planters who may have been, as Gabriel Manigault was, educated in Europe and exposed there to sophisticated design ideas and decorating schemes. The grounds, marked out according to their original uses, make for a cohe-sive site.

**MAGNOLIA
PLANTATION
AND GARDENS**
803-571-1266.

Two houses, one of them burned by Sherman's army, preceded the current building on this property which was floated here by barge in 1873.

Hwy. 61, 10 miles NW of
  Charleston.
Daily 9–5:30.
Admission: Adults $8 (an
  additional $3 to tour the
  Audubon Swamp);
  teenagers $6; children
  4–12 $4. Admission to
  the house $4.

The entire tract dates back to the time of the earliest settlers, the Barbadian planters who relocated on the Ashley River. The legacy here is gardens, acres of them, reflecting (in layout and specimen planting) two centuries of horticulture. The gardens include 250 varieties of *Azalea Indica* and 900 varieties of *Camellia Japonica*; there are bike and walking paths, a petting zoo, a canoe trail, and picnic areas. House tours and nighttime programs in the illuminated garden.

Wade Spees

In March, a broad hillside of flowering azaleas borders the rice mill pond at Middleton Place.

MIDDLETON PLACE
803-556-6020.
Hwy. 61, 14 miles NW of
  Charleston.
Daily 9–5.
Mon.–Sat. 10–5, Sun. 25.
Admission Mar.–June:
  Adults $10; children $5.
  July–Feb.: adults $9;
  children $4.50. House
  tours: additional $5 per
  person.

The formal gardens, laid out in 1741 and constructed by 100 slaves over a period of a decade, feature terraces, camellia allées, butterfly lakes, hillside drifts of azaleas, and acres of landscaped paths. The site is so grand in conception that it can be appreciated even when little is in bloom: the geometry of the original plan itself is breathtaking. The main house was sacked by Union forces; tours of a remaining wing evoke Revolutionary and antebellum life, as do the working stable yard and outbuildings. A gift shop and restaurant are on the premises.

**NATHANIEL RUSSELL
  HOUSE**
803-723-1623.
51 Meeting St.
Mon.–Sat. 10–5, Sun. 25.

People have no doubt been admiring this house from the day it was completed (ca. 1808), and with good reason. It represents the high point of the Adam style in the city — its stairway appears to float, a lovely combination of function and fantasy

Admission $5; $8 with combination ticket to the Edmondston-Alston House.

— and it is one of the most th and exquisitely executed neocl the nation. A property of the I Foundation.

**ST. MICHAEL'S
EPISCOPAL CHURCH**
803-723-0603.
Meeting St. at Broad St.
Daily 9–4:30.

This church is still the center of many Charlestonians' lives, as it has been since 1761. With its old bells and gleaming steeple, it is part of the famous "Four Corners of Law" in downtown Charleston, an intersection that represents, in religious, civic, judicial, and federal buildings, the order imposed on society. There is a tranquil walled graveyard to explore, too.

**ST. PHILIP'S
EPISCOPAL CHURCH**
803-722-7734.
146 Church St.

Constructed in 1835–38, facing a central park, and flanked by its graveyard, St. Philip's seems out of the Old World of Europe. The building is sheathed in a mottled, tan stucco material that reflects the gradual shifting in light over a day. The church is open for morning services Sunday and Wednesday. Evening services take place on Wednesdays and on the second Friday of each month.

THOMAS ELFE HOUSE
803-722-2142.
54 Queen St.
Tours: Mon.–Fri. at 10, 11, and 12.
Admission: $3.

A meticulously restored, classic Charleston "single house," this dwelling was built before 1760 by the renowned cabinetmaker, who came to Charleston from England in the mid-18th century and left his mark in homes and furniture throughout the city. The carved fretwork that embellishes mahogany tables and chairs makes his work artistically distinctive; his abundant record-keeping has enabled historians to understand his life and times. The small house shows signs of his craftsmanship and knack for fitting things in. The cypress panelling brings a soft glow to the interior. Also on display are tools and artifacts.

Beaufort Area

**BAPTIST CHURCH OF
BEAUFORT**
803-524-3197.
600 Charles St.

This is an 1844 Greek Revival beauty. The ceiling plasterwork and ornamented cornices seem to match — in their absolute, solid mass of decoration — the abundant self-confidence of the prosperous little town of Beaufort in its heyday.

. OF EASE
_n Luther King, Jr.
Dr., St. Helena Island.

The ruins of this planters' church, built in the 1740s to serve worshippers far from town, are of brick and *tabby*, a construction material that blends oyster shells with lime, sand, and water. The site is wonderful for photographs.

JOHN MARK VERDIER HOUSE
803-524-6334.
801 Bay St.
Tues.–Sat. 10–4.
Admission: Adults $3;
children $2.

Built circa 1790 for a local merchant according to the plan and Adam-influenced decoration of the day, this house includes a formal parlor and ballroom, ornamental fireplace friezes, carved moldings, and antiques that are original both to the family and to the period of the house. Lovely herb garden in back. Headquarters of the Historic Beaufort Foundation.

Wade Spees

Old Sheldon Church, built in the style of a Greek Temple, was a casualty of the American Revolution, as British fought desperately to hold on to the Lowcountry.

OLD SHELDON CHURCH RUINS
Secondary Rd. 21, off
Hwy. 17, NW of
Beaufort.

Beautiful brick columns, fragile arches, and sill slabs remain from a church that was burned twice, first by the British in 1779 and then by the Union Army in 1865. A little temple in the woods.

PENN CENTER
803-838-2432.
Martin Luther King, Jr.
Dr., St. Helena Island.
York W. Bailey Museum
open Tues.–Fri. 11–4.
Admission free.

Founded in 1862 by two Pennsylvania women as a school for freed slaves, Penn has remained a vital institution to promote education, self-sufficiency, and cultural expression among native islanders. In the days of segregation, it was one place where blacks and whites could meet together, as they did when the Rev. Dr. Martin Luther King planned his march on Washington. The York W. Bailey Museum holds a collection of cultural artifacts, African objects, and paintings. Community sings featuring gospel choirs and spirituals, a cherished island tradition to which visitors are welcome, take place in Frissell Hall on the third Sunday of each month, Sept.–May, at 7:30 p.m.. The entire campus is a National Historic Landmark.

The 19th-century interior of St. Helena's Episcopal Church in Beaufort offers 20th-century worshippers serenity and a sense of history

Wade Spees

ST. HELENA'S EPISCOPAL CHURCH
803-524-7595.
507 Newcastle St.

This church, built of brick from England in 1724, is adorned inside with graceful columns, upstairs galleries, and tall, multi-paned windows on the deep sills of which rest buckets of blossoming magnolia, daffodils, or narcissi in season. Its shaded, walled churchyard makes for a lovely stroll.

TABERNACLE BAPTIST CHURCH
803-524-0376.
907 Craven St.

A lovely, white clapboard building with bell tower; in its churchyard lies the grave — and stands a fine bust — of Robert Smalls, who was born a slave, engineered a daring ship capture during the Civil War, and was later a congressman.

Savannah Area

ANDREW LOW HOUSE
912-233-6854.
329 Abercorn St.

This is a city house in the high style, although adapted to the rigors of Savannah's summer heat by means of jalousied rear porches. By 1848, when the house was built, Savannah was in its prime: this

Mon.–Wed., Fri.–Sat.
10:30–4; Sun. 12–4;
closed Thurs.
Admission: Adults $3.50;
children $1.00.

is how the wealthy cotton merchants lived. It was from this house that Juliette Gordon Low founded the Girl Scouts and where she died in 1927.

**FIRST AFRICAN
BAPTIST CHURCH**
912-233-6597.
23 Montgomery St.
Fri. 10–12, or by appt.

The oldest church for black worshippers in North America. Within the church (circa 1859) is a small museum and archive.

The Gift

"To His Excellency President Lincoln, Washington, D.C.: I beg to present you as a Christmas-gift the city of Savannah, with one hundred and fifty heavy guns and plenty of ammunition, also about twenty-five thousand bales of cotton."

— W.T. Sherman, Major-General. From Savannah, Dec. 22, 1864

**GREEN-MELDRIM
HOUSE**
912-233-3845.
1 W. Macon St., Madison
Square.
Tues. and Thurs.–Sat.
10–4.
Admission: $3.

Used as headquarters by General W.T. Sherman during his 1864 Christmas occupation of Savannah, this Gothic Revival mansion was considered the city's most expensive house when it was built in 1850. Wonderful exterior ironwork and porches.

**ISAIAH DAVENPORT
HOUSE**
912-236-8097.
324 E. State St.
Mon.–Sat. 10–4:30, Sun.
1:30–4:30.
Admission: Adults $4;
children $3.

The proposed demolition of this landmark in 1954 galvanized Savannah preservationists. Today it's a museum, adorned with furnishings and decorative arts of the Federal Period in which it was built.

**JULIETTE GORDON LOW
GIRL SCOUT CENTER**
912-233-4501.
142 Bull St.
Daily (except Wed.) 10–4,
Sun. 12:30–4:30.
Admission: Adults $4;
children $3.

A Regency townhouse decorated in postbellum period style, this building commemorates the childhood of the founder of the Girl Scouts, who was born here in 1860. Gift shop with special things for Scouts.

Juliette Gordon Low, the accomplished daughter of an elite Savannah family and founder of the Girl Scouts, in a self-portrait.

Wade Spees

KING-TISDELL COTTAGE
912-234-8002.
514 E. Huntingdon St.
Mon.–Fri. 10:30–4:30,
Sat.–Sun. 1–4.
Admission: Adults $1.50;
children $0.75.

This charming, original Victorian cottage houses a museum of the black history and culture of Savannah and the Sea Islands. Three walking or driving tours, highlighting events and significant sites that pertain to black history, can be arranged in advance. Additional exhibition space and displays are at the **Beach Institute** (912-234-8000; 502 E. Harris St.), which was established in 1865 by the American Missionary Association to educate the newly freed slaves, and which today continues as a black cultural center. Of special interest is the collection of woodcarvings, including likenesses of U.S. Presidents, by acclaimed folk artist and Savannah barber Ulysses Davis. (Institute open Mon.–Fri. 12–5, Sat.–Sun. 1–5. Admission: Adults $1.50; children $0.75.)

MICKVE ISRAEL TEMPLE
912-233-1547.
20 E. Gordon St.
Mon.–Fri. 10–12.

The Gothic-style synagogue was built in the 1870s, more than 100 years after the congregation was established. The museum and library house the oldest Torah in America, as well as letters, books, and historical documents.

OWENS-THOMAS HOUSE
912-233-9743.
124 Abercorn St.
Tues.–Sat. 10–5, Sun.–Mon. 2–5.
Admission: Adults $5;
children $2.

Designed in 1816 by Englishman William Jay and considered the best example of his Regency style for an urban villa, this house contains a collection of European and American decorative arts and has a formal garden.

TRUSTEES GARDEN
E. Broad at Bay St.

The site of the first experimental garden in America, the cultivation of this spot was key to the early colonists' efforts at self-sufficiency through the development of crops for export. On-site herb shop.

WORMSLOE HISTORIC SITE
912-353-3023.
7601 Skidaway Rd., Isle of Hope.
Tues.–Sat. 9–5, Sun. 2–5:30.
Admission: Adults $1.50; children $0.75.

The tabby ruins, an avenue of oaks, and artifacts excavated from the site are all that remain of the colonial plantation built by Noble Jones, a physician and carpenter who came with the first settlers on the ship *Anne* and survived to establish the Georgia colony. An audio-visual show and interpreters of colonial life make the period vivid for visitors.

MILITARY SITES

The presence of the military — invaders and defenders — has enriched the history of the Lowcountry since the time of the American Revolution, and it is still felt today at military bases, schools, and training centers. You needn't be a veteran, or even a Civil War buff, to enjoy the installations, monuments, forts, and military museums that are so plentiful in the region. Children — with their innate appreciation of danger and adventure, their love of costume and accessories, and their highly developed sense of winning, losing, and just causes — especially seem to twig to these sites and installations.

Charleston Area

AMERICAN MILITARY MUSEUM
803-723-9620.
40 Pinckney St.
Mon.–Sat. 10–6, Sun. 1–6.
Admission: Adults $2; children $1. No fee for military in uniform.

Hundreds of artifacts, uniforms, and documents detailing the contribution of members of all branches of the armed forces, from the Revolution to Vietnam.

THE CITADEL MUSEUM
803-792-6846.
171 Moultrie St.
Sun.–Fri. 2–5, Sat. 12–5.
Admission free.

Located on the campus of the Military College of South Carolina, founded in 1842, the museum tells the history of the school and the Corps of Cadets through documents, photographs, and uni-

The Friday dress parade of the Citadel's Cadet Corps is another venerated Lowcountry tradition.

Wade Spees

forms. An Events Line (803-792-6726) will keep you up to date on Citadel doings; dress parades take place most Fridays at 3:45 p.m. during the academic year.

THE CONFEDERATE MUSEUM
803-723-1541.
188 Meeting St.
(currently under repair due to Hurricane Hugo damage; call for information).

There's a Gullah expression in the Lowcountry that sums up the feeling of this museum: when you ask someone on the telephone "Is that you?" the person may reply, in a weary tone laced with irony, "That's what's leff' of me." This may be what's left of the old Confederacy: uniforms, tattered flags, documents, and artifacts.

FORT SUMTER NATIONAL MONUMENT
803-722-1691.
Departure points at City Marina on Lockwood Dr. (handicapped access) and Patriots Point.
Daily trips year-round except Christmas Day; five or six trips Mar. 1–Nov. 30, fewer in winter months.
Admission: Adults $8.50; children under 12 $4.25.

A relaxing ferry trip, which offers splendid views of the harbor and peninsula, takes you to the place where the Civil War began. Rangers are on hand at the fort to answer your questions; there are gun emplacements to explore and a museum with artifacts to help you imagine scenes of the siege, which lasted approximately two years and ended in the abandonment of the fort by Confederate soldiers. The entire tour lasts just over two hours.

Fort Sumter, where the stark choices faced by a splintered Union were played out in bloodshed in April 1861.

FORT MOULTRIE
803-883-3123.
W. Middle St., Sullivan's
   Island.
Daily 9–5, to 6 in summer
   months.
Admission: Free.

The primary site of Charleston's seacoast defense system, from its first test in the American Revolution until 1947. The palmetto-log fort that repelled the British fleet is gone, but buildings and earthworks dating from 1809 convey the sense of fragility and isolation the early patriots must have felt. A 20-minute film in the Visitor Center provides an excellent introduction to military life over the years. Operated by the National Park Service.

PATRIOTS POINT
803-884-2727.
Hwy. 17 in Mt. Pleasant,
   just over the Cooper
   River Bridge.
Daily 9–5, to 6 in summer
   months.
Admission: Adults $8;
   children $4.

Big ships are berthed here — the aircraft carrier *Yorktown*, the nuclear merchant ship *Savannah*, the World War II sub *Clamagore*, the destroyer *Laffey*, and cutter *Ingham* — and on self-guided tours you can see their aircraft, guns, and missiles, as well as views of how their personnel lived and worked on board. The view of peninsular Charleston from the signal bridge and platform of the *Yorktown* is unbeatable. Snack bar and gift shop, seating areas for the rest and air you'll need: there's a lot of walking, some of it in close quarters.

Beaufort Area

**PARRIS ISLAND
   MUSEUM**
803-525-2951.
War Memorial Building.
Marine Corps Recruit
   Depot.

The museum is a showcase for the history and development of the area on which the famous "boot camp" stands, from its earliest settlement through contemporary recruit training. The Spanish village of Santa Elena, which dates from 1566, is

Daily 10–4:30.
Admission: Free.

undergoing excavation. Exhibits of uniforms, arti-facts, weapons, drawings, and documents trace the history of the Marine Corps in its worldwide engagements. Maps for a self-guided driving tour around the depot are available. If you're interested in observing morning colors or a graduation, contact the Visitor Center (803-525-3650). You may also picnic in designated areas or eat at a base restaurant.

Savannah Area

FORT JACKSON
912-232-3945.
1 Fort Jackson Rd., 3 miles
from downtown Savan-nah.
Daily 9–5, to 7 in summer
months.
Admission: Adults $2;
children $1.50.

The oldest standing fort in Georgia, Fort Jackson saw action during both the Revolution, when an outbreak of malaria forced its abandonment, and the Civil War, when it was central to the Confederate network of river batteries. A self-guided tour takes you to military exhibits in the fort's casemates. Special military history programs enliven the fort several times each year.

**FORT MCALLISTER
HISTORIC PARK**
912-727-2339.
Hwy. 144, Richmond Hill.
Tues.–Sat. 9–5, Sun. 2–5:30.
Admission: Adults $1.50;
children $0.75.

The fall of Fort McAllister, on the Ogeechee River, signaled the end of Sherman's "March To The Sea." Unlike other forts in the area, it is not made of masonry; therefore its earthen walls (which could be repaired after a round of fierce bombardment) outlasted the others. There are self-guided tours, rangers on hand, and a good, small museum. Picnicking in the park is popular, but bring insect repellant.

*Massive and moated, Fort
Pulaski at the mouth of the
Savannah River survived
30 hours of Federal bombard-ment before succumbing in
1862.*

**FORT PULASKI NATIONAL
  MONUMENT**
912-786-5787.
Hwy. 80 east, about 30 minutes
  from Savannah.
Daily 8:30–5:15, to 6:45 in
  summer months.
Admission: $1.

A young officer named Robert E. Lee had his first military assignment here, soon after the fort was built. It's a masterpiece of engineering, a huge and heavy brick building, surrounded by a moat, sitting on an unstable marsh. And yet during the Civil War, rifled cannons blasted holes in the masonry of such forts, and they became obsolete. Interpretive programs explain life at the fort during the Civil War, and you are free to roam its ramparts. An excellent selection of books is available at the gift shop.

**TYBEE MUSEUM/FORT
  SCREVEN**
912-786-4077.
30 Meddin Dr., Tybee Island,
  18 miles E of Savannah.
Apr.–Sept.: Mon.–Fri. 10–6,
  Sat.–Sun. 10–4; Oct.–Mar.:
  Mon., Wed., Thu., Fri. 12–4.
Admission: Adults $1.50;
  children $0.50.

Located within Fort Screven, which was acquired by the federal government in 1808 and used as a post through World War II, the Tybee Museum and the Tybee Lighthouse (912-786-5801) offer visitors a glimpse of life at a beach outpost over the years. The museum has an assortment of objects, Indian and Civil War weaponry, as well as illustrated newspaper accounts of the Civil War and memorabilia. A lighthouse has marked this site since 1736. Today you can climb this 19th-century version (over 150 feet tall) for a wonderful view of the river.

MUSEUMS

Charleston Area

**AVERY RESEARCH
  CENTER FOR AFRICAN-
  AMERICAN HISTORY
  AND CULTURE**
803-727-2009.
125 Bull St.
Tours Mon.–Fri., 2–4.

Housed in one of the first schools dedicated to educating freed slaves, the center is today a repository of printed and picture materials and objects related to the heritage of the region's African-Americans. It was built by the Freedman's Bureau in 1868 to meet the needs of 1,000 eager students who had been receiving instruction from teachers sent by the American Missionary Association and other organizations. The reading room of the Center's archives and library is open Mon.–Fri., 1:30–4:30.

Displays at the Charleston Museum offer an excellent overview of plantation work and the lives of slaves.

Wade Spees

CHARLESTON MUSEUM
803-722-2996.
360 Meeting St.
Mon.–Sat. 9–5, Sun. 1–5.
Admission: Adults $5; children $3; combination tickets to Museum and its historic properties available at discount.

The museum, founded in 1773, is the oldest in America. This means that both the ideas that gave the collection its intellectual underpinnings and the very objects themselves, many from Charleston's oldest families, reflect more than two centuries of the city's self-consciousness. Exhibits interpreting subjects as diverse as flora and fauna, fashion, the art of silversmithing, Indian life, and plantation life come together to provide a seamless image of a special place. The section on African-American slavery — texts, artifacts, photographs, charts — is superb. There is a wonderful "hands-on" room especially for children.

CHARLES TOWNE LANDING 1670
803-556-4450.
Hwy. 171 between I-26 and Hwy. 17.
Daily 9–5, to 6 in summer months.
Admission: Adults $5; children $2.50. Free to handicapped.
Rental bicycles $2/hour with $2 deposit.

Consider this 80-acre park an outdoor museum, where the lives of the Lowcountry's earliest European settlers are interpreted in several ways: in an village setting; on a 17th-century replica of a typical coastal trading vessel; and in "wilderness," as found in the Animal Forest, where birds and beasts common to the area in 1670 roam in a secured habitat.

Beaufort

ARSENAL MUSEUM
803-525-7471.
713 Craven St.

The arsenal itself, completed in 1852, and the collection of documents stored there (having to do with local history — everything from artifacts to stuffed birds) are under restoration, but the museum should reopen in late 1993. Call for further information.

Reenactments of candle-making at Charles Towne Landing show the self-sufficiency of early settlers.

Wade Spees

NORTH STREET AQUARIUM
803-524-1559.
608 North St.
Thurs.–Sat. (Mon.–Wed. for school groups by appt. only).
Admission: Adults $1; children $0.50.

This new attraction, opening in 1993, will feature tanks of marine life — some of which will be touch tanks — and a gift shop.

Savannah Area

OATLAND ISLAND EDUCATION CENTER
912-897-3773
711 Sandtown Rd.
Mon.–Fri. 8:30–5, second Sat. of each month 10–4.
Admission: Can of Alpo dog food.

Children will love walking the woodland trails of this 175-acre preserve, where they can watch for the animals, which are abundant and roam in their natural habitat. Sheep, goats, ponies, and swans may cross your path; bald eagles and hawks soar overhead. There is a farmyard, too.

RIVER STREET TRAIN MUSEUM
912-233-6175.
315 W. River St.
Mon.–Sat. 11–6, Sun. 1–6
Admission: Adults $1.50; children $0.50.

Antique model train layouts, including miniature villages and lots of "O" gauge and other train memorabilia.

Wade Spees

Youngsters learn of the region's natural history and its diverse habitat at Lowcountry wildlife and science centers.

SAVANNAH HISTORY MUSEUM
912-238-1779.
303 Martin Luther King, Jr. Blvd.
Daily 8:30–5.
Admission: Adults $2.75; children $1.00.

Two sight-and-sound presentations, exhibits, and objects relating to Savannah's history, housed in the old Central of Georgia railway depot train sheds, by the Visitors Center.

SAVANNAH SCIENCE MUSEUM
912-355-6705.
4405 Paulsen St.
Tues.–Sat. 10–5, Sun. 2–5.
Admission: Adults $2.50; children $1.50.

If you want to see one of the Southeast's largest collections of amphibians and reptiles, living and dead, as well as comprehensive collections of shells, rocks, minerals, and a wonderful pressed herbarium of indigenous plants — or if someone in your party actually *prefers* this kind of exhibit to a house museum (gasp!) — spend time here. There's a great planetarium, too.

SHIPS OF THE SEA MUSEUM
912-232-1511.
503 E. River St.
Daily 10–5.
Admission: Adults $3; children $1.50.

Ship models on display tell the exciting story of maritime adventure, war, commerce, and exploration in the world's oceans, from the time of the Vikings forward. There is a fascinating collection of ships-in-a-bottle on permanent display.

UNIVERSITY OF GEORGIA MARINE EXTENSION SERVICE AQUARIUM

This is a working research lab and facility, but visitors are welcome to visit the aquarium and exhibits, which depict underwater marine and plant life of coastal Georgia. Fossils of sharks' teeth

912-598-2496.
Diamond Causeway, Skid-
away Island, ca. 15 miles
from downtown Savan-
nah.
Mon.–Fri. 9–4, Sun 12–5;
closed Sat. temporarily.
Admission: $1.00 sug-
gested donation.

and whale skulls are prominently displayed. A self-guided visit takes about an hour. Afterward, you can picnic. From here it's but a short hop to **Skidaway Island State Park** (912-598-2300), where you can walk through a maritime forest, bird-watch, and observe the teeming life of the marsh.

MUSIC

Like most self-respecting cities, Savannah and Charleston have symphony orchestras and chamber groups that play regularly throughout the year. Charleston, of course, has *Spoleto*, which brings boys' choirs, operatic soloists, and instrumentalists to the city each May and June. The region is rich in indigenous music, too: blues, jazz, spirituals, gospel. As new audiences for these styles develop, concerts to showcase them are emerging. The *Charleston Blues Festival* in February and the *MOJA Arts Festival* in the fall are two of them. Often, concerts of gospel music and spirituals take place in conjunction with spring and fall house tours and may be held at a historic site. You should check local newspapers for schedules or, once you arrive in the Lowcountry, contact the organizations below for information.

Charleston

Charleston Symphony Orchestra (803-723-9693; 14 George St., Charleston, SC 29401) Performances take place in the Gaillard Auditorium (77 Calhoun St.) throughout the year, under the direction of David Stahl. In any season, concert series might include selections from the classical repertoire, pops, and chamber works.

Lowcountry Blues Society (803-722-3263; at Erwin Music, 52 1/2 Wentworth St., Charleston, SC 29401) The **Charleston Blues Festival** runs for about 11 days every February and features performances at sites all over the city, from small clubs to larger theaters. The shows are first-rate — musicians come from Chicago, North and South Carolina, anywhere the blues are played. You have a range of styles among which to choose, from guitar soloists playing traditional Mississippi Delta blues to bands fronted by harp players who really cook. Gary Erwin's terrific music store is command central for festival information and schedules. The festival is one of the best things that's happened on the Charleston cultural scene.

MOJA Arts Festival (803-724-7305; 135 Church St.) This 16-day festival, whose name is Swahili for "one" or "unity," takes place in the fall and celebrates the African and Caribbean cultural influences on the Lowcountry. It includes many musical performances. Administered by the city's Office of Cultural Affairs.

Beaufort Area

Hallelujah Singers (803-524-3163; Chamber of Commerce, 1006 Bay St., Beaufort, SC 29902) The group of singers under the direction of Marlena McGhee Smalls, a talented vocalist who has earned a national reputation, performs throughout the year, often in a downtown church at the time of annual house tours. Call or write for specific schedules.

Penn Center Community Sings (803-838-2432; P.O. Box 126, St. Helena Island, SC 29920) Community groups, quartets of senior citizens, gospel choirs, spur-of-the-moment vocalists, and soloists who deacon out lines of spirituals to the audience can be heard at 7:30 p.m. on the third Sunday of each month from September to May, in Frissell Hall on the historic Penn Center campus. The popularity of the sings — and the feelings of fellowship they engender — are a moving testament to the pride of Sea Islanders in their culture and heritage. Contributions are welcome.

Savannah

Savannah Symphony Orchestra (912-236-9536; 225 Abercorn St.) The orchestra presents regularly scheduled symphony performances; chamber music ensembles often play on Sunday afternoons at the Telfair Academy.

Community sings held monthly at Penn Center keep the heritage of spirituals and gospel music alive.

Wade Spees

Sunday chamber music concerts held in spacious 19th-century rooms are a favorite of Lowcountry audiences.

Wade Spees

NIGHTLIFE

The after-supper activities of music, dancing, and general schmoozing in a crowded bar take place in fairly centralized areas of Lowcountry cities. In Charleston, there is the **Market Area** and **East Bay Street**, where you are as likely to find a ice cream parlor open late, or an indefatigable tee-shirt vendor still selling his wares, as you are to find a jazz club. In Savannah, the action centers along **River Street**, scattered in places that have taken up residence in the old cotton warehouses, and at the **City Market**. In both places, you'll rub shoulders with straight-laced bankers, good ol' boys, students, artists: it's a heady mix. Farther afield, on the resort-oriented islands, restaurants, and bars often feature bands in the summer: remember, this is the land of the "shag," the highly stylized dance set to beach music that originated in South Carolina.

Savannah's River Street by day attracts strollers and shoppers; after dark, it's the center of the city's nightlife.

Wade Spees

What follows is a list of the better known or easily accessible spots for night owls to enjoy. Cover charges vary widely, depending on the entertainment. Check local newspaper listings when you're in town for special shows.

Charleston Area

Bert's Bar (803-883-9646; 2213-B Middle St., Sullivan's Island) Rock-and-roll and blues music draw a nighttime crowd, who may have spent their day on a beach or a boat. It's a place for beer, burgers, and live bands on Friday and Saturday nights.

Best Friend Lounge (803-577-2400; 115 Meeting St.) Located in the Mills House Hotel, this is a quiet piano bar where you can relax and visit. A good place to gather for an after-dinner drink. Open to 10 p.m.

Cafe 99 (803-577-4499; 99 S. Market St.) In the warm evenings from April to October, you can sit outside and watch street performers; or listen to music and eat selections from a great raw bar inside.

Chef & Clef (803-722-0732; 102 N. Market St.) Live jazz nightly to about 1 a.m.; full meals or simple burgers served until midnight.

Fulford-Egan (803-577-4553; 231 Meeting St.) The culture of beatniks is coming back into fashion — poetry readings, "designer" leather sandals, acoustic music, low-key coffeehouse atmosphere — and you'll find its expression here. No alcohol served, but coffees, teas, and desserts. Blues performances are especially good.

Louis's Charleston Grill (803-577-4522; in the Omni Hotel) A solid, elegant bar such as you'd find in an old big-city hotel where locals drop in to snack and hear nightly jazz — sometimes a combo, sometimes a chanteuse. When the weather's warm some Friday after work, the Charleston Blues All Stars might be playing in the courtyard. (See the review in Chapter Five, *Restaurants and Food Purveyors*.)

Myskyn's Tavern (803-577-5595; 5 Faber St.) Late-night rocking and dancing; blues bands, reggae, and nationally known performers. What it lacks in intimacy it makes up for in spirit, especially for popular shows.

Safari's (803-723-1164; at the Fish Market Restaurant, 12 Cumberland St. at East Bay St.) A long, comfortable room flanked by the bar on one side, sofas and chairs on the other; jazz played up front. Head to the back if you want to talk. Good music, relaxed atmosphere. Open Thursday, Friday, and Saturday nights.

Beaufort

Banana's (803-522-0910; 910 Bay St.) Jazz combos on Wednesday and Saturday nights.

The Gullah House (803-838-2402; Hwy. 21, St. Helena Island) Live jazz and blues performances on Friday, Saturday, and Sunday nights.

Johnson Creek Tavern (803-838-4166; Hwy. 21, Harbor Island) A modest beach bar about 25 minutes from town, where you'll find campers from Hunting Island State Park and young couples, as well as "after-party" groups who come for the last set. A variety of music is offered on the weekends, from bluegrass to rock.

Plums at Night (803-525-1946; 904 1/2 Bay St.) During the day, this is a popular lunch spot for locals, the best place for homemade ice cream. On Thursday through Saturday nights, it's transformed: blues bands, trios, sometimes an open mike, patrons drifting in from the Waterfront Park to catch up with friends. Loose and not highfalutin', an inevitable stop for Beaufort's night crowd.

Savannah

The Bottom Line (912-232-0812; City Market, 206 W. St. Julian St.) Live jazz and swing music; dancing.

Crossroads (912-234-5438; 219 W. St. Julian St.) This place features blues to 3 a.m., nightly except Sunday. Art students and young Savannah crowd.

Hard Hearted Hannah's (912-232-9000; 15 E. Liberty St., inside the DeSoto Hilton) Great jazz bands and soloists, first set starts nightly at 9. The patrons know their music — sophisticated but relaxed.

Kevin Barry's (912-233-9626; 117 W. River St.) Irish bar serving sandwiches. Live Irish music, usually on weekends. Locals frequent the place, as a nice spot for relaxing after hours.

SPOLETO

It is said that the first professional dramatic production in America of a play written here was performed in Charleston in the 18th century by a shipwrecked poet, who was washed ashore, as he put it, "full of lice, shame, poverty, nakedness and hunger."

No such description could conceivably apply to the outstanding performers

Each spring, the Spoleto Festival transforms Charleston into an ultra-sophisticated city for the arts. Les Ballets de Monte Carlo is one of the many dance, musical, theatrical, choral, and jazz groups that have appeared here before an international audience.

Wade Spees

who come to the city today for Charleston's most famous festival (though perhaps some might allow that, like many artists, they are not as well off as they could wish!)

For 18 days at the end of spring, a time of budding oleander, fading azalea and unapologetically fragrant magnolias, *Spoleto* comes to Charleston, and Charleston becomes the city it has long imagined itself to be: an artistic mecca, where expressions of high culture find a setting among people who believe they understand the meaning of civilized life.

Spoleto gave Charlestonians a chance to prove their culture and sophistication, and prove it they have done. Emboldened by the unwavering artistic vision of Gian Carlo Menotti (who fell in love with Charleston and organized the first festival in 1977) and egged on by an indefatigable mayor, Charleston's cultural and business communities have consistently — and with full attention — adapted themselves and their city to the idea that first-class art of many kinds can inhabit, enrich, and be enriched by the lively, unique qualities of this old city. Spoleto instilled new vigor into the town, giving rise to building projects and renovations, new restaurants and shops: it linked the pride of the Lowcountry's past to confidence in its future. Perhaps more than anything, it opened the doors of Charleston to the nation.

Spoleto took its name from the town in Italy where, in the 1950s, Mr. Menotti had organized another festival, the Festival of Two Worlds. Spoleto in Charleston is the American counterpart to that successful European venture. In any one season, it offers more than 100 scheduled events, including premieres of opera and dance as well as dozens of chamber-music, choral, jazz, and orchestral performances. Performances take place indoors and out — in parks, plantation gardens, amphitheaters, and auditoriums.

If that's not enough, the regular Spoleto events are augmented by some 600 *Piccolo Spoleto* performances (often free), organized by the city's Office of Cultural Affairs. These events can include organ, choral, and madrigal recitals in churches; mime shows, outdoor concerts, and numerous theater productions. (Tickets and schedules for Piccolo Spoleto are available in Charleston at the Spoleto Box Office, 14 George St., and at the Gaillard Auditorium, 77 Calhoun St.)

There are several ways to purchase tickets to the main Spoleto festival. The best is to request, by mail or telephone, *in early spring*, the festival ticket brochure, a near-tabloid size schedule of events with a pre-printed order form. Contact:

Spoleto Festival U.S.A
P.O. Box 704
Charleston, SC 29402
803-722-2764

You'll find that the variety and number of events, when and at what hour they are scheduled, can be overwhelming. Nevertheless, poring over the brochure and making plans can offer, to those in search of sophisticated culture, the same sort of pleasurable anticipation that stirs avid gardeners as they read beautiful seed catalogues. In 1993, for example, the lineup included such highlights as the world premiere of Mr. Menotti's one-act opera *The Singing Child*; Rossini's *Le Comte Ory*, in honor of the composer's 200th birthday; and Eisenstein's film *Alexander Nevsky*, with a live performance of Prokofiev's accompanying score. Also on the schedule: the Martha Graham Dance Company and Nikolais and Murray Louis Dance; the Barry Harris Trio, Bobby Watson and Horizon, Jon Hendricks and Company, and the Gil Evans Orchestra performing *Porgy and Bess*. The season's opening gala with the Spoleto Festival Orchestra and the closing open-air concert and fireworks display are traditional favorites.

Early planning really pays off: you'll get the best choice of seats and performances, and the chance, if you prefer, to select a special Spoleto ticket package, which gathers together in one bundle many events occurring over several days. As an advance ticket holder, you may also be eligible for discounted air travel.

Having chosen to fill your days, you must now secure lodgings for the night: again, the earlier the better for best selection. (See Chapter Three, *Lodging*, for ideas.)

If you are a bit lax in planning, there may still be tickets available; to seek them out in the weeks before the first performances, the basic Spoleto festival ticket brochure is critical. With it in hand, you may, *starting April 1st until festival's end*, order tickets by telephone. Call: **803-577-4500, 24-hours a day; fax number 803-723-6383.** Charge to Visa or MasterCard (or fax the completed ticket order form) There's a $1 handling charge levied per ticket.

In person, visit the *Spoleto Office* at 14 George St., which is open year round but extends its hours from April until the festival closes. There is also a box office at the *Dock Street Theater* (135 Church St.), open daily during the festival from 10 a.m. until 30 minutes after the final performance of the day.

Even if you arrive in Charleston and find yourself without tickets at the last minute, there's no need for despair. Tickets often are available up to one hour before curtain time; remaining tickets go on sale at performance sites 30 minutes before curtain. Chairs or standing room for sold-out performances at the **Dock Street Theater** and the **Garden Theater** go on sale at 10 a.m. on the day of performance.

Wade Spees

Founder Gian Carlo Menotti directed this production of The Marriage of Figaro *at the Spoleto Festival.*

THEATER

By the middle of the 18th century, theatrical performances were well established in the cultural life of Charleston; by century's end, they were making their way into Savannah. In the antebellum years, theater was but one jewel in the crown of culture, offset by the brilliant setting provided by a society that lived for pleasure and sought it in balls, concerts, seasonal celebrations, and lavish home entertaining.

In this century, it wasn't until 1927 — when DuBose Heyward's novel *Porgy*, the story of a lame Charleston street vendor and his love for Bess, was adapted and performed on the Broadway stage — that drama native to Charleston came alive. Theatrical performances in the Lowcountry still reflect their indigenous stories — they are often showcased during Piccolo Spoleto — but a growing audience also supports new works from nationally known dramatists and selections from the classical repertory. When visiting, call ahead for performance schedules and tickets.

Charleston

Amazing Stage Company (803-577-5967; 133 Church St.) Productions that offer special enjoyment for families, plays like *Cheaper By the Dozen* or *A Christmas Carol*; also original works, children's theater, and workshops.

Charleston's Chopstick brings a whimsical slant to the classics.

Wade Spees

Charleston Actors Theater Society (803-767-8731; 20-B Blake St.) A new traveling troupe specializing in staged readings of scripts with emphasis on the African-American experience.

Chopstick Theater (803-556-8025; 1023 Wappoo Rd.) Original work and, in summer months, a delightful "Festival of Classics" at the Dock Street Theater.

Dock Street Theater (803-723-5648; 135 Church St.) This is a lovely interpretation of a Georgian-style theater, of the sort 18th-century Charlestonians would have patronized. Rebuilt during the Depression within the old Planters Hotel (circa 1809) as a project of the Works Progress Administration, the theater's cypress interiors, intimate box seats, and terrific acoustics make it a wonderful place to attend performances. It's the site of the immensely popular Chamber Music Series during Spoleto and festival plays, as well as a stage for roving companies.

Footlight Players (803-722-8809; 107 East Bay St.) An old, established theater company dedicated to community-theater repertory.

Premiere Theater at the College of Charleston (803-792-5600; Simons Center for the Arts, George St.) New plays. Casts include professional actors as well as students and faculty from the College of Charleston.

Beaufort

Beaufort Little Theater (803-522-2000; 3060 Mink Pt. Blvd.) Beaufort's popular community theater performs well-known works — musicals, comedy, and drama — several times each year.

Savannah

City Lights Theatre Company (912-234-9860; 12 W. York Lane) Productions in a small 75-seat theater; "Shakespeare-In-The-Park" in Washington Square in spring.

Murder Afloat (912-925-2586; Hyatt Regency Dock; 2 W. Bay St.) Solve a murder mystery while you're on the dinner cruise. Saturday nights, Mar.—Oct., adults $15, children $12.

Savannah Theater Company (912-233-7764; 222 Bull St.) Seasonal productions of contemporary drama, musicals, and comedy.

SEASONAL EVENTS IN THE LOWCOUNTRY

The following list is intended to draw your attention to annual special events in the Lowcountry that might coincide with the time of your visit. (For seasonal festivals revolving around food, see "Lowcountry Food Festivals" in Chapter Five, *Restaurants and Food Purveyors*.) Some of them, like outdoor concerts in a park, offer informal pleasures that you can enjoy on a whim with your family. Others, like house tours, Spoleto performances, or tennis and golf tournaments, require a bit of planning: purchasing your tickets in advance is a good idea, as is securing lodgings, especially in the busy spring tourist season. For specific information regarding dates, schedules, performance times, admission or ticket prices (if applicable), call or write in advance, or check local newspaper listings. For lodging suggestions, see Chapter Three.

FEBRUARY

Charleston

Charleston Blues Festival (803-722-3263; 52 1/2 Wentworth St., Charleston, SC 29401) Eleven days of performances by top blues players.

Southeastern Wildlife Exposition (800-221-5273; Dept. R., P.O. Box 20159, Charleston, SC 29413-0159) A comprehensive, multi-site exhibition of wildlife art in various media, and presentations promoting habitat conservation and wildlife appreciation. A huge, three-day event that draws collectors, artists, hunters, and bird-watchers. Tickets can also be purchased in Charleston at the Southeastern Wildlife Exposition Gallery (803-723-1748; 211 Meeting St., Charleston SC 29401).

Savannah

First Saturday Festival (on the Waterfront, Saturdays, February to November, 10 a.m.–6 p.m.) From spring to fall, continuous family entertainment, live bands, and vendors bring excitement to River Street.

Georgia Heritage Celebration (912-233-7787, Historic Savannah Foundation; 912-651-7022, Massie Heritage Center) A 12-day celebration of the founding of Georgia and the Savannah colony which features tours, reenactments of Colonial life, lectures, art exhibits, music, dance, and crafts. At various city locations.

MARCH

Beaufort

St. Helena's Episcopal Church Spring Tours (803-522-1712; 507 Newcastle St., Beaufort, SC 29901) Tours of historic homes, gardens, and churches in Beaufort and on the Sea Islands.

Charleston

Drayton Hall Candlelight Concert (803-766-0188; 3380 Ashley River Rd., Charleston, SC 29414) When this house is lit only by candles, it seems at its height of serene beauty. The concert featured works from the classical repertoire; and there might be a little Gershwin thrown in, too.

Festival of Houses (803-723-1623; P.O. Box 1120, Charleston, SC 29402) The Historic Charleston Foundation's tours of private homes, plantations, gardens, and churches usually start toward the end of the month and last four weeks. A superbly organized event — a tradition for over 40 years — it will enrich your understanding of the Lowcountry.

Sunday Art in the Park (Hampton Park, 4–6 p.m.) Every Sunday from March to October, this beautifully landscaped park is the site of band concerts, performances that showcase local talent, and art shows. Bring your picnic, ball and glove, Frisbee, bike or running shoes and enjoy the outdoors.

Hilton Head

Family Circle Magazine Cup Tennis Tournament (803-363-4502; P.O. Box 7000, Hilton Head Island, SC 29938) For nine days, usually starting at the end of the month, the world's top women players compete at Sea Pines Plantation. Excellent tennis in a relaxed atmosphere.

Savannah

Savannah Tour of Homes and Gardens (912-234-8054; 18 Abercorn St., Savannah, GA 31401) For four days, Savannah's historic homes, churches, and gardens are open to visitors.

St. Patrick's Day Parade (912-920-8228, subject to change annually; Parade Committee, P.O. Box 9224, Savannah, GA 31412) Savannah claims a substantial Irish heritage and celebrates it with abandon on this holiday. Mobs of people turn out to watch the parade, which starts at 10 a.m. downtown and dominates practically all other city activity for the day and night.

APRIL

Hilton Head

MCI Heritage Classic (803-671-2448; 79 Lighthouse Rd., Suite 414, Hilton Head, SC 29928) Falling about a week after the Masters at Augusta, this premiere golf tournament brings thousands of people and the top PGA players to Hilton Head.

MAY

Beaufort

Gullah Festival (803-524-3163; Beaufort Chamber of Commerce, Box 910, Beaufort, SC 29901) Held on the last weekend in May, the festival features performances, plays, concerts of spiritual and gospel music, films, and lectures related to the Gullah heritage of the Sea Islands. Open-air market of crafts and food in the Waterfront Park.

Bluffton

Bluffton Village Festival (803-757-3855; Bluffton Town Hall, Bluffton, SC 29910) A very small, old-fashioned street festival featuring artisans, food, and entertainment, usually held the second Saturday of May.

Charleston

Confederate Memorial Day Observance (803-722-8638; Magnolia Cemetery Trust, P.O. Box 6214, Charleston, SC 29405) Join the United Daughters of the

Confederacy and other groups in a program honoring the Confederate War dead.

Spoleto Festival U.S.A. (803-722-2764; P.O. Box 704, Charleston, SC 29402) Beginning in late May and lasting for about 18 days, Spoleto brings the best of international theater, music, and dance to Charleston.

Savannah

Arts on the River (912-651-6417; Office of Cultural Affairs, Savannah, GA 31401) Savannah's arts community turns out in force for a celebration that doesn't end until after dark. Jazz and symphony concerts, dance, theater, and art.

Beach Music Festival (912-786-5444; Tybee Beach) Spend a weekend at the beach, listen to lots of bands playing beach-music oldies, and even learn to shag.

Scottish Games and Highland Gathering (912-964-4951; P.O. Box 13435, Savannah, GA 31401) Scottish dancing, pipe bands, and traditional games honoring Scotch heritage, usually held the first weekend in May.

JUNE

Colleton County

Edisto Riverfest (803-549-9595; Walterboro-Colleton Chamber of Commerce, P.O. Box 1763, Walterboro, SC 29488) Join a guided canoe and kayak flotilla as it winds down the Edisto River. Food, entertainment, and displays of equipment featured at two state parks along the way. Usually held the second weekend of the month.

Edisto Island

Edisto Summer Festival (803-869-3867; Chamber of Commerce, P.O. Box 206, Edisto Island, SC 29438) A weekend of family-oriented fun on the beach, in the water, and on the links. Street dances, local food specialities, and entertainment.

Savannah

Concerts in Johnson Square From June to August, enjoy two-hour lunchtime concerts every Wednesday and Friday, starting at 11:30 a.m., in one of the city's loveliest settings.

JULY

Fourth of July Fireworks take place in several Lowcountry resorts as well as these locations: **Brittlebank Park (Charleston), Parris Island (Beaufort), Hilton Head, Bluffton, Savannah's Riverfront,** and **Tybee Beach.**

Beaufort

Beaufort County Water Festival (803-524-0600; P.O. Box 52, Beaufort, SC 29901) A week-long festival starting in mid-July that features special events each day and night: croquet, fishing, tennis, Ping-pong and golf tournaments, a juried art show, antiques show, kid's day, parade, and several outdoor dances. The air shows and acrobatic water-ski demonstrations are especially fun to watch.

Savannah

Maritime Festival (912-236-3959; P.O. Box 9347, Savannah, GA 31412) Boat races, fishing tournaments, and various competitions, both serious and fun. Scheduled to coincide with annual pre-Olympic sailing regattas in July and August. Savannah is the site of the yachting events — 10 in all — for the 1996 Summer Olympics.

SEPTEMBER

Charleston

House and Garden Candlelight Tours (803-722-4630; The Preservation Society, P.O. Box 521, Charleston, SC 29402) More than one dozen different candlelight walking tours of private homes and gardens are offered over a period of about four weeks by the city's oldest preservation organization.

Scottish Games and Highland Gathering (P.O. Box 21109, Charleston, SC 29413) Competitions in dancing and athletics held in a fairlike atmosphere at Boone Hall Plantation.

Hilton Head

Hilton Head Celebrity Golf Tournament (803-785-3673; Chamber of Commerce, P.O. Box 5647, Hilton Head Island, SC 29938) Held Labor Day weekend, the tournament draws lots of celebrities who play with a keen sense of fun.

Savannah

Savannah Jazz Festival (912-232-2222; Coastal Jazz Assoc., P.O. Box 8004, Savannah, GA 31412) All styles of jazz played in spots throughout the city.

OCTOBER

Beaufort

Historic Beaufort Foundation Fall Tour of Homes (803-524-6334; P.O. Box 11, Beaufort, SC 29901) A weekend of candlelight and daytime tours of homes and gardens in and around Beaufort; the final day often features tours of outlying plantations, such as the rarely seen *Auldbrass*, designed by Frank Lloyd Wright and meticulously restored inside and out.

Charleston

MOJA Arts Festival (803-724-7305; Office of Cultural Affairs, 133 Church St., Charleston, SC 29401) The festival runs for about two weeks and celebrates — in lectures, art exhibits, music, dance, and theater — the cultural roots of the African-American experience.

Edisto Island

Edisto Historic Preservation Society Tour of Homes (803-869-1954; P.O. 206, Edisto Island, SC 29438) Day-long tour of homes.

Hilton Head Island

An Evening of the Arts (803-785-3673; Chamber of Commerce, P.O. Box 5647, Hilton Head Island, SC 29938) A festive charity auction featuring work by local artists.

Ridgeland

Gopher Hill Festival (803-726-8126; P.O. Box 1267, Ridgeland, SC 29936) A one-day celebration with arts and crafts, music, and food. The Ridgeland area long was known as Gopher Hill, named for the gopher tortoise, a species which lives a protected life in the sand hills of Jasper County.

Savannah

Savannah Greek Festival (912-236-8256; St. Paul's Greek Orthodox Church, 14 W. Anderson St., Savannah, GA 31401) A three-day-long celebration of Savannah's Greek heritage with food, music, and dancing.

NOVEMBER

Charleston

Drayton Hall Arts and Crafts Festival (803-766-0188; 3380 Ashley River Rd., Charleston, SC 29414) A two-day marketplace of fine arts and crafts on the grounds of Drayton Hall.

Plantation Days (803-556-6020; Middleton Place, Hwy. 61, Charleston SC 29414) The spirit of harvest days on a Lowcountry plantation is recreated through activities such as blacksmithing, wool dying and spinning, candle-making, and pottery. Traditional music and crafts, too, in the stable yards and green at Middleton Place.

Holiday Festival of Lights (803-762-2172; James Island County Park) See more than 100,000 holiday lights strung in the park, a dazzling display in a place that rarely knows a white Christmas. Family entertainment and special events scheduled through Christmas.

St. Helena Island

Heritage Days (803-838-2432; Penn Center, P.O. Box 126, St. Helena Island, SC 29920) Held the second weekend in November on the historic Penn Center campus, Heritage Days celebrates Sea Island culture in its many forms. Thursday there is a special community sing; Friday there are lectures and presentations followed by an old-fashioned fish fry with musical entertainment; on Saturday, a parade and performances which include Gullah games

Dancers from Sierra Leone — a country with linguistic and cultural similarities to St. Helena Island — perform at Penn Center's Heritage Days Festival.

Wade Spees

and storytelling, dance, music, and demonstrations of traditional Sea Island crafts such as basket-making, net-weaving, and boat-building. Unique in the Lowcountry.

Gathering and Corn-shelling, St. Helena Island

"When they go into the field to work, the women tie a bit of string or some vine round their skirts just below the hips, to shorten them, often raising them nearly to the knees; then they walk off with their heavy hoes on their shoulders, as free, strong, and graceful as possible. The prettiest sight is the corn-shelling on Mondays, when the week's allowance, a peck a hand, is given out at the corn-house by the driver. They all assemble with their baskets, which are shallow and without handles, made by themselves of the palmetto and holding from a half a peck to a bushel. The corn is given out in the ear, and they sit about or kneel on the ground, shelling it with cleared corn-cobs. Here there are four enormous logs hollowed at one end, which serve as mortars, at which two can stand with their rude pestles, which they strike up and down alternately. . . . They separate the coarse and fine parts after it is ground by shaking the grits in their baskets; the finest they call corn-flour and make hoe-cake of, but their usual food is the grits, the large portion, boiled as hominy and eaten with clabber."

— Harriet Ware to her family in Boston, from St. Helena Island May 22, 1862
From Letters from Port Royal, *1862-1868, Elizabeth Ware Pearson, Editor*

Savannah

Crafts and Cane Grinding (912-897-3773; Oatland Island Education Center, 711 Sandtown Rd., Savannah, GA 31412) On the second Saturday in November, more than 50 artisans from the Southeast come to sell their work and demonstrate how it's done; farmers grind cane to make syrup; folk musicians play outside.

DECEMBER

Beaufort

Christmas at the Verdier House (803-524-6334; 801 Bay St., Beaufort, SC 29902) The late-18th century planter's home is decorated during Christmas week as it might have been during holidays of long ago.

Night on the Town (803-525-6644; Main Street Beaufort USA) Join an informal, local street party as the downtown merchants welcome patrons to partake of holiday snacks and libations. There are decorations everywhere; jazz musicians, carolers, and even Santa make special appearances. An evening of small-town fun.

Charleston

African-American Spirituals (803-766-0188; Drayton Hall, 3380 Ashley River Rd., Charleston, SC 29414) "The Senior Lights" singing group of Johns Island presents a moving concert of music of the Sea Islands at Drayton Hall, usually just after Christmas.

Christmas in Charleston (803-853-8000; P.O. Box 975, Dept. VG, Charleston, SC 29402) The season brings special tours and holiday events, such as a parade of boats strung with lights and open-air marketplaces. Many restaurants and hotels offer holiday specials, too.

The decorations at the Manigault House recall the festivities of Christmas past.

Wade Spees

Savannah

Christmas in Savannah (912-944-0456; Convention & Visitors Bureau, P.O. Box 1628, Savannah, GA 31402-1628) All month long, Savannah comes alive with special holiday events: tours, performances, 19th-century style holiday presentations in old homes, crafts shows, and celebrations at the beach and on the river.

CHAPTER FIVE
Grits, Game, and Gumbo
RESTAURANTS & FOOD PURVEYORS

As early as 1745, visitors to the Lowcountry were impressed with the abundance and variety of its foods, the sophisticated way they were prepared, and the splendid manner in which meals arrived at the table. The habit of lavish, at-home dining had established itself as a mark of high status in a society committed to living well. Given the region's plentiful supply of game and fish, its gentlemen of leisure who enjoyed the chase, and its slaves to tend gardens and kitchens, it was an easy habit to support.

Old accounts tell of hunting and fishing parties that delivered marsh hens, dove, quail, and crab by the dozens; that brought in pigeons and deer hunted by torchlight; that landed huge drum, a beast of a fish that pulled at hook and line and dragged a bateau as a whale might. Add to these hunters' trophies the harvest from garden and field — okra, corn, peas and beans, turnips, beets, greens, and of course rice, first introduced to the Lowcountry in the late 1600s — and you had then,

Wade Spees

Sightseers on a carriage tour admire Anson's, where the freshest ingredients are lightly sautéed moments before they reach your table.

and have to this day, a traditional Southern meal, flavored as always with meat marked by "a streak of lean and a streak of fat."

It was not only the natural bounty of the land and the availability of labor to harvest several crops each season that led to sumptuous, uniquely prepared Lowcountry meals. The sheer management of the plantation and its physical layout — including individual kitchens and smokehouses — gave rise to a separate world of cooking. It was managed by slaves who contributed to recipes their own sense of spicing, texture, ingredients, and method. The influence of their African and West Indian heritages, combined with European preferences, produced a distinctive regional style that is being redefined by authors and chefs like John Martin Taylor and Edna Lewis.

Even among more modest people, and when times got hard, dining remained an important ritual. Schoolchildren released for an hour from class and fathers home from the office would reunite at the midday meal. It honored family and tradition; it was one standard most people could afford to keep up. As Edna Lewis has said: "The birds are just the beginning. In the South you put everything you have on the table." Such resourcefulness is the trademark of Southern cooking.

Like the rest of the South — slow to industrialize and lacking many large cities — the Lowcountry for much of this century offered its residents few places to dine out and few reasons to do so. The culture centered around home, family, the connections of friends and neighbors, and a convivially shared history. You could conduct your business in a restaurant, but not your social life. The dozens of restaurant listings in this chapter show how that has changed.

Today, the cities of Charleston and Savannah are filled with plain and fancy places to eat, designed to serve a local population more eager than ever to dine out (and with the means to do so), as well as visitors who arrive with high culinary expectations. Small towns that may have had but one restaurant now boast several of good quality. In addition, the nutrition and cooking fad that seems to have swept the nation has spawned specialty food stores and rekindled interest in farmers' markets and other fresh-food outlets, which in the Lowcountry tend to be pickup trucks parked on the roadside and filled with baskets of tomatoes, greens, shrimp, crab, boiled peanuts, and watermelon.

The restaurants reviewed in this chapter represent a wide sampling of what's available in various price ranges. Since new places are opening all the time, since chefs move and styles change, the listing cannot be regarded as complete nor as having the last word. We'd like to think it's authoritative, though, based as it is on numerous visits by several people over time. If anything, it should provide a sense that while fried seafood is in no danger of falling off a menu, more innovative dishes have found a secure place for themselves, too.

Hours of operation, prices, methods of payment, and policies regarding reservations have been noted and checked as close to the date of publication as possible, but a call ahead to confirm is always wise. The general price range we list is meant to reflect the cost of a single meal, usually dinner, featuring an appetizer, entree, dessert, and coffee. Cocktails, beer and wine, gratuity, and tax are not included in the estimated price.

Dining Price Code	Inexpensive	Up to $10
	Moderate	$10 to $20
	Expensive	$20 to $30
	Very Expensive	$30 or more

Credit Cards	AE — American Express
	CB — Carte Blanche
	D — Discover Card
	DC — Diner's Club
	MC — MasterCard
	V — Visa

Food purveyors of all sorts — delis, gourmet and health-food stores, open-air markets, roadside farm stands — are listed at the end of the review section by geographic area.

RESTAURANTS

Charleston

During Spoleto, most Charleston restaurants relax their hours, serving lunch as late as 3 p.m., early supper at 5:30 p.m., and full meals at midnight. The crowds pile up, so make reservations. If you're rushing between performances, enjoy a picnic in the open-air pavilions at the Waterfront Park at the foot of Queen Street, in the shady grove of Washington Square, or on a bench at the Battery.

ANSON
803-577-0551.
12 Anson St.
Open daily.
Price: Expensive.
Cuisine: American.
Serving: L, D.
Credit Cards: AE, D, DC, MC, V.

New in 1992, just in time for the dressy Spoleto crowds, Anson practically glows from the street. Run by longtime Lowcountry restaurateurs, the cooking technique here is last-minute sautéing: the dish arrives at your table sizzling hot, with crispy vegetables, meat, fish, or fowl glistening with juice. The meticulous presentation matches the decor — lots of attention to the tiniest detail of color and contrast. There are comfy banquettes and lots of smaller tables for four or six, done up in heavy linens. The fish entrees are fresh from the boat, and the she-crab soup laced with sherry probably the best you'll taste. Follow your meal with a glass of brandy or port.

BAKER'S CAFE
803-577-2694.
214 King St.
Open daily.
Price: Inexpensive.
Cuisine: American.
Serving: B, L.
Credit Cards: DC, MC, V.
Special Features: Take-out
   bakery items.

If you're bracing for a day of window shopping and antiquing along King Street, stop in here first for breakfast, including delicious croissants. It's bigger than a bakery, but hasn't lost the early-morning freshness that makes such places so cheerful. Classical music plays in the background, the light pours in the storefront-style display windows, and watercolors, prints, and posters enliven the pale walls. Weekend brunch is very popular, but you'll find your wait to be a friendly one, among others who may be relaxing with the newspaper on an outdoor bench or strolling until some tables clear.

CAROLINA'S
803-724-3800.
10 Exchange St.
Open daily.
Price: Expensive to Very
   Expensive.
Cuisine: American.
Serving: L, D.
Credit Cards: AE, DC, MC,
   V.

Late-night crowds converge on Carolina's, at the two dozen tables lining the main passageway or in back by the bar, amidst oversized antique French posters and crowded banquettes. You could have a light meal of omelets or pasta, more substantial local delicacies like grilled smoked Carolina quail with spicy greens and tasso grits, or sit at the bar and make a meal of appetizers like shrimp and crabmeat wontons with ginger sauce. The juicy baby back ribs are not for the meek. The restaurant occupies the site of the former Perdita's, in its day the best formal, old-fashioned — and many would say only — place to eat in Charleston for many years. If there's one place that shows how far the city has come toward a vision of itself as a sophisticated enclave, a place to see and be seen, this is it.

CELIA'S PORTA VIA
803-722-9003.
49 Archdale St.
Closed Sun.
Price: Moderate to Expen-
   sive.
Cuisine: Italian, Sicilian.
Serving: L, D.
Credit Cards: AE, MC, V.
Reservations suggested.

A family heritage of four Italian grandparents has bestowed a cozy, old-world feeling to the restaurant, where you will often see local chefs sitting down to a meal as well as downtown regulars. There's not really a bar for lingering, nor a foyer: in you come, and it's as if you're home for Sunday dinner. Indeed, some of the paintings and chandeliers are from Celia Cerasoli Manske's parents' house. Fresh homemade mozzarella is a big draw; the pasta dishes are inventive; the wine list is broad and deep. Dining upstairs — in a room that looks like an old tavern, dressed up with an Oriental rug and white tablecloths — feels more intimate. Spoleto performers often drop by to play, and sometimes there's a jazz pianist.

Enter the courtyard to Fulton Five and imagine you're in an intimate family restaurant in sunny Italy.

Wade Spees

FULTON FIVE
803-853-5555.
5 Fulton St.
Closed Sun. and Mon.
Price: Moderate to Expensive.
Cuisine: Italian.
Serving: L, D.
Credit Cards: AE, CB, DC, MC, V.

It's said that one reason Gian Carlo Menotti chose Charleston as the site for his Spoleto Festival USA is that the city had a Mediterranean feel, a serene charm as easy to appreciate and as softly worn as stucco walls in a seaside village. Fulton Five wasn't open then, but it, more than any Charleston restaurant, fits the description. Sylvia Meier's small place exudes quiet confidence and lack of pretension. The appetizers are the finest around, among them field greens with fennel, carpaccio, calamari with peppers. The pasta dishes, usually three, are simply adorned or just tossed with excellent olive oil and herbs. The decor is both sumptuous and comfortable: green walls that seem murky and lustrous, recessed windows set off by dark brown shutters, brocade fabrics flecked with gold, sunflowers set in silver urns.

GARIBALDI'S
803-723-7153.
49 S. Market St.
Open daily.
Price: Moderate to Expensive.
Cuisine: Italian; seafood.
Serving: D.
Credit Cards: AE, MC, V.

Garibaldi's established itself in Charleston at a time when the city was first feeling its oats, when it was being "rediscovered" as a tourist destination. As patrons entered from busy Market Street, which was itself just beginning to boom with fancy ice-cream shops and streetside cafes, you could read on their faces a look of surprise that seemed to say: Charleston, suddenly hip! The murals, outdoor courtyard, and the clusters of the interesting-looking people endowed the simplest dinner — fettuccine Alfredo, say, with salad and a glass of wine — with a sweet giddiness. Even as Charleston has grown up, Garibaldi's doesn't seem jaded.

**GAULART &
MALICLET**
803-577-9797.
96 Broad St.
Closed Sun.
Price: Inexpensive to Moderate.
Cuisine: French.
Serving: B, L, D.
Credit Cards: AE, MC, V.

Not big enough to be called a bistro, much more pleasant than a bar, "Fast and French" as it is nicknamed is unlike any eatery in town. You sit on high chairs at a black-topped counter that juts out into tiny bays, and your neighbors are as likely to be Broad Street lawyers as local artists. Platters of pâté, sausages, selections of cheeses, and French bread are served; hearty soups; fondues; excellent wine. The smoked salmon is great, finished off with fruit. The menu is full of variety, and it's available at wonderfully odd times, late at night, for example, or if you're hungry at 5:30 and want to make an early theater performance.

LAFAYETTE
803-723-0114.
276 King St.
Open daily.
Price: Moderate to Expensive.
Cuisine: French.
Serving: L, D.
Credit Cards: MC, V.
Reservations suggested.

Chef Thierry Goulard has brought his Manhattan cooking talents to bear on indigenous species like shrimp and baby greens. His crab cake with lobster sauce has captivated even the most been-everywhere locals; the delicious smell of the open grill and kitchen area will whet your appetite, too. It's a small, bright restaurant located on a busy corner, where window tables offer excellent people-watching relaxation.

**LOUIS'S CHARLESTON
GRILL**
803-577-4522.
In the Omni, 224 King St.
Open daily.
Price: Very Expensive.
Cuisine: American, Southern.
Serving: D.
Credit Cards: AE, MC, V.

There's nothing understated about this place: located in the Omni, it has the strut and bluster of a big-city restaurant and the dark woodwork, marble floors, popular bar-scene, and table-trimmings to match. Chef Louis Osteen has been called one of the most gifted chefs in America: his restaurant has been dubbed "hot." The menu is ambitious and learned — but also includes the helpful caveat that "fish can be prepared simply grilled, if desired." If he's cooking, you're likely to have a superior meal, which might include a warm bean salad with grilled shrimp and roasted monkfish wrapped in caul. The buttermilk tart with fresh raspberries makes a fine ending.

MAGNOLIA'S
803-577-7771.
185 East Bay St.
Open daily.

You might think that a big and breezy place like this one, which seems to epitomize the willing-to-please personality of the New South, would run

Price: Moderate to Expensive.
Cuisine: "Nouvelle" Southern.
Serving: L, D.
Credit Cards: AE, MC, V.

out of energy, but it hasn't. In fact, Charleston seems to have mellowed its Atlanta edge. The service is snappy but not bothersome, the menu smart but not smart-alecky. It's terrifically popular and deserves to be so, for it has kept up good standards with everything from simple burgers to jumbo scallops with grain mustard and basil butter. The custard desserts, and there are several to choose from, are the best around.

> "Nothing helps scenery like ham and eggs."
>
> — Mark Twain

MARINA VARIETY STORE
803-723-6325.
City Marina, Lockwood Dr.
Open daily.
Price: Inexpensive to Moderate.
Cuisine: Southern.
Serving: B, L; D (no dinner served on Sun.).
Credit Cards: AE, MC, V.

As the rest of Charleston is getting more dressy all the time, this place isn't. Style still matches substance. Come here with your family for a terrific, classic Lowcountry breakfast — eggs, grits with shrimp gravy, biscuits, loads of coffee — and watch the day unfold over the harbor. Sandwiches and soups at lunch are simple and hearty; dinner offers solid, reliable chow, especially local seafood.

PALMETTO CAFE AT CHARLESTON PLACE
803-722-4900
130 Market St. (in the Omni).
Open daily
Price: Expensive to Very Expensive
Cuisine: American.
Serving: B, L, D.
Credit Cards: AE, CB, D, DC, MC, V.
Handicapped access.

The spacious, bright Palmetto Cafe opens early and stays lively all day as hotel guests and King Street shoppers drift through. The Sunday brunch offers live jazz and an abundant meal.

PAPILLON
803-723-6510.
41 Market St.
Open daily.
Price: Inexpensive.
Cuisine: Italian.
Serving: L, D.
Credit Cards: AE, MC, V.

You can eat an amazing variety of pizzas — whole-wheat crust, too — from a buffet, or choose from pasta dishes, salads, and sandwiches. Speedy service, informal atmosphere suitable for kids, and a central downtown location make it a comfortable, convenient place to grab a bite. Open to midnight on the weekends, for that last snack.

PRIMEROSE HOUSE
803-723-2954.
332 East Bay St.
Open daily.
Price: Expensive.
Cuisine: American.
Serving: L, D, Sun. B.
Credit Cards: AE, D, MC, V.
Reservations recommended.

There's an enthusiasm for cooking that enlivens this restaurant and brings to the menu wonderful innovations: chicken breasts grilled and topped with mozzarella and sun-dried tomatoes, then dashed under the broiler and served on capellini; oysters drizzled with carmelized shallot and tabasco butter; vegetable bisques sparked by dill and ginger; tasty blended vinegars. The Sunday brunch features nearly two dozen egg dishes with varieties of tops, bottoms, and insides you'd never dreamt of. The setting is the Charleston-style basement — that is, ground level — of a huge old house.

The informal feel of Pinckney Cafe is prized by local Charlestonians who know good food.

Wade Spees

PINCKNEY CAFE AND ESPRESSO
803-577-0961.
18 Pinckney St.
Closed Sun. and Mon.
Price: Inexpensive to Moderate.
Cuisine: American eclectic.
Serving: L, D.
Credit Cards: None.
Special Features: Take-out available.

A pale yellow, flower-bordered cottage with a porch full of tables and chairs would be an inviting site even if it were a dress shop. As it is, the cafe attracts crowds of young booksellers, artists, students, lawyers, and families who come for the casual air (the proprietors live upstairs and there are only about a dozen tables inside) and fresh, unaffected food. The antipasto salad is great for lunch, but the regulars may talk you into the black bean burrito — order both from the kitchen counter. Dinner is full-service, and grilled fish, flavored with mint or pecan butters, is a favorite. Loads of coffee selections and a variety of sweet desserts to go with them.

RESTAURANT MILLION
803-577-7472.

Luxury and formality of the sort found here, combined with superb French haute cuisine, is rare:

2 Unity Alley.
Closed Sun.
Price: Very Expensive.
Cuisine: French.
Serving: D.
Credit Cards: AE, DC, MC, V.
Reservations required.

the prestigious French guide to international dining, *Relais & Chateaux*, cites Million among its 18 United States listings. You can choose from two *prix fixe* dinners ($45–$70 per person) or select individual dishes, which might include squab enriched with goose liver and truffles, duckling with juniper berries, rack of lamb with fennel mousse, medallions of peppered tuna, prepared by chef Jose De Anacleto. The dining room is hung with antique tapestry; the tables are large and set at generous distances from one another; the service is impeccable. An incomparable meal anywhere.

ROBERT'S OF CHARLESTON
803-577-7565/800-729-0094.
112 N. Market St.
Closed Sun. and Mon.
Price: Very Expensive (approximately $67 per person including tax and tip).
Cuisine: French.
Serving: D.
Credit Cards: AE, MC, V.
Reservations required.
Special Features: Singing.

Robert Dickson succeeds where few could, not only by providing diners with superb food but by entertaining them as well. As you feast on a *prix fixe* six-course gourmet meal, which will include fish, game, his special beef tenderloin, and prodigious amounts of red and white wine, he and other talented performers sing selections from the Broadway and operatic repertory. His professionally trained voice is every bit as good as the food, which is why an evening's single seating may be booked weeks in advance.

Ornate Moorish-influenced architecture, unique in Charleston, provides a dramatic setting at Saracen's.

Wade Spees

SARACEN
803-723-6242.
141 East Bay St.
Closed Sun. and Mon.
Price: Expensive.
Cuisine: French.
Serving: L, D, tea on Wed.
 3–5.
Credit Cards: AE, MC, V.

Saracen is located in a building that would be considered elegantly unusual for a restaurant, but when it was established as the Farmers and Exchange Bank in 1853, it must have been positively shocking. Huge arched windows held in place by massive decorated woodwork reflect architectural styles that have been called, all at once, Moorish, Gothic, Hindu, and Persian. The menu changes according to season and the availability of fresh market ingredients, but the style is French, and the results, especially the soups, are sublime.

SPIRIT OF
 CHARLESTON DIN-
 NER CRUISE
803-722-2628.
City Marina, 17 Lockwood
 Dr.
Open Tues.–Sat. except in
 winter months.
Price: Expensive. ($32.95
 per person including tax
 and tip; bar beverages
 extra).
Cuisine: American.
Serving: D.
Credit Cards: AE, MC, V.
Reservations required.

You can extend your touring day and take advantage of the warm evening breezes by eating and relaxing aboard a 102-foot cruise boat that motors around the harbor and scenic rivers. A four-course meal is served, and there is dancing and live entertainment. Secure reservations with a credit card. If you must cancel, do so by 1 p.m. on the day of the cruise for a refund. Boarding begins at 6:30 p.m.

Charleston Area and the Sea Islands

If you are staying at a Sea Island resort, you will find a variety of dining choices offered in a range of prices and styles; but most of them, like the resorts themselves, are characterized by a sense of unsurprising order and solid predictability. If you are more adventurous and want to eat with local people, you might try some of the following restaurants.

BOWENS ISLAND
 RESTAURANT
803-795-2757.
Hwy. 17, about 8 miles
 south of the Ashley
 River bridge. Sign on the
 right points you down a
 dirt road. Bear right and
 drive to the dock.
Open Thurs.–Sat.

If Huck Finn lived in the Lowcountry, this is where he'd eat. He'd feel at home — newspapers for tablecloths, soda or beer straight from the cooler, barely any silverware, wooden tables scarred with penknifed initials, walls covered with autographed scrawls. He'd appreciate the food, too, for it's the real thing: hushpuppies, fried shrimp, and the house specialty, roasted oysters. Lowcountry oysters are so sweet and small they

Price: Inexpensive to Moderate.
Cuisine: Lowcountry seafood.
Serving: D.
Credit Cards: None.

make other oysters look fat and vulgar by comparison. Here, they're prepared the old-fashioned way — dug from the marsh flats, thrown across a piece of sheet metal above an open fire, and covered with wet rags. When they've steamed open, the cook will shovel a smoking load onto your table. The restaurant has been open nearly 50 years and seems so far to have resisted, as Huck might, any banal attempt at self-improvement.

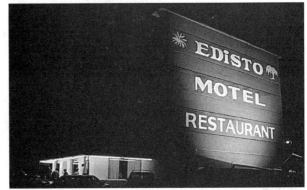

Customers line up at the Edisto Motel on Hwy. 17 for local shad roe, a house speciality.

Wade Spees

EDISTO MOTEL RESTAURANT
803-893-2270.
Hwy. 17 at Jacksonboro.
Open Thurs.–Sat.
Price: Inexpensive to Moderate.
Cuisine: Southern.
Serving: D.
Credit Cards: None.

The restaurant is not on Edisto Island, but part of a plain old motel complex on Hwy. 17, like dozens of others that serviced travelers heading south before the days of I-95 and national lodging chains. The reason customers line up outside to wait for a table is a Lowcountry legend: the shad-roe served in the spring, taken from locally caught shad, is creamy-delicious. Call ahead to make sure it's on the menu.

JOE'S ON SHEM CREEK
803-884-3410.
130 Mill St., Mt. Pleasant.
Open daily.
Price: Moderate.
Cuisine: Seafood, steaks.
Serving: L, D.
Credit Cards: AE, MC, V.

There are more places to eat right at the dock here than anywhere else, and the views of Charleston and the skyline are terrific. Friendly and casual, easy for children, who will love to watch all the marina-related activity. Oysters are a speciality, and the grilled fish is super-fresh.

OLD POST OFFICE RESTAURANT
803-869-2339.
Hwy. 174 at Point of Pines Rd., Edisto Island.
Closed Sun. and Mon.
Price: Moderate.
Cuisine: Southern.
Serving: D.
Credit Cards: MC, V.

This is the place for a fine, upscale dinner on Edisto, where you can escape the ubiquitous fried fare so popular at island restaurants. It's a small, elegant place that seats about 50 people. Soft jazz or classical music might be playing as the sun sets over the marsh and you relax and enjoy such dishes as veal or seafood sautéed with a light touch.

SHEM CREEK BAR AND GRILL
803-884-8102.
508 Mill St., Mt. Pleasant.
Open daily.
Price: Moderate to Expensive.
Cuisine: American, seafood.
Serving: L, D, B (Sat., Sun.).
Credit Cards: MC, V.

This place draws a big boating crowd, especially on summer nights. There's a bar at the dock, a very popular raw bar inside, and views aplenty. It's very much a local scene: beer-in-the-bottle casual, noisy, and fun.

Local blue crab, picked by hand, makes its way to nearly all Lowcountry menus.

Wade Spees

STONO CAFE
803-762-4478.
2008 Wappoo Dr., at Five Points, James Island.
Closed Mon.

The basic ingredients for a good meal and one you can linger over are here: fresh-from-the-garden-and-sea fish, oysters, crab, and vegetables, and a very low-key atmosphere. The recipes take tradition one step further, but not self-consciously, to include vege-

Price: Inexpensive to Moderate.
Cuisine: American, Southern.
Serving: L, D, Sun. B.
Credit Cards: None.

SULLIVAN'S
803-883-3222.
2019 Middle St., Sullivan's Island.
Open daily.
Price: Inexpensive.
Cuisine: Southern.
Serving: L, D (no Sun. eve. dinner).
Credit Cards: MC, V.

SUNSPOT
803-588-6624.
10 Center St., Folly Beach.
Closed Mon.
Price: Inexpensive to Moderate.
Cuisine: French.
Serving: D; Sat. and Sun. B.
Credit Cards: None.

Beaufort Area

THE ANCHORAGE
803-524-9392.
1103 Bay St.
Closed Sun.
Price: Moderate to Expensive.
Cuisine: Continental.
Serving: L, D.
Credit Cards: AE, D, MC, V.

tarian entrees, pasta dishes, and salads. Lunch is especially nice, served from 11:30 to 2:00, if you're getting a late start on your touring.

In the pictures taken by photographers working for the Farm Security Administration in the 1930s, the ones featuring Lowcountry families at the dining table show how habits have changed. At lunch — often the main meal of the day in those days — you'd see two vegetables, a main meat dish, white bread, dessert, and coffee. Fewer families serve in this style than used to, but you can still find this variety of fare at Sullivan's, where portions are generous, simply prepared, and served in a family-friendly atmosphere.

Smack on a downtown street corner in unassuming Folly Beach, the Sunspot has become a favorite brunch hangout for Charlestonians, who might follow it up with a walk on the beach. Baked grits, sausages, eggs-many-ways, and breads make for solid Lowcountry fare with a French touch. It's a funky, brightly painted place, the best choice in the neighborhood.

Located in an 18th-century mansion overlooking the Beaufort River, the Anchorage and its cozy back bar are a favorite lunch spot for local business people and their guests. The atmosphere at dinner is more elegant, quiet enough to sustain long conversation. During the day, the rooms are filled with light, softening the heavy and intricate plaster and wood detailing added to the home in the Victorian period; at night they glow. The menu features seafood and good salads, as well as classically prepared meat and veal dishes with appropriate sauces.

Locals celebrate special occasions at Beaufort's elegant Anchorage House.

Wade Spees

BANANA'S
803-522-0910.
910 Bay St.
Closed Mon.
Price: Inexpensive.
Cuisine: American.
Serving: L, D.
Credit Cards: MC, V.

John and Lynn Jersild came to town with the idea of establishing a restaurant like the one they had in Puerto Rico — loose, tropical in feeling — and they have. The floors are bare wood, ceiling fans whir overhead, and baskets of hanging flowers sway in the breeze. The menu is mostly sandwiches and burgers — prime rib is the weekend special — but lots of locals go for a beer or frozen drink and homemade potato chips after work. Jazz combos play Wednesdays and Saturdays.

DOCKSIDE
803-524-7433.
11th St. West, Port Royal.
Closed Mon.
Price: Moderate.
Cuisine: American; seafood.
Serving: D; L (on Sun. only, buffet-style).
Credit Cards: MC, V.

A casual restaurant right on Battery Creek, where shrimp boats tie up and the sunsets pour color in the sky. The menu offers fried and broiled seafood specialities, as well as steak and pasta. Before dinner, work up your appetite by a visit to the town's marsh boardwalk and observation tower located at "The Sands," a beach near the Port at the foot of Paris Avenue. Sharp eyes can find lots of fossilized sharks' teeth here, too.

EMILY'S
803-522-1866.
906 Port Republic St.
Closed Tues.
Price: Moderate to Expensive.
Cuisine: Continental.
Serving: L, D.
Credit Cards: AE, D, MC, V.

At Emily's you can settle on one entree or be creative and put together a meal from "tapas" items — small dishes of hot and cold appetizers, which may have light sauces or seafood stuffing. The small restaurant is dark and cozy, attracting local lawyers, young business people, new downtown residents, and sailors cruising through on the Intracoastal Waterway. Easy to get to and open late, a great place for a nightcap.

GADSBY TAVERN
803-525-1800.
822 Bay St.
Open daily.
Price: Moderate to Expensive.
Cuisine: American.
Serving: L, D.
Credit Cards: AE, D, MC, V.

Perhaps it took a born-and-raised-in-Beaufort architect to express in one renovation job both the formality and spontaneity of his hometown. Gadsby's has both. The main dining area — illuminated by attractive sconces, furnished in comfortable chairs, colored from a palette of mauves, deep greens, and browns — runs the length of the restaurant: here is the place for a quiet meal. At its end is a bright bar with tables and booths, and beyond that, a porch overlooking the Waterfront Park. Late-afternoon and evening music enlivens the bar; the television may be turned to sports. A seafood salad or steak sandwich makes a great lunch; four-course meals featuring beef, or from time to time a lobster special, are standard at dinner.

Home cooking Sea-Island style features the classics: grits, crab casserole, greens, and some fantastic iced tea.

Wade Spees

GULLAH HOUSE
Hwy. 21, St. Helena Island, about 7 miles south of Beaufort.
803-838-2402.
Closed Mon.
Price: Inexpensive to Moderate.
Cuisine: Lowcountry.
Serving: B, L, D.
Credit Cards: D, DC, MC, V.

The Gullah House, run by St. Helena Islanders, is a friendly center of island life. At breakfast, which starts at 6 a.m., you might see several residents gathering for an early meeting before work. At lunch and dinner, and especially on the weekends, when there is live jazz and blues entertainment, people ride out from town and the nearby resort areas. There's generally an after-church crowd, too. The cooking is the best of the Lowcountry: greens, creamy grits, gumbo, "From the Dock" platters, shrimp casserole, grilled chicken, fritters, oysters, and crab.

Dining outside at Plums, on the Waterfront Park, is as relaxed as eating a sandwich on your own front porch.

PLUMS
803-525-1946.
904 1/2 Bay St.
Closed Sun.
Price: Inexpensive.
Cuisine: American.
Serving: B, L.
Credit Cards: MC, V.
Special Features: Home-
  made ice cream and
  take-out service.

THE STEAMER
803-522-0210.
Hwy. 21, Lady's Island.
Closed Sun.
Price: Moderate to Expen-
  sive.
Cuisine: Lowcountry.
Serving: L, D.
Credit Cards: AE, D, MC,
  V.
No Reservations.

Plums, with its checkerboard floor and pale wood banquettes, has been a runaway success ever since it was started by two local women. Now with its "second family," it still satisfies customers with hot sandwiches like grilled turkey or reubens, multi-layered clubs, peanut butter and jelly for kids, and salads. The soup's homemade and so are the desserts. Full bar service available; and a swell little outdoor porch.

Beaufort's most consistently popular spot — there's usually a wait for dinner, and it's even hard to find a place at the bar while you're doing so. Broiled local seafood and shellfish platters are the main dishes, although you may have a steak if you wish. It's noisy, crowded, and very informal (toss your old oyster shells into a bucket at the center of your table), but the food is worth it. If you're curious about Frogmore Stew, an indigenous dish that features sausage, corn on the cob, shrimp, and potatoes, in a spicy broth, this is the place to try it.

Wade Spees

Frogmore Stew at The Steamer gathers the best of land and sea: sausage, corn, potatoes, slaw, and all that firm, pink shrimp

**WHITEHALL PLANTA-
TION INN**
803-521-1700.
Hwy. 21, Lady's Island,
   just over the Woods
   Bridge.
Closed Sun.
Price: Moderate to Expen-
   sive.
Cuisine: Continental.
Serving: L, D.
Credit Cards: D, MC, V.
Reservations recom-
   mended.

A wonderful setting under a canopy of live oaks by the river, and a dining room that has windows on three sides, make eating here so relaxing and enjoyable that it's usually the place local people bring their visiting guests. It has a nicely settled-in feeling. No one seems to be in a big hurry. The menu offers some surprises: roast lamb, lightly sauced sliced veal, and crispy duckling are worth trying.

**WILKOP'S WHITE
HALL INN**
803-521-1915.
Hwy. 21, Lady's Island, at
   the corner of Meridian
   Rd.
Closed Mon.
Price: Moderate to Expen-
   sive.
Cuisine: American, South-
   ern.
Serving: L, D; B (Sun.).
Credit Cards: AE, DC,
   MC, V.

Wilkop's has moved into a brand new building that has less charm than the old place, but the menu still features the favorites local people have been choosing for nearly 20 years: shrimp salad or softshell crab sandwiches at lunch, homemade soups, and their classic, mini spice-and-blueberry muffins. For dinner, try the baked flounder stuffed with crabmeat or sautéed scallops.

Savannah is a small city full of confidence and easy sophistication, and so is the Bistro.

Wade Spees

Savannah

BISTRO SAVANNAH
912-233-6266.
309 W. Congress St.
Open daily.
Price: Moderate to Expensive.
Cuisine: American, Southern.
Serving: D.
Credit Cards: AE, MC, V.
Reservations recommended.
Handicapped Access.
Special Features: All food available to go.

The Bistro opened in March 1989 and has steadily drawn a mix of residents and visitors staying at the downtown B&Bs. Repeat customers come for the homemade desserts, the catfish (dramatically filleted tableside), the great New York strip steak, and the casual, upbeat atmosphere: you could turn up in a tux or shorts and feel at home. Lots of art by local talent hangs on the walls. If you love garlic, try the appetizer that features it roasted and squeezed on goat cheese with Vidalia onion relish. Extensive wine list, specializing in California vineyards.

CHUTZPAH & PANACHE
912-234-5007.
251 Bull St.
Closed Sun.
Price: Moderate.
Cuisine: American.
Serving: L; D (Fri. and Sat.).
Credit Cards: MC, V.

A charming place to eat, located in a boutique featuring hand-printed and woven women's clothing. There's a limited menu with soups and hearty salads, a meat dish (often lamb), and seafood. Wines are reasonably priced, and the desserts are made by a local baker. Eat here before a Civic Center performance and then walk to the show.

CITY MARKET CAFE
912-236-7133.

Matthew Maher's popular and unpretentious restaurant, open since 1991, covers a lot of

224 W. St. Julian St.
Open daily.
Price: Moderate.
Cuisine: American.
Serving: L, D.
Credit Cards: AE, CB, D,
    MC, V.
Special Features: Kids'
    menu.

bases well. His menu includes pasta, sandwiches, rotisserie chicken and ribs, ice-cream sundaes and fountain concoctions, desserts from the Silver Palate cookbook, Cokes in the bottle, and 16 brands of beer. The place itself seems full of fizz: brick walls, a black tin ceiling, fresh tablecloths, and indoor and outdoor dining. The staff is unfazed by children and won't even blink if you order a hefty grilled sandwich for dinner while your companion has beef tenderloin and fine wine.

Feel like a plain ol' local at Clary's, where you can read the newspaper in the warm spring air and watch the passing parade of tourists, students, and downtown neighbors.

Wade Spees

CLARY'S CAFE
912-233-0402.
404 Abercorn St. at Jones St.
Open daily.
Price: Inexpensive.
Cuisine: American.
Serving: B, L.
Credit Cards: AE, MC, V.
Wheelchair accessible seating.

A bacon-and-egg sandwich on wheat and coffee is a typical order at Clary's, a downtown eatery where your cup stays refilled and the food is simple and good. At lunch, the Greek salad is big enough to share; or if you're hungry, you might try the meatloaf special, which includes vegetables, biscuits, and mashed potatoes. Top it off with a root-beer float.

**CRYSTAL BEER PAR-
LOR**
912-232-1153.
301 W. Jones St.
Closed Sun.
Price: Inexpensive.
Cuisine: American.
Serving: L, D.
Credit Cards: AE, D, MC,
    V.

Located at the end of one of Savannah's prettiest residential streets, the Crystal is a bar with leather banquettes and frosted mugs that has been serving for 60 years. It's not undiscovered — it's been written up time and again — but fame has not altered its unprepossessing style and probably never will. It would be like urging a sleepy dog lying in the sun to move on. The fried oyster or

A cold glass of beer enjoyed in an upholstered leather booth: what better way to escape the Lowcountry heat.

Wade Spees

shrimp salad sandwiches are among the best around; the crab stew is thick and filling. Fine for youngsters, too.

Meals prepared by Elizabeth Terry at her namesake restaurant have been singled out for praise in the South, and the country.

Wade Spees

ELIZABETH ON 37TH
912-236-5547.
105 E. 37th St. (at Drayton, in the Victorian District).
Closed Sun.
Price: Expensive to Very Expensive.
Cuisine: American; gourmet Southern.
Serving: D.
Credit Cards: AE, MC. V.
Reservations recommended.

Dinner is served in four beautifully decorated dining rooms with lovely table settings and attentive service (two captains and many of the wait staff have been with chef Elizabeth Terry for 10 years). Selected in 1992 as one of the 25 best restaurants in the country, the menu features several signature dishes, among them such seasonal items as (in fall and winter) medallions of venison marinated in a cider and clove mixture and grilled, then served with sautéed red cabbage with an earthy cumin flavor and a sweet potato cake. In spring and summer, try crabcakes rolled in almond crumbs, baked and served with a white wine butter sauce, accompanied by a corn relish. Wine list ranges from moderate to very expensive.

45 SOUTH
912-233-1881.
20 E. Broad St.
Closed Sun.
Price: Very Expensive.
Cuisine: Continental;
  gourmet Southern.
Serving: D.
Credit Cards: AE, MC, V.

A softly lit place, lots of dark green in the decorating, almost like a row house, with elegant tables situated in three sections and a small bar. The service is here in abundance, but not rushed: there seemed to be one waiter to attend to the water glasses alone and another to operate the battery-powered pepper-grinder. Wonderful soft breadsticks accompany well-prepared and presented food, especially a crabcake appetizer with roasted red pepper remoulade and shrimp-and-endive on the side; the scallops of veal with garlic potatoes and spicy mustard; and the grilled swordfish.

Wade Spees

Politicians at one table, a big family at another, Savannah's young set at the bar provide a high-spirited mix of people at Garibaldi's

GARIBALDI'S
912-232-7118.
315 W. Congress St.
Open daily.
Price: Moderate to Expensive.
Cuisine: Italian.
Serving: D.
Credit Cards: AE, MC, V.
Handicapped Access.
Reservations recommended.
Special Features: Take-out available.

Two things should draw your attention as you enter this very busy place: the blackboard with its daily specials, and the crowd, likely to include a sampling of civic leaders, politicians, writers, and artists. Even if you have to wait for a table — or for your meal if it's really crowded — the people-watching will be fun. The pasta dishes come as simple as fettuccine Alfredo, to which you can add a spinach salad. But if you're more adventurous, start with eggplant and chevre and move on to veal, cooked five ways. Or just come for dessert and coffee and after-dinner drinks.

JOHN & LINDA'S
912-233-2626.
313 W. St. Julian St.
Open daily.
Price: Moderate to Very
  Expensive.
Cuisine: American; South-
  ern.
Serving: L, D; B (Sun.)
Credit Cards: AE, MC, V.
Reservations recom-
  mended.

The folks who updated Clary's Cafe have scored another victory here in the City Market, a restaurant with an open kitchen, an airy dining room full of potted plants, and a cozy corner bar often enlivened by a jazz trio. There's outside seating, too, which makes Sunday brunch a treat. The menu is a mixture of standards, like steaks and fresh fruit splashed with Grand Marnier, and surprises like Buffalo Oysters (think Buffalo wings) and ravioli Olivia (cheeses and sausages in a pesto sauce). The atmosphere is easy and good-humored: the chefs sport berets but no self-consciousness.

Your dining companions may become your friends when you eat family-style at Mrs. Wilkes'.

Wade Spees

**MRS. WILKES' BOARD-
  ING HOUSE**
912-232-5997.
107 W. Jones St.
Open Mon.–Fri.
Price: Inexpensive.
Cuisine: Southern.
Serving: B, L.
Credit Cards: None.
Handicapped Access.
Special Features: Take-out
  available from back
  door.

This is truly homemade cooking served as it would be at home: the diners seated around large tables, with heaping platters of fried chicken, baskets of biscuits, and bowls of slaw, vegetables, red rice, and black-eyed peas or green beans. Located in the basement of an old red-brick house, you'll know it when you see the line forming at mealtime.

NACHO MAMA'S
912-236-1000.
W. St. Julian St, in the City
  Market.

It's not at the beach, but it has the feel of a funky, barefoot place. Art students, tourists, and downtown regulars come here to eat and watch the world go by at the City Market; the folks behind

Closed Sun.
Price: Inexpensive.
Cuisine: Mexican.
Serving: L, D.
Credit Cards: None.
Special Features: Take-out available.

the counter are friendly and efficient. It offers an informality new to Savannah, a city long felt by many to be too sleepy to capitalize on its assets. Sit inside at the bar — it's more of a counter and furnished like a student's apartment with odd table lamps and flaky brick walls with posters — or, better yet, relax outside at picnic tables. When you order, your slip gets shot to the grill along a wire; listen for your name and collect your basket of food. It's great Mexican fare, as hot as you prefer, and lots of it: one burrito is enough for lunch. Fillings for meat-eaters and vegetarians. Wash it all down with a cold beer.

RIVER HOUSE
912-234-1900.
125 W. River St.
Open daily.
Price: Moderate to Expensive.
Cuisine: American; Seafood.
Serving: L, D.
Credit Cards: AE, MC, V.
Reservations recommended.
Handicapped Access.

Eat in a converted cotton warehouse overlooking River Street and the boat traffic, too. Fresh fish is the speciality; service is very efficient even if there are crowds, which there may be: it's in a great location, just down the street from the Hyatt, and a favorite of visitors. Try some take-out from the Pecan Pie and Cookies Co. located on the premises to satisfy a late-night craving.

SAVANNAH RIVER QUEEN DINNER CRUISE
912-232-6404.
9 E. River St.
Hours: Fri., Sat., Sun at 7 p.m.
Price: Expensive to Very Expensive.
Cuisine: American.
Serving: D.
Credit Cards: AE, MC, V.

Enjoy a complete meal of fish or prime rib, salad, vegetables, and dessert while your cruise boat plies the Savannah River, upstream and down. There's live entertainment and a dance floor; the band even plays requests. Tickets for the two-hour cruise are $30.70 for adults and $18 for children, including tax. Tip and bar beverages are extra. Fully prepaid reservations are required, and there are no refunds. A change of date will be honored, given 48 hours' notice. Call ahead to confirm schedule; fewer trips in colder months.

SMITTY'S DIXIE CHEF
912-353-8000.
7080 Hodgson Memorial Dr. at Eisenhower, midtown Savannah.
Open Tues.–Sat.

There are no frills at Smitty's — five booths, ten stools, get-the-job-done waitresses, and as the menu points out, "no chandeliers, no carpet" — but it's known for the best cheeseburger in the Lowcountry, the kind that takes both hands to hold and eat, and lots of napkins to catch the juice. Splurge

Price: Inexpensive.
Cuisine: Southern.
Serving: L.
Credit Cards: None.
Special features: Take-out
available.

on calories and get the steak fries. Excellent iced tea: you can even buy it by the gallon, with a bag of ice, to go.

VINNIE VAN GOGO'S
912-233-6394.
317 W. Bryant St.
Open daily.
Price: Inexpensive.
Cuisine: Pizza, Italian specialities.
Serving: L (Sat.); D (from 4
p.m.)
Credit Cards: None.
Special Features: Delivery
by bicycle courier to
downtown area.

Calzones and thin-crust pizza by the slice or pie (14″ or 18″) made from dough prepared on the premises during the day and rolled and tossed while you watch from the counter. These cooks are having fun. Nineteen toppings including Italian sausage made in Chicago (by an Italian, we're told) and shipped south. Large selection of imported beers and a concoction called spodeeodee (cheap red wine, 7-Up, splash of orange soda), which sells by the glass or pitcher as fast as they can mix it up. A perfect example of the new life that has ingrained itself into the old city.

WINDOW'S
912-238-1234.
2 W. Bay St.
Open daily.
Price: Moderate to Very
Expensive.
Cuisine: Continental.
Serving: L, D; B (Sun.).
Credit Cards: AE, D, MC,
V.

Though it's located in the Hyatt and has the fresh, glossy look that characterizes the hotel, it feels more like an upscale urban restaurant. Sunday brunch is the best around — a full buffet, where your eyes are guaranteed to be bigger than your appetite. Wonderful views and a staff that lets you take the time to enjoy your meal and linger over coffee.

Savannah Area

**CRAB SHACK AT
  CHIMNEY CREEK**
912-786-9857.
40 Estill Hammock Rd.,
Tybee Island.
Open daily.
Price: Inexpensive to Mod-
erate.
Cuisine: Seafood.
Serving: L (Sat. and Sun.
only); D (daily).
Credit Cards: MC, V.

You won't find a more informal place outside your own kitchen: wooden tables inside and out, beer in the bottle, diners in bathing suits and sandy feet welcome. The food is strictly off-the-boat: delicious fat crab served in cakes or blended with spices and cheese, and boiled shrimp. Kids will love to select their own crabs out of the tank. The view, at a bend in the creek, is the Lowcountry at its best.

The Lowcountry's old houses may put on airs, but its old dockside restaurants sure don't.

Wade Spees

THE BREAKFAST CLUB
912-786-5984.
1500 Butler Ave., Tybee
   Beach.
Open daily.
Price: Inexpensive.
Cuisine: Southern.
Serving: B, L.
Credit Cards: MC, V.

Get a real feel of the kicked-back life of Tybee Beach at The Breakfast Club, where you can eat ham and eggs as early as 6 a.m. You might run into the shrimpers coming in or the early anglers just setting out. If you want to get a jump on the day, or take a quiet walk on a deserted morning beach, this is a great place to start.

FOOD PURVEYORS

BAKERIES

Charleston Area

Michel's Cafe and Bakery (803-724-3815; 372 King St., in the Marion Sq. Mall) You could make a meal of fresh pastries and breads here, but don't limit yourself to breakfast: take some to go.

Saffron (803-722-5588; 333 East Bay St.) The glass cases filled to brimming with pastries and the racks of fresh bread should promote thoughts of a gourmet picnic; or you can eat here, in the sleek cafe with a checkerboard floor. A small gourmet grocery features vinegars, cheeses, jellies, and other treats.

Upper Crust (803-763-0654; 1124 Sam Rittenberg Blvd.) A good spot for a light meal or snacks like scones, desserts, and homemade breads.

Beaufort Area

Sweet Temptations (803-524-6171; 205 West St.) Breads, cookies, croissants, and cakes baked on the premises.

Savannah Area

Express Cafe and Bakery (912-233-4683; 39 Barnard St.) Charles and Aileen Snyder have made an upscale Art Deco–style bakery out of a downtown storefront: the breads and desserts are homemade, the bagels come from Brooklyn. Fresh garden produce makes for excellent sandwiches and soups, too.

Gottlieb's (912-236-4261; 1601 Bull St.) Many varieties of breads, seeded rolls, cookies, and sweets from Savannah's traditional purveyor.

CANDY AND ICE CREAM

Charleston Area

Cacao's Chocolates (803-722-3921; 344 King St.) Homemade chocolates in several dozen amazing varieties and ice creams, too.

Charleston Chocolates (803-577-4491; 190 East Bay St.) It's Valentine's Day year-round here with hand-dipped chocolates and fancy trimmings.

Lucas Neuhaus (803-722-0461; 73 State St.) If you're in the Market Area and overwhelmed by all the shops and all the merchandise for sale, drop in for one fabulous Belgian chocolate or confection.

Häagen-Dazs (803-723-9326; 23 S. Market St.) Sometimes it's even too hot in the Lowcountry for ice cream — it's a melted mess after a few licks — but this old favorite stays open after the sun goes down.

Beaufort Area

Chocolate Tree (803-524-7980; 507 Carteret St.) A family-run emporium selling many kinds of chocolates, truffles, and dipped fruits made right on the premises, plus candy-making accessories. Watch for their "all you can eat" days — for serious chocoholics only.

Ice Creams and Coffee Beans (803-525-6115; Old Bay Marketplace, 917–919 Bay St.) Take a seat by the window and take a breather. Flavorful scoops by the cone or cup; espresso, cappuccino, sweet desserts, and sandwiches.

Lollipop Tree (803-524-3223; 504 Scott St.) Sweet, whimsical candies in unusual flavors — if they could only grow on trees!

Savannah Area

Peaches 'n Cream (912-233-3131; 5 E. River St.) If you're watching your waistline, go for the yogurt; but if you can convince yourself that you'll walk off the calories on a riverfront stroll, go for ice cream and toppings.

Savannah's Candy Kitchen (912-233-8411; 225 E. River St.) You could gain weight on the smell of this shop, which features delectables like soft fudge, pralines, glazed pecans, and chewy chocolate turtles.

DELIS AND FAST FOOD

Charleston Area

Bookstore Cafe (803-720-8843; 412 King St.) Breakfast all day and blue-plate specials served an arm's length away from lots of fine books.

Doe's Pita Plus (803-577-3179; 334 East Bay St.) A small, bustling place offering sandwiches of chopped vegetables, chicken, or meat stuffed in soft pita bread pockets and seasoned with dressing or light sauces. Side orders of tabouli, hummus and potato salad.

Mediterranean Deli (803-766-0323; 90 Folly Rd., South Windermere Shopping Center) Cases of imported beers and wines divide the room; the tables are covered in white butcher paper; the chairs and booths are upholstered in vinyl. Many people who know the fancy places still call this their favorite for lunch. A classic, friendly deli.

Mike Calders Deli and Pub (803-577-0123; 288 King St.) Feast on Dagwood Bumstead—style sandwiches filled with premium deli fare like liverwurst and corn beef. Top it off with ale and beer from the British Isles. Popular college hangout.

Reubens (803-722-6883; 251 Meeting St.) Bagels and lox, knishes, sauerkraut, chopped liver, and hot Italian sausage make this place feel like a West Side deli in New York. Right downtown.

Beaufort Area

Bay Towne Grill (803-522-3880; 310 West St.) Don't overlook this tiny spot in a building at the edge of a parking lot. Great and hefty sandwiches, soups, salads, and lemonade. Open 11–5, closed Sunday.

Dick and Jane's Dog Spot (803-522-9100; Hwy. 21, Lady's Island) A small, basic American grill open for lunch until 4 p.m. daily except Sunday. Excellent hot dogs and hamburgers with sides of slaw, beans, chili and fried cheese. The chicken fajita is sizzling and juicy. Beer and wine available.

Maryland Fried Chicken (803-524-8766; 1100 Ribaut Rd.) Best fried chicken in Beaufort, by the piece, dinner, or bucketful.

Shrimp Shack (803-838-2962; Hwy. 21, St. Helena Island, about 11 miles south of Beaufort) Fresh seafood from the family dock — you can see the shrimp boats from the porch — slaw, red rice, hush puppies, and beans. You'll wish more places served the terrific shrimp burger (a fat patty on a bun). Informal dining on a screened porch or gazebo.

Upper Crust (803-521-1999; Hwy. 21, Lady's Island) Plain and fancy pizzas, chili, submarine sandwiches, and hot grinders.

Savannah Area

Alan Gottlieb's (912-355-1765; 5500 Abercorn St.) Kosher favorites including smoked fish, lots of salads, and rich desserts.

Eli's Deli (912-355-3287; 4430 Habersham St.) Here in this sunny corner location, you can get sandwiches to eat in or to go out. Imported Greek products, fancy cheeses, and "Buckhead Bread."

Fannies on the Beach (912-786-6109; 1613 Strand, Tybee Island) You're on the beach and you're hungry: get a burger and fries or fried chicken and onion rings here.

606 East (912-233-2887; 319 W. Congress St.) Creative sandwiches like "muffaletta" (grilled ham, marinated olive salad, and melted mozarella) served on grilled Greek pita bread, and veggie "wraps" of broccoli, zucchini, mushrooms, yellow squash, and tomatoes.

Truffles Cafe (912-354-5368; 7804 Abercorn St., in the Oglethorpe Mall) A bright place where you can have a delicious meal of quiche, soups, or full salads after shopping. The warmed-up blond brownies topped with ice cream and pecan sauce are justly famous.

GOURMET AND HEALTH FOOD STORES

Charleston Area

Carolina Wine and Cheese (803-577-6144; 54 1/2 Wentworth St.) Fresh German bread, excellent deli meats, coffees and teas, gourmet items, and all the makings for homebrewed beer.

Fulford-Egan Coffees & Teas (803-577-4553; 231 Meeting St.) Coffee and tea and all the accessories to brew it share space in this coffeehouse, which also serves pastries and desserts.

Gita's Gourmet (803-722-8207; Market St., in the central building) Charleston's oldest gourmet shop with Southern specialities to take home, like benne biscuits, pepper jelly, watermelon pickle, and relishes. Large selection of cheeses, coffees and teas, dried pastas.

Hoppin' John's (803-577-6404; 30 Pinckney St.) A wonderful culinary bookstore that also sells fresh stone-ground grits and food-related items such as cards and kitchen accessories. If you're interested in Lowcountry cooking, this store is a must.

Raspberry's (803-556-0076; 1331 Ashley River Rd.) Natural, unprocessed foods, including grains, herbs, bulk flour, and organic produce. Vitamins and body care items, too.

Beaufort Area

Blackstone's (803-524-4330; 915 Bay St.) A gourmet grocery and deli for Beaufort residents and an informal "chandlery" for sailors coming through on the Intracoastal Waterway. Deli items include meats, pâtés, cheeses, and side dishes. Beer and wine, and staples, too. Good pre-picnic stop.

Sea Island Mercantile & Provisioning, Ltd. (803-522-3000; 800-735-3215; 928 Bay St.) Savor Lowcountry flavors as well as memories by ordering soups, condiments, sauces, and speciality books by mail. Shrimp, oysters, clams, scallops, and soft-shell crab can be delivered overnight. Drop by for more information.

Vita Villa Ltd. (803-522-0583; Hwy. 21, Lady's Island Square) Herbs, grains, candies, books, vitamins, local honey, and sugar-free and preservative-free health foods.

W.H. Gay Seafood (803-524-8637; 2340 Boundary St.) Fresh fish, shellfish, and shrimp from local waters, packed in ice to last on the road. Utensils, shirts, and "shrimp boots" in the classic white, low-cut style.

Savannah Area

Brighter Day (912-236-4703; 1102 Bull St.) A health-food store featuring a full line of natural foods and health-care products, as well as excellent sandwiches to go, breads, and organic produce.

Callaway Gardens Country Store (912-236-4055; 301 E. River St.) Accessories for the kitchen and Southern goods to stock the shelves — items like grits, muscadine grape preserve, and smoked meats.

Sophisticated Palate (912-355-6160; 238 Eisenhower Dr.) Gourmet foods like wines, cheeses, canned goods, and coffees; also the tools to make your cooking gourmet, too: pasta machines, coffee grinders, small appliances, and the like.

Smith Brothers (912-234-2204; 2502 Habersham St.) A complete grocery with an excellent butcher and a wide variety of gourmet foods. A longtime Savannah institution.

FARMERS' MARKETS AND SEASONAL FOOD FESTIVALS

Wade Spees

Early shoppers get the best pick of local produce at Charleston's Saturday Farmers' Market.

The growing season in the Lowcountry lasts from February to the first frost in November, with many crops being planted more than once. A visit to an outdoor market on Saturday morning may yield anything from herbs to watermelon. In general, the vendors do most of their selling on Saturday mornings between April and October. Central Markets are located at **Marion Square** in **Charleston**, the **Waterfront Park** in **Beaufort,** at the **Gullah Market** on **Hilton Head**, and at the **State Farmers' Market** in the **Savannah Area** (Hwy. 80, Garden City).

If you're traveling on the Sea Islands, Johns Island and St. Helena in particular, you might stop by the farms themselves, where you can buy from a stand or pick your own tomatoes, peppers, melon, blueberries, and strawberries. The hours may be informal, and there are no telephones in the fields, so a bit of exploring is called for. Look for notices in the local paper announcing the opening of fields, ask at a gourmet shop, or call the local Chamber of Commerce for information.

Wade Spees

Fields of the Lowcountry have produced indigo, rice, cotton, and now tea.

For an unusual treat, you may want to visit the **Charleston Tea Plantation** (803-559-0383), the only one in the nation, located on Wadmalaw Island about 20 miles south of the city. Free tours lasting about an hour are scheduled one Saturday per month (usually the first Saturday) starting at 10 a.m. The last tour of the day is at 1:30 p.m. and they are canceled in case of rain. To get there, drive south on Hwy. 17 to S.C. 171. Turn east (toward Folly Beach), and soon after turn south on S.C. 700, Maybank Highway. The plantation is located at nearly the end of this road.

Another way to sample the freshest produce and seafood is to attend any one of the many regional festivals dedicated to food. Many of them are long-established and county fair in feeling, featuring parades, rides, and family-style entertainment. Here is a list of some of them.

Wade Spees

Thousands turn out for annual oyster roasts at Boone Hall Plantation.

Lowcountry Oyster Festival (803-853-8000; Charleston Trident Convention and Visitors Bureau, P.O. Box 975, Charleston, SC 29402.) A huge oyster feast, held on the grounds of Boone Hall Plantation near Charleston every February.

Colleton County Rice Festival (803-549-9595; P.O. Box 426, Walterboro, SC 29488.) Arts and crafts, cooking demonstrations, and rice-husking celebrate the Lowcountry's rice-growing heritage. Held the last full weekend in April, in Walterboro, the county seat.

Mt. Pleasant Seafood Festival (803-884-2528; P.O. Box 745, Mt. Pleasant, SC

29464) Held in April to honor the "farmers of the sea" and showcase their catch and the way they get it.

Hampton County Watermelon Festival (803-943-3784; Chamber of Commerce, P.O. Box 122, Hampton, SC 29924) The oldest festival in the state celebrating the county's best crop. Held at the end of June and lasting a week, featuring seed-spitting contests, beauty queens, and a big parade.

Mullet Day Festival (803-757-4399; c/o Bluffton Marine Rescue Squadron, Bluffton, SC 29910) This big fish fry, street dance, and crafts show is held at All Joy Landing, Brighton Beach, around the 4th of July.

Catfish Festival (803-784-3606; Chamber of Commerce, P.O. Box 307, Hardeeville, SC 29927) Family entertainment, boat races on the Savannah River, and of course catfish are the focus of this festival, which takes place the third weekend in September.

Taste of Charleston (803-577-4030; Greater Charleston Restaurant Association, 185 East Bay St.) Every October, more than 50 city restaurants, including many of the best chefs in town, participate in a food and tasting festival featuring Lowcountry and international cuisine.

CHAPTER SIX

Having Fun On Land And Sea

RECREATION

Wade Spees

An hour's worth of digging yields a bucketful of conch.

For centuries, Low-country people have depended for nourishment on the reliable bounty of land and sea. By now they are so accustomed to going forth to gather and returning home with full baskets that the *work* of gathering and the *pleasure* to be had in it are easily interchanged. From the very beginning, the waters, woods, and marshes have yielded harvest and pleasure in equal amounts; many's the hunter or fisherman or Sunday painter who took to the outdoors seeking the one, only to come home with the other, as if he couldn't help it. Such is the natural abundance of the Lowcountry, and the dozens of opportunities to explore it — by power boat or windsurfer, with canoe or crab net, paintbrush or pup tent — that visitors still have this experience today.

The weather in the Lowcountry conspires to make outdoor activity a year-round endeavor. Points of access are numerous and convenient, the distances not long, the preparation minimal, with no mountains to climb or lift lines to endure. There are guides to lead you, captains to ferry you, campgrounds to shelter you, and trails to show you the way.

The addition in recent times of first-class resorts has created opportunities for recreation of a more studied sort. There are dozens of premiere golf courses and several outstanding tennis layouts, facilities that attract national tournaments and top teaching pros. (For information specific to Hilton Head Island, see Chapter Eight.) Many municipalities have public courts and courses. There are minor-league baseball teams. Old plantation lands and hunting clubs have been revived to foster the sport of shooting dove, duck, and quail, as well as larger game such as deer and wild pig. Savannah itself is making necessary preparations to host all the Olympic yachting activity scheduled for the summer of 1996.

The Pleasures of Abundance

April 14, 1905: "It is not a cheap thing to live in this country. One must have horses, one must have servants — but once given a moderate income to cover these things and there is no spot on earth where one can have so much for so little. Wild ducks abound all winter, also partridges, snipe, and woodcock; rabbits and squirrels run over everything. Our streams are filled with bream, Virginia perch and trout. If anyone wants better living than these afford, he can have wild turkey and venison for the shooting, as the woods abound in these, and he can have shad daily during two months if he goes to the expense of a small shad net and a man to use it. It is a splendid country for poultry."

— From *A Woman Rice Planter* by "Patience Pennington"
[Elizabeth Waties Allston], Cornelius O. Cathey, Editor
(Cambridge: The Belknap Press of Harvard University Press, 1961)

While guessing what a novelist had in mind in his work can be a risky business, perhaps when DuBose Heyward wrote "It is always Sunday on Sea Islands," he was thinking that there is in every day a piece of Sunday in the Lowcountry, a piece of time as yet unplanned and unscheduled, in which to enjoy the best of your surroundings both naturally and simply, with as few complications as possible. This is the definition of recreation in the Lowcountry.

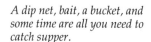

A dip net, bait, a bucket, and some time are all you need to catch supper.

Wade Spees

So here are some options. If your recreational pursuits require clothing or equipment you didn't bring with you, see the shops listed later in this chapter under "Sporting Goods and Clothing."

BASEBALL

Two Class A teams play regularly in the Lowcountry. The *Charleston Rainbows*, a farm team of the San Diego Padres, play at College Park. For tickets and information call 803-723-7241. The *Savannah Cardinals*, a farm team of the St. Louis Cardinals, play their home games at Grayson Stadium. The ticket number is 912-351-9150.

BEACH ACCESS

There are hundreds of miles of coastline between Charleston and Savannah and on the barrier islands. At many points, the public can reach the coast at designated access sites. Some of these offer changing areas, restrooms, showers, and picnic tables. Others are mere paths in the sand. Some, like the beaches on pristine barrier islands, are accessible only by boat.

The beaches on this coast are flat and wide, without rocks, overlooked by dunes or maritime forest. The surf ranges from placid to roiling (the Washout at Folly Beach is considered a top surfing spot). Lifeguards are *not* on duty at every beach access point, and swimming may be extremely hazardous in their absence. It is not wise to swim in unmonitored areas. Walking on the dunes, picking the sea oats, and driving on the beach are forbidden.

A few suggestions follow for reaching the beach by land or water. For more detailed information about specific access points, contact the chambers of commerce or tourism commissions listed at the end of Chapter Nine, *Information*.

Boardwalks and stiles lead the way to flat Lowcountry beaches and warm ocean waters.

Wade Spees

EASY ACCESS

Some of the best beach access points, and certainly the most convenient ones, are located in shorefront towns, where you can shop or eat as part of your outing and park in designated or metered areas.

In the *Charleston area,* you'll find *Sullivan's Island* and *Isle of Palms* lying north of the city on Hwy. 17 and S.C. 703. Located to the south, off Hwy. 17 on S.C. 171, is *Folly Beach*, where in addition to simple dune walkovers, you can enjoy the fully outfitted *Folly Beach County Park* (803-588-2426), offering 4,000 feet of oceanfront access, lifeguards, changing rooms, showers, and pay parking. A bit farther south off Hwy. 17, at the entrance to Kiawah Island, is *Beachwalker Park* (803-768-2395), another well-developed public beach destination with facilities, lifeguards, and limited pay parking.

Still farther south lies *Hilton Head*, with beach access off Hwy. 278 (the main island road) at *Folly Field Beach Park* and *Coligny Circle*.

The only accessible beach on Georgia's northern coast, *Tybee Island* lies 18 miles east of *Savannah* on Hwy. 80, the Islands Expressway. In addition to its commercial and residential area, there is a museum (912-786-4077) and a lighthouse that you can climb.

BEACHFRONT STATE PARKS

The Lowcountry has two large, well-maintained and very popular beachfront parks. *Edisto Beach State Park* (803-869-2756) is located 50 miles southeast of *Charleston* on Hwy. 174, at the southern tip of Edisto; *Hunting Island State Park* (803-838-2011) is on Hwy. 21, about 30 minutes from *Beaufort.*

These two parks, each of which covers more than 3,000 acres, offer campsite and shelter accommodations (see the "Camping" section later in this chapter), nature trails, dressing rooms and showers, picnic areas, playgrounds, and surf or pier fishing. The 19th-century *Hunting Island Lighthouse* offers an expansive view of the confluence of ocean waters and St. Helena Sound.

SHORE REFUGES

Charleston Area

By water, and with advance arrangements, you may visit *Cape Romain National Wildlife Refuge* (803-928-3368; 390 Bulls Island Rd., Awendaw, SC 29429), a 64,229-acre site managed by the U.S. Fish and Wildlife Service.

The refuge consists of four parts: *Bulls Island*, a 5,000-acre barrier island; *Cape Island*, a favorite spot for loggerhead turtles to nest; *Moore's Landing*, the site of ferry services, refuge offices, and an observation pier just right for birders; and *Raccoon Key Island*, a popular spot for shelling.

The lighthouse at Hunting Island State Park, a cool spot to visit after a hot day on the sand.

Wade Spees

Several companies operate beach excursion and shelling trips to the refuge, including *Cape Romain Island Charters* (803-884-5523 or, after 6 p.m., 1-800-528-2041); *Capt. Ken Kirchner* (803-884-6509); and *Wild Dunes Yacht Harbor* (803-886-5100). The 1992 ticket prices ranged from $20 for adults ($10 for children under 12) on large tour boats, up to $175 for six passengers for a five-hour excursion aboard a smaller boat. Some deep-sea fishing charters (See "Fishing" in this chapter) offer sightseeing services as well.

Another refuge in the Charleston area is *Capers Island*, a classic, undisturbed barrier island managed by the *South Carolina Wildlife and Marine Resources Department*. Contact them (803-795-6350; P.O. Box 12559, Charleston, SC 29412) regarding public use restrictions, instructions for anchoring and beaching boats, and camping permits.

An alligator at home in the Cape Romain National Wildlife Refuge.

Wade Spees

Savannah Area

Wassaw Island, located east of Savannah and Skidaway Island, can be reached by either private or charter boat arranged through the *U.S. Fish and Wildlife Service*, Savannah Coastal Refuges Office (912-652-4415; P.O. Box 8487, Savannah, GA 31412). Within its 10,000 acres, there are more than 20 miles of inland island trails to explore and a seven-mile beach to walk.

Though not strictly a refuge, *Daufuskie Island*, where novelist Pat Conroy taught school (the experience he described in *The Water Is Wide*) is of special interest. It is no longer the isolated hamlet it was; resort development has come to its shores. Nonetheless, a visit will provide a glimpse of Sea Island living as it was for generations in a place of haunting beauty. Boats leave from River St. in Savannah (in front of the Hyatt Hotel) Tues., Thurs., Sat. at 11 a.m. for a trip lasting four hours, including about two hours on shore. The cost with tour and lunch on Daufuskie is $25 per person. If you wish to spend a day on Daufuskie, board the excursion boat on Hilton Head at the Broad Creek Marina on Marshland Rd., departures daily at 11 a.m., returning at 4 p.m. The fare is $15 round-trip per person. On the island, you can rent golf carts for touring ($40 per day including a map), and lunch (costing about $6) is available. Call 1-800-398-7687 for more information.

BIRD-WATCHING

The barrier islands mentioned above provide the least disturbed habitats for birds and wildlife you're likely to find in the Lowcountry; if you're a serious birder, a visit to any one of them should be included in your trip.

But even if you can't make it to the islands, you will not be disappointed in what you can find in more accessible places. Because of its situation on the North American flyway and its diverse natural environment, the Lowcountry attracts scores of wading, shore, and songbirds, some of them as unusual as the roseate spoonbill and parasitic jaeger. Woodcocks flock in plowed fields, owls hover in roadside forests, and hawks soar over open grassland. In February, you are likely to see thousands of robins and cedar waxwings swarming in country yards, picking the cherry laurel trees clean.

Local Audubon societies, conducting an annual Christmas count, have reported over 200 types of birds from scrub areas to shorefront. Visitor-friendly sites for birding — where you may find boardwalks, observation areas, and informational slide shows or displays — are scattered throughout the Lowcountry and are listed under "Nature Preserves" later in this chapter.

More informal birding sites recommended by local birders include the following:

Charleston/Beaufort Area

Mt. Pleasant: the area leading to the old **Pitt St. Bridge**. Here sightings of mar-bled godwits, oystercatchers, grebes, and mergansers have been reported. Activity is best at half tide, especially in fall and winter. A spotting scope is useful here.

Sullivan's Island: around the beach and groins behind **Fort Moultrie**. Here, in fall and winter, you might see peeps, or an occasional purple sandpiper.

I'on Swamp, 15 miles north of Mt. Pleasant off Hwy. 17 on U.S. Forest Service Rd. 228. Here spring brings warblers — possibly even the shy Bachman's — and the resident upland birds, including red-cockaded woodpeckers, make their homes.

U.S. Highway 17, by the **Ashepoo and Combahee river crossings**. Anhinga, rails, and gallinules nest in the remnant rice fields.

Savannah Area

Savannah National Wildlife Refuge. More than 200 species of birds have been sighted here; huge flocks of migratory waterfowl make it their home in winter months.

BOATING

SAILING

For a sailor unfamiliar with Lowcountry coastal waters, the tides and cur-rents can be strong and tricky to navigate. If you're interested in renting a sailboat, either for a day's excursion or for a trip along the Intracoastal Water-way, it's best to check out local conditions thoroughly, discussing your plans with the rental outfitter before you go. For a listing of marinas, some of which may offer sailboat rentals, see Chapter Two, *Transportation*.

In addition, sailboats in a range of sizes are available for hire from the fol-lowing:

Charleston Area

Bohicket Yacht Charters & Boat Rentals (803-768-7294; 1880 Andell Bluff Blvd., Johns Island, SC 29455).

Ocean-racing yachts streak across the broad harbors and inlets of Charleston.

Wade Spees

Charleston Charter Co. (803-762-7900; P.O. Box 1427, Charleston, SC 29402).

Wild Dunes Yacht Harbor (803-886-5100, ext. 34; P.O. Box 527, Isle of Palms, SC 29451).

Time Out Sailing (803-577-5979; City Marina, Lockwood Dr., Charleston, SC 29401). Offers instruction.

Savannah Area

Sail Harbor (912-897-2896; 618 Wilmington Island Rd., Savannah, GA 31410).

You can even tend sail while you sightsee aboard the 84-foot schooner *Pride* (803-795-1180; 2044 Wapoo Hall, Charleston, SC 29412). Ticket prices in 1992 were $15 for adults and $10 for children, for a two-hour tour Apr.–Dec.

LANDINGS

If you're towing your own boat, there are dozens of landings, most often simple ramps, where you can park your trailer and launch. Parking is free, but generally unmonitored.

Listings or maps that show the locations of public boat landings in **South Carolina** are available from the **Marine Resources Division** (803-795-6350; P.O. Box 12559, Charleston, SC 29412) and the **Lowcountry Resort Islands and Tourism Commission** (803-943-9180; P.O. Box 366, Hampton, SC 29924).

In **Georgia**, you can find out about landings in the **Historic Savannah Visitor's Guide**, published by the Convention and Visitor's Bureau (912-944-0456; P.O. Box 1628, Savannah, GA 31402). In addition, there's an excellent, highly readable guide to public access points in north coastal Georgia, *"A Guide to the Georgia Coast,"* by the Georgia Conservancy (912-897-6462; 711 Sandtown Rd., Savannah, GA 31410).

CANOEING AND KAYAKING

If canoeing and kayaking are more to your taste, you can experience calm waters and observe birds and other wildlife along the 56-mile stretch of the *Edisto River*, thought to be the nation's longest free-flowing black-water stream. As you meander along, you're likely to see great blue herons wading by the oak-lined riverbank, or hummingbirds feeding at wildflowers. The trail follows an ancient waterway used by Indians and earliest settlers. *Colleton State Park* (803-538-8206; Canadys, S.C., U.S. Rte. 15, 12 miles north of Walterboro; I-95 exit 69) and *Givhan's Ferry State Park* (803-873-0692; Hwy. 61 and S.C. 30) are along the route. You can put in there, and also camp and picnic.

To inquire about conditions on the Edisto (canoeing and kayaking are not recommended there when the water level is above 7.5 feet), call 803-538-3659. The *Walterboro-Colleton Chamber of Commerce* (803-549-9595; P.O. Box 426, Walterboro, SC 29488) can assist you in renting canoes or kayaks, or securing a guide at certain times of the year.

Nearer *Charleston*, canoeing is also permitted at *Magnolia Gardens* (803-571-1266; Hwy. 61) and *Palmetto Islands County Park* (803-884-0832; Long Point Rd., Mt. Pleasant).

Near *Savannah*, access points along the *Savannah River* allow you to travel through tidal creeks leading into the *Savannah National Wildlife Refuge* (912-652-4415). *White's Canoe Rentals* (912-748-5858; Bush Rd.) may also have outing ideas and maps.

Kayaking is a simple, quiet way to get eye-level with the marsh.

Wade Spees

JET SKIS

Jet skis are a cross between the smallest and the fastest outboard boat you can imagine. Powered by engines upward of 500ccs, they are a thrilling — if noisy — way to blast around the harbor, beyond the waves, or through the marshes. They rent by the hour and half hour and have a two-person capacity. In *Charleston*, they are available downtown at the *Ashley Marina* (803-722-1996) In *Savannah*, contact *Sunny Daze Water Sports* on Wilmington Island (912-897-4003).

BOWLING

Bowling league activity flourishes in the Lowcountry, with teams for all ages and abilities, so finding available space in local lanes in the evenings can be a challenge. On a rainy afternoon, you're likely to find some open lanes around *Charleston* at the *Ashley Lanes* (803-766-9061; 1568 Sam Rittenberg Blvd.); in *Beaufort* at the *Ribaut Lanes* (803-524-3111; 700 S. Ribaut Rd.); in *Savannah* at the *Major League Lanes* (912-925-0320; 115 Tibet Ave.). The lanes have video games and snack bars for those on the sidelines, too.

CAMPING

In the old days, a camping expedition in the Lowcountry usually involved sailing or rowing — or being sailed or rowed — in boats as heavily loaded as barges to the uninhabited barrier islands. Upon arrival there, the party would set up housekeeping at a "fish camp" for several days. These same spots would be revisited year after year, although they might consist of nothing more than driftwood chairs, a palmetto-log windbreak, and a fire pit. The tradition was rustic, the site well off the beaten track. Many Lowcountry residents still camp this way, though stories they bring home definitely outclass their accommodations!

Today's visitor can approximate this experience (but near running water, toilets, a campground store, and gnat repellent) at *public campgrounds* at the following sites:

Charleston Area

Buck Hall, Francis Marion National Forest (803-887-3257; Wambaw Ranger District, P.O. Box 106, McClellanville, SC 29458) 15 sites; hiking trails, boat ramp, and fishing.

In a campground clearing, your "bed" will be soft and sandy, and your bedtime music the rustle of the wind in the dry palmetto fronds.

Wade Spees

Edisto Beach State Park (803-869-2156; 8377 State Cabin Rd., Edisto Island, SC 29438) 103 sites, 5 cabins; hiking trails, interpretive programs, boat ramp, playground, general store, showers, water and electrical hookups.

James Island County Park (803-795-9884; 871 Riverland Dr., Charleston, SC 29412) 125 sites, 10 cabins; paved bike trails, fishing and crabbing docks, playground, RV hookups.

Beaufort Area

Hunting Island State Park (803-838-2011; 1775 Sea Island Pkwy., St. Helena Island, SC 29920) 200 sites, 15 cabins; nature trails, showers, store, water and electrical hookups.

Savannah Area

Skidaway Island State Park (912-598-2300; Savannah, GA 31411) 88 sites; laundry, pool, bath house, nature trail, water and electrical hookups.

Reservations are not available at all parks for campsites, and in the crowded summer months the parks can reach capacity very quickly. It's wise to call ahead to check on availability, or you'll risk finding yourself without shelter and some 20 miles from a motel. Cabin rentals are often booked a year in advance. The camping season in the Lowcountry can start as early as February and stretch into November.

For information on *private campgrounds* on Hilton Head, see Chapter Eight; for others near the coast, contact the following:

Near Charleston

Oak Plantation Campground (803-766-5936; Hwy. 17, 4 miles south of the intersection with S.C. 7 near the Johns Island Road) Full hookups with 15-, 30-, and 50-amp. service; 100 tent sites, 150 camper sites, propane, laundry, groceries, bathrooms.

Lake Aire RV Park and Campground (803-571-1271; S.C. 162, just off Hwy. 17) 100 sites including full hookups, primitive sites, and camper sites. Seven-acre fishing lake, swimming pool, paddleboat and canoe rental, showers, laundry, recreation area, bike and foot trails.

Pelican Cove RV Resort (803-588-2072; 97 Center St., Folly Beach) Located on the Folly River within walking distance of the beach and public boat ramp, 37 spaces, full hookups, laundry, small pool, showers.

Wood Brothers Campground (803-844-2208; Hwy. 17, 37 miles south of Charleston) Wooded and open sites for RVs, campers, and tents; grocery, propane, showers, fishing pond.

Near Beaufort/Savannah

Kobuch's (803-525-0653; Hwy. 302, Burton, minutes from Marine Corps Recruit Depot at Parris Island) 14 sites, full hookups.

Point South KOA (803-726-5733; Exit 33 off I-95 at Hwy. 17) 54 sites, full hookups, swimming pool, hot tub, electrified camping cabin that sleeps six, rec room with movies shown every night, groceries, fishing lake, Laundromat, campsites. Extensive tourist information available about little-known historic sites in area.

River's End Campground and RV Park (912-786-5518; Polk St., Tybee Island) 150 sites, full hookups, water and electric, and tent sites, three blocks from beach, rec room, groceries, propane.

Stoney Crest Plantation Campground (803-757-3249; Hwy. 46, Bluffton) 30 sites, full hookups, tent sites, playground, propane, groceries, swimming pool, laundry.

DIVING

If all the people who wear the wristwatches divers wear — thick black band, fluorescent numbers, dial rimmed with rings and buttons — ever actually suited up and went under, they'd clog the inshore waters of the Lowcountry; offshore, they might be taken for manatees.

Several outfitters provide rentals, guides, ocean charters, and instruction in the sport. Some in the *Charleston area* are *Aqua Ventures* (803-884-1500), *Charleston Scuba* (803-722-1120), and *The Wet Shop* (803-744-5641).

In Beaufort, call Dive Masters (803-524-9372) or Low Country Divers (803-522-9430).

In *Savannah,* contact *Divers Supply* (912-748-8004) or the *Diving Locker and Ski Chalet* (912-927-6604).

Prices vary according to services, length of instruction, and the nature of exploratory dive you wish for.

FAMILY FUN

The Lowcountry's long summer nights, when dusk comes as late as nine o'clock, mean there's always extra time for that round of miniature golf or walk on the beach. By day, there are waterslides to offer cooling thrill rides. Here are some activities that adults and kids can enjoy together. See the Hilton Head chapter for family amusements there.

Charleston Area

Classic Golf (803-881-9614; 1528 Ben Sawyer Blvd.) Miniature golf landscaped and lit for night play.

To the Ducklings: "Make Way For People!"

Wade Spees

Frankie's Fun Park (803-767-7888; 5000 Ashley Phosphate Rd.) Two 18-hole mini-golf courses, go-cart tracks, game rooms, batting cages, and bumper boats. Open daily, 10 a.m. to midnight. A great reward for kids who have been sightseeing all day.

Beaufort Area

Beaufort County Water Slide (Hwy. 21 near Hunting Island State Park) A three-run slide and snack bar operated by the County Recreation Commission. $5 day pass, open daily to 6 p.m.

Savannah Area

Putt-Putt Golf Course (912-355-4795; 202 Mall Blvd.) Three courses, lit for night play, open to midnight. $4 per round; $8 for 3 rounds. Play Monday-Friday during the day for $5.

Savannah Skate Inn (912-238-0000) Roller skating, $2.75 per person including rental.

Tybee Water Park and Mini-Golf (912-786-5552; Tybee Island).

FISHING

Fishing was and is such a common, pleasurable pastime in the Lowcountry, so thickly woven into the fabric of local life, that in describing it, one is likely to end up talking about the entire culture itself: the way its residents

---

Herring Run

June 1, 1903: "During the run of herring in the spring they crowd up the little streams in the most extraordinary way, just piling on top of each other in their haste to reach the very source of the stream, apparently. I suppose one little leader must wave its little tail and cry 'excelsior' to the others. At a small bridge over a shallow creek near here a barrelful has been taken with a dip-net in an afternoon. But it takes a meditative, not to say an idle person, to watch for the special day and hour when the herring are seized by the impulse to ascend that particular stream."

— From *A Woman Rice Planter* by "Patience Pennington"
[Elizabeth Waties Allston], Cornelius O. Cathey, Editor
(Cambridge: The Belknap Press of Harvard University Press, 1961)

Bait-To-Go on Lady's Island.

Wade Spees

cook, the stories they choose to tell, the skills they wish to pass on, where they live, what they do on weekends, what kinds of politicians they elect, how they judge character, what their values are for their children. Like the Myth of the Old South and Old Families, the lore of fishing confers a kind of lineage by which people know themselves. And where the Old Families might have Old Houses, people who fish have Old Cars, "fishing cars" as they are widely known — dinged-up rustbuckets that make it to the boat landing (not much farther) with the faithfulness of a hunting hound.

In fact, the opportunities for fishing are so numerous, the catches still plentiful, the waterways still generally pristine, the tradition so revered, that a book written in 1856, *Carolina Sport By Land and Water* by William Elliott, can be read as a nearly modern account.

Today's enthusiast can choose freshwater or saltwater sites, fishing from piers, bridges, boats or banks, from the beach or by trolling an artificial offshore reef. The state's longest fishing pier (1,120 feet) is **Paradise Pier** (803-838-5455), located on Hunting Island near **_Beaufort_** and open 24 hours. The

Paradise Pier reaches across Fripp Inlet, where dozens of species run with the tides.

Wade Spees

catch can range from small bream, porgy, and spot — of the family commonly known as "sailor's choice" — to flounder, to big-game fish like wahoo, drum, shark, and cobia. In general, the best part of the season extends from April through November, but small panfish remain active beyond those dates.

Licenses are required for freshwater fishing. Most visitors interested in recreational fishing will not need one; they're not necessary for recreational shrimping and crabbing. Licenses are sold in many hardware and hunting stores, K-Marts, and tackle shops. For further information on licenses, and size and catch limits, contact the *South Carolina Wildlife and Marine Resources Dept.* (803-795-6350; P.O. Box 12559, Charleston, SC 29412) or the *Georgia Dept. of Natural Resources* (912-651-2221). The South Carolina agency also sells a *Guide to Saltwater Recreational Fisheries* ($4.50).

For a comprehensive map indicating recreational fishing facilities in the Lowcountry, including marinas, boat landings, bridges and catwalks, shellfish grounds, and offshore reefs, write the *Lowcountry Council of Governments* (803-726-5536; P.O. Box 98, Yemassee, SC 29945).

SPORT-FISHING CHARTERS

A sport-fishing charter can take you to the Gulf Stream or to any of the dozen or so artificial reefs offshore. While the first artificial reefs that appeared in this area to attract sheepshead over 150 years ago were hutlike structures about six feet high, made of logs and then sunk, today's reefs are far more elaborate affairs that attract dozens of species. Given that much of the sea floor off the coast is sandy, these reefs provide the hard substrate necessary to create a "live bottom" of invertebrates, small fish, coral, crabs, and sponges. They are active feeding stations for the big fish, and experienced guides know them well. Trips of this sort generally take a full day. Trips closer to shore, in smaller boats, can be easily enjoyed by the half day.

A listing of some of the many *charter boat services* available follows. Others may be available at Lowcountry marinas listed in Chapter Two, *Transportation.* (For Hilton Head fishing, see Chapter Eight.) Rods, reels, bait and tackle are provided; lunch or snacks are usually available, but you should check in advance; boats are equipped with safety equipment and licenses; all but the smallest have heads. It is wise to bring sunscreen, windbreakers, and a towel.

Many charters will design a trip to suit your particular interest or prepare a boat for a fishing tournament. Boats generally carry four to six passaengers and can be hired by the half or full day. Small motor boats can be rented by the hour also. If bad weather is forecast, call ahead to confirm that the trip is on. Trips range widely in price. A full day of Gulf-Stream fishing aboard a 40-foot boat that carries six people could run $950. Some 1992 prices were as follows:

— 30–60-foot boats capable of carrying six people: full day $840–$1,155, half-day $420–$575.

You can charter a boat to explore distant islands, fish, dive, troll, or just follow the gulls and sightsee.

Wade Spees

— 25-foot boats suitable for 4 passengers: full day $500, half day $250.

— small skiffs powered by motors (7.5–40 h.p.): $25–$50 per hour.

Charleston Area

Bohicket Charters/Rentals (803-768-7294; Bohicket Marina Village, Johns Island) Large selection of boats from 14 to 55 feet for inshore bass and trout fishing, jetty fishing, and offshore fishing for shark, mackerel, tuna, and marlin. Full- and half-day trips.

Carolina Clipper (803-884-2992; Shem Creek, Mt. Pleasant) Captain Randolph Scott piloting a large boat outfitted with a snack bar and sundeck. Beginners welcome.

Captain Ivan's Island Charters (803-588-6060; Charleston) Captain Ivan Schultz. Thirty-foot, wide-beam boat with 21-passenger capacity, full- and half-day excursions to offshore reefs, trips to Gulf Stream (12 hours).

Captain Ken Kirchner (803-884-6509; Mt. Pleasant) Light tackle and saltwater fly fishing, catch and release fishing, up to three anglers aboard 21-foot Boston Whaler.

Happyniss Sportfishing Charters (803-881-1575; Toler's Cove, Mt. Pleasant) Maximum party of six aboard 42-foot Bertram. Full day for marlin and tuna; half day for sailfish, wahoo, king mackerel.

J.J. Deep Sea Fishing (803-873-2065; City Marina) Thirty years' experience in area waters, beginners welcome. Offshore to about 30 miles.

Edisto/Beaufort

Fishing Fever (803-869-3216; Edisto Marina, 803-869-3504) Captain Jim Herlong. Full- and half-day offshore trips and river trips.

Capt. Howard Hicks (803-869-3096; Edisto Marina, 803-869-3504) Cruises aboard the *Indigo*.

Low Country Fishing (803-522-8066; Beaufort) Captain Doug Gertis. Light tackle inshore fishing for jack crevalle, trout, tarpon and other species on a 19-foot Maverick Master Angler. Tag and release fishermen get a discount.

Capt. Eddie Netherland (803-838-5661; Fripp Island Marina) Offshore and inshore trips by day and half-day on 25-foot Grady-White Sailfisher. King mackerel a specialty.

Sea Wolf IV (803-525-1174; Port Royal Landing, Beaufort) Captain Wally Phinney, Jr. USA, Ret. Deep-sea fishing, diving, cruising, by day or half day aboard 29-foot boat.

Savannah

Al Klein's Bottom Line Charters (912-897-6503; Wilmington Island) 30-foot deep-sea boats; 35-foot Bertram; 60-foot vessel for group charters.

Chimney Creek Charters (912-786-9857; Tybee Island) Trips for up to six persons aboard 32-foot craft; for 1–3 persons on smaller Boston Whalers, McKees, and English Dories.

Miss Judy the Charter Boat (912-897-4921; 124 Palmetto Dr., Savannah) Deep-sea, bottom fishing and trolling, Gulf Stream trips.

Salt Water Charters (912-598-1814; Landings Harbor, Skidaway) Captain Bob Morrissey. Inshore and deep-sea fishing for bass, grouper and other species by full day or half day.

FITNESS FACILITIES

Contemporary travelers may leave their troubles behind when they're on vacation, but few of them forget to pack their workout clothes. The explosion of interest in fitness, and in facilities to encourage it, hasn't bypassed the Lowcountry, although historically physical fitness for its own sake hasn't ranked as high on the list of the area's preferred pastimes as, say, hunting or being on the river, or talking about fishing or politics, or just having a drink and meal with friends.

Nonetheless, the idea of working out by joining an aerobics class, lifting weights, running on a motorized tread, or using a stair machine in an air-conditioned gym or studio has its appeal, especially in the summer, when even a short walk will produce beads of sweat. Lowcountry fitness centers range from community facilities to private clubs, and many of them offer day rates for visitors. The front-desk manager of your hotel or your bed-and-breakfast host may be able to steer you toward their favorites, or recommend personal trainers; and, of course, if you're staying in a resort, it is likely to have its own facilities.

The 1992 fees for daily use ranged from $6 to $35 depending on what services were provided. Special three-day rates are also available starting at $15 per couple.

Charleston

Bodyworks (803-763-6760; 1401 Sam Rittenberg Blvd.) Nautilus, free weights, aerobics, body analysis equipment, fitness instruction, fitness cycles, stairs and treadmills.

Family Fitness (803-569-3611; 8085 Rivers Ave.) Aerobics, free nursery, Nautilus, tanning beds, whirlpool, women's gym.

Health Quest (803-554-0052; 2205 Leeds Ave.) Charleston's largest health club. Many aerobics and fitness classes, weight training, personalized programs, spa facilities, body-sculpting with weights, various fitness machines.

St. Andrew's Family Recreation Center (803-763-3850; 1642 Sam Rittenberg Blvd.) Aerobics, racquetball, squash, indoor pool, free weights, nursery, fitness machines.

Beaufort

Aero Gym (803-522-1080; Sam's Point Rd.) Aerobics, step classes, body-sculpting, weights.

Ray's Gym (803-524-8351; Hwy. 170) Complete gym, fitness training, body-sculpting, Nautilus, weights, fitness machines.

Savannah

Downtown Athletic Club (912-236-4874; 7 E. Congress St.) Step training, aerobics, spa facilities, classes, fitness machines.

Gold's Gym (912-355-3393; 301 Mall Way) Aerobics and step classes, free weights, machines, tanning salon, fitness testing, whirlpool and sauna, child care.

La Vida Health Club and Sports Clinic (912-927-7486; 525 Windsor Rd.) Exercise classes, sauna, whirlpool, evaluation and injury rehab, private coaching.

Racquet Plus (912-355-3070; 4 Oglethorpe Professional Blvd.) Racquetball, aerobics, free weights, Nautilus.

GOLF

The presence in the Lowcountry of so many golf courses, public, private, and semiprivate — so many beautiful ones, and so many that are consistently ranked by golf professionals as among the top 100 in the world — means that visitors can and do spend every day for a week playing one or two courses without ever repeating themselves. The Lowcountry probably has more golf courses per person than any other region in the country, and probably more courses with holes offering expansive ocean or marsh views, or such scenic hazards as deer, heron, and the occasional alligator.

Whether you're a duffer or scratch golfer, the pleasure you can derive from simply being on a course — early in the morning as the heavy dew dries and the temperature rises, or late in the day as the chuck-will's-widows commence their plaintive call — is worth the planning and expense that today's golf excursions require. Lowcountry weather allows for year-round play and (in

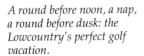

A round before noon, a nap, a round before dusk: the Lowcountry's perfect golf vacation.

the summer) late-afternoon starting times. The high-season months are in fall and spring, so it is wise to schedule your playing time well in advance.

On some courses, carts are required at peak playing times. For resort play, it is usually necessary to be an overnight guest. Golf packages that include lodging are numerous, so ask about them. Club rentals and instruction are available at all courses.

Greens fees/cart rentals reflect 1992 prices. For information about courses on Hilton Head Island, consult that chapter.

PUBLIC AND SEMIPRIVATE COURSES

Charleston Area

Charleston Municipal Course (803-795-6517; 2110 Maybank Hwy.) 18 holes, par 72, 6,400 yards. Pro: Jimmy Murray. Greens fees $9–$14 weekdays, $11–$16 weekends. Carts $8.50 per person.

Crowfield Golf & Country Club (803-764-4618; Goose Creek) 18 holes, par 72, distances for three sets of tees from 5,600 yards to 7,000 yards. Pro: Marty Mikesell. Greens fees $17 weekdays, $22 weekends, cart rental $9.50.

Fairfield Ocean Ridge (803-869-2561; Edisto Beach) 18 holes, par 71, 6,312 yards. Pro: Kevin Craig. Greens fees $40 with cart.

Kiawah Oaks (803-768-7431; Johns Island) 18 holes, par 72, three sets of tees: 6,156 yards, 6,544, yards, and 6,764 yards. Pro: Martin Shorter. Greens fees including cart $30 plus tax.

Links at Stono Ferry (803-763-1817; Hollywood) 18 holes, par 72, 6,006 yards. Pro: Pam Weeks. Greens fees including cart $17 weekdays, $25 weekends.

Patriots Point Golf Links (803-881-0042; Mt. Pleasant) 18 holes, par 72, 6,850 yards. Pro: Jim Hahn. Greens fees $17 weekdays, $19 weekends, cart rental $9.50 per person.

Shadowmoss Plantation Golf Club (803-556-8251; Hwy. 61) 18 holes, par 72. Four sets of tees: 5,169 yards, 6,129 yards, 6,399 yards, 6,701 yards. Pro: Michael Friend. Greens fees including cart $22 weekdays, $29 weekends, including Friday play.

Beaufort Area

Cat Island Club (803-524-0300; Cat Island) 18 holes, George Cobb design, par 71. Four sets of tees: 4,933 yards, 5,470 yards, 6,125 yards, 6,518 yards. Pro: Tony Biati. Greens fees including cart $24–$34 according to season.

Country Club of Beaufort (803-522-1605; Lady's Island) Russell Breedon design, 18 holes, par 71. Three sets of tees: 4,880 yards, 6,089 yards, 6,489 yards. Pro: Pamela Phipps. Greens fees including cart $24–$36.

Golf Professionals Club (803-524-3635; Lady's Island) Championship Course, par 72, 6,700 yards; Players Course, par 72, 6,100 yards. Pro: Dick Tremblay. Greens fees including cart $22–$25.

Savannah Area

Bacon Park Golf Course (912-354-2625; Shorty Cooper Drive) 27 holes, par 72, 6,333 yards, driving range, putting green. Pro: Murle Breer. Greens fees for 18 holes including cart $20.30, without cart $11.15.

Sheraton Savannah Resort (912-897-1612; Wilmington Island) 18 holes, par 72, 7,100 yards, driving range, putting green. Pro: Craig Hartle. Greens fees including cart $48.10.

Southbridge Golf Club (912-651-5455; Southbridge Blvd.) Rees Jones–designed 18 holes, par 72, 6,990 yards, driving range, putting green. Full staff of teaching pros. Greens fees including cart $28.50 weekdays, $35 weekends and holidays.

PRIVATE COURSES

If you wish to plan your vacation around golf, you might save yourself travel time by staying in resorts or private residential communities where the game is the center of focus. Accommodations range from deluxe hotel rooms to villas, condominiums, and rental homes. These resorts also have complete recreational layouts which include swimming pools, tennis courts, and marinas. Here's a list of some well-known resort golf courses in the Lowcountry.

Charleston Area

Kiawah Island (803-768-2121; P.O. Box 12357, Charleston, SC 29422-2357) Four championship courses designed by Pete Dye, Jack Nicklaus, Gary Player, and Tom Fazio, par 71 and 72, ranging from 6,203 to 7,250 yards. Seamlessly integrated golf and landscape features make for some of the prettiest golf anywhere. Host of the 1991 Ryder Cup.

Seabrook Island (803-768-1000; 1002 Landfall Way, Seabrook Island, SC 29455) Named by *Golf Magazine* as a Silver Medal Resort, features two par-

72 18-hole courses (yardage from 6,549 to 6,880) designed by Robert Trent Jones and Willard Byrd.

Wild Dunes (803-886-2164; Isle of Palms) Located within a first-quality beach resort, two Tom Fazio–designed 18-hole courses featuring holes playing across Morgan Creek and along the Atlantic: The Links, par 72, 6,722 yards; The Harbor Course, par 70, 6,402 yards. Non-resort guests welcome. Pro: Terry Florence. Greens fees including cart $68–$88 (Links Course), $49–$68 (Harbor Course).

Beaufort Area

The Country Club of Callawassie (803-785-7888; Hwy. 170, Beaufort, SC 29902) Tom Fazio–designed course with range of yardage: 5,201-yard ladies' course to 7,064-yard championship course.

Dataw Island (803-838-3838; Club Road, Dataw Island, SC 29920) Two 18-hole courses designed by Arthur Hills and Tom Fazio are the centerpieces of a beautifully groomed, low-key, well-planned residential community.

Fripp Island Ocean Point Golf Links (803-838-2309; Fripp Island, SC 29920) Set on the rim of the Atlantic and Fripp Inlet, an 18-hole course, par 72, 6,590 yards, open to guests of the family-oriented beach front resort.

HORSEBACK RIDING

The first racecourse in the Lowcountry was built near Charleston in 1735, and the South Carolina Jockey Club was founded there in 1758. Through the years, the breeding of horses has been a major pursuit, and equestrian showmanship has been a popular form of recreation.

Today visitors can ride in the ***Charleston area*** at the *Seabrook Island Resort* (803-768-1000), which features trails, an equestrian center, and beach rides; at *Shady T* (803-871-7770), where trail and Western-style pleasure riding is a specialty; at the *Stono River Riding and Boarding Stable* (803-559-0773), which offers the experienced rider cross-country trails and a stadium arena; and at *Stono Ferry Stables* (803-763-0566).

In the ***Beaufort area***, Dorinda Mark's *Broomfield Stables* (803-521-1212), Lee Sutcliff's *D&L Stables* (803-524-6455), and the *Equestrian Center at Rose Hill* (803-757-3082) welcome inquiries from visitors seeking instruction within the ring. *Waterside Rides at Lowcountry Farms* (803-689-3423) offers guided trail rides along the Intracoastal Waterway and the marsh.

Recreational riding, dressage, and competitive polo keep equestrians busy.

Wade Spees

In *Savannah*, instruction is available at **Sa-Hi Riding Academy** (912-232-6797).

HUNTING

In the Lowcountry you can hunt a wide variety of quarry, including deer, wild turkey, dove, quail, feral hog, duck, fox, rabbit, woodcock, snipe, and clapper rail. What's more, you can do so during seasons that start as early as

Hunting deer the old-fashioned way, by firelight. Credit: Georgia Historical Society. Hunting Scene from Harper's Weekly, 2-19-1859. Courtesy of the Georgia Historical Society.

Georgia Historical Society, GHS Prints

late summer (deer) and last through fall and winter until late spring (turkey). The Lowcountry has the longest deer season in the country and is considered the premiere spot on the East Coast to bag marsh hens.

There are six Game Management Areas in the Lowcountry, and hunters at work within them are required to have a variety of licenses and permits, abide by strict size and bag limits, obtain landowners' permission before hunting on private lands, and observe safe and ethical hunting practices in the field. For information, maps, and regulations concerning *South Carolina* hunting areas, contact the *Wildlife and Marine Resources Dept.* (803-734-3888; P.O. Box 167, Columbia, SC 29202). In *Georgia*, contact the *Game and Fish Division* of the Dept. of Natural Resources (912-651-2221; Rte. 2, Box 219R, Richmond Hill, GA 31324). Outdoor recreation stores that specialize in hunting (see "Sporting Goods and Clothing" below) may also provide tips, information, and licenses.

Some of the most popular public hunting grounds in the Lowcountry are located in the *Francis Marion National Forest* (803-825-3387; Berkeley County), *Webb Wildlife Center and Palachucola* (803-625-3569; Hampton and Jasper counties), *Bear Island* (803-844-2952; Colleton County), *Turtle Island* and *Victoria Bluff* (in Jasper and Beaufort counties — 803-844-8957), and in the *Savannah National Wildlife Refuge* (912-652-4415).

If you prefer a more managed hunt, consider the guiding, cleaning, and transportation services of plantations that specialize in various kinds of game hunting, according to the season. Some offer overnight accommodations. For information contact the *Lowcountry Tourism Commission* (803-943-9180; P.O. Box 366-W, Hampton, SC 29924).

The *Southeastern Wildlife Exposition*, which takes place every February in Charleston, is the region's largest and best gathering of fishermen, hunters, outfitters, and artists who specialize in subjects of interest to sportsmen. Display sites scattered throughout the Charleston area feature Lowcountry and Western collectibles, crafts, decoys, antiques, and posters. A free shuttle bus service can take you to them. In addition, there are presentations and demonstrations. Write: *EXPO Information*, 211 Meeting St., Charleston, SC 29401 (803-723-1748).

NATURE PRESERVES

Many small islands, swamps, or boggy necks nestled in the creeks and riverways of the Lowcountry offer natural camouflage and a near-wild habitat to the wildlife that live or migrate there. Some are more developed than others — with boardwalks or marked trails — but none require strenuous activity or advanced knowledge for enjoyment. If you are interested in the ecology of the Lowcountry, the life cycle of the marsh, the effects of tidal flow on vegetation, and the interdependence of plant and animal life, then these sites will give you a feel for the rhythms of the Lowcountry beneath the surface.

Charleston Area

ACE Basin (Access off Hwy. 17 at Green Pond, S.C. 26, Bennett's Point, Bear Island.) A consortium of private individuals and state and federal groups have joined together to preserve some 350,000 acres of incredibly diverse habitat, including several islands, at the center of the Lowcountry. It is one of the largest undeveloped estuarine sanctuaries left on the East Coast. ACE takes its name from the area it embraces: the lands and waters amidst the Ashepoo, Combahee, and Edisto rivers on both sides of St. Helena Sound, a fishery so rich and pristine it accounts for nearly 10 percent of the state's shellfish harvest. Seventeen endangered species make their home here. Bring binoculars and cameras.

Audubon Swamp Garden (803-571-1266; Hwy. 61 at Magnolia Plantation.) Comprising 60 acres of blackwater cypress and tupelo swamp, with trails through virgin pine forests, wild flowers, and exotic plants, this garden impressed John J. Audubon 150 years ago. Admission $4, $3 with combination ticket to Magnolia Plantation.

Cypress Gardens (803-553-0515; Goose Creek. I-26 west to Exit 208, then to Hwy. 52 north.) Take a guided tour or paddle a flat-bottom boat yourself through an old rice plantation reserve, now a protected natural swamp garden. A succession of blooms, from the earliest camellia and narcissus to trumpet vine and azalea, brightens the shadowy cypress forest. Open 9–5 daily. Adults $5, children $2, under 6 free.

Francis Biedler Forest in Four Holes Swamp (803-462-2150; Harleyville. From I-95 take I-26 east to Exit 177, then south on S.C. 453 to U.S. 178. Follow signs east on 178. From Charleston, take I-26 west to Exit 187, then south on U.S. 27 to U.S. 78, then west on U.S. 78 to U.S. 178.) The 5,415-acre forest, managed by the National Audubon Society, contains the largest remaining virgin stand of bald cypress and tupelo gum trees in the world. There's a self-guided boardwalk and Visitor Center, but the point here is to walk quietly and observe well, to absorb what you can on your own without the experience being "packaged" in any way. Open 9–5 daily except Mondays. Adults $3.75, children $1.75, under 6 free.

Wade Spees

In the aftermath of Hurricane Hugo, Lowcountry naturalists study the recovery taking place in forests, swamps, and preserves.

Hilton Head/Savannah Area

Pinckney Island National Wildlife Refuge (803-652-4415; Hwy. 278 at foot of Hilton Head bridge.) This is a 4,053-acre complex of small islands and hammocks set in the marsh. Only Pinckney Island, interwoven with 14 miles of trails, is open to visitors. A good place to spend an hour walking and birding.

Savannah National Wildlife Refuge (912-652-4415; Take I-95 Exit 5 to Hwy. 17 south; 8 miles south of Hardeeville.) The refuge consists of 25,608 acres spread across land once used for growing rice. Get a map at the Visitor Center and drive along the five-mile Laurel Hill Wildlife road for a good introduction to an area which includes fresh-water marsh, river-bottom hardwood swamp, and tidal rivers and creeks. Hiking trails (39 miles in all) are well marked, many of them following the path of the old rice dikes. A naturalist could easily arrive at sunrise, when it opens, and spend the day.

Victoria Bluff Heritage Preserve (803-844-8957; Sawmill Creek Rd., off Hwy. 278, 3 miles from the Hilton Head bridge.) This serenely beautiful parcel of some 1,000 acres on the Colleton River has long been eyed for residential or industrial development, but local residents finally seem to have secured its protection as a passive recreation area. Some trails are marked, some hunting is permitted. It is adjacent to the **Waddell Mariculture Center** (803-837-3795; tours by appt.), a leading research facility in the field of aquaculture; and the University of South Carolina's **Coastal Zone Education Center** (803-837-4848; tours by appt.), which sponsors programs to educate the public in marine science.

POLO

Spectators can pack a tailgate picnic and enjoy Sunday afternoon polo games in September and October, April and May at *Stono Ferry* (South of Charleston off Hwy. 17 to S.C. 162, Hollywood; 803-766-6208) and at *Rose Hill Plantation* (Hwy. 278, Bluffton; 803 757-3082). The games begin at 2 p.m. Admission is $5 per person, children under 12 free.

SPORTING GOODS AND CLOTHING

If, when you arrive in the Lowcountry, you find that you've left some vital bit of gear or clothing at home (or if you're eager to take up a new sport and need the right stuff in a hurry), the following stores will help you. They also, quite often, can provide information about sporting possibilities and locales in their area.

Charleston Area

Audubon Shop and Gallery 803-723-6171; 245 King St.
Bicycle Shoppe 803-722-8168; 280 Meeting St.
M. Dumas & Sons 803-723-8603; 294 King St.
Henry's Sporting Goods 803-881-0465; 1662 Hwy. 17 North, Mt. Pleasant.
Island Bike & Surf Shop 803-768-1158; Bohicket Marina Village.
Outdoor Outfitters 803-763-9115; 1662 Savannah Hwy.
Timeout 803-577-5979; 3 Lockwood Dr., Suite 204.

Beaufort

Island Outfitters 803-522-9900; Hwy. 21, Lady's Island.
High Tide Surf Shop 803-524-2334; 905 Bay St.

Savannah

Pro Bass Outfitters 912-927-6654; 7929 Abercorn St.
Thompson's Sporting Goods 912-354-7184; 904 E. 69th St.
Wilderness Outfitters 912-927-2071; 103 Montgomery Crossroads.

TENNIS

L ike golf, tennis is a popular Lowcountry sport around which an entire vacation could be designed. There are courts in city parks, tennis centers, and county recreation areas. Your hotel or bed-and-breakfast host should be able to direct you to the best-maintained, most accessible ones; or call the town halls for the location of their recreation centers.

In _Charleston_, the _Charleston Tennis Center_ (803-724-7402; Farmfield Ave., west of Charleston on Hwy. 17) has 15 outdoor hard courts, lit for night play. $2.50 per hour per person. Visitors should call ahead to check availability, or may reserve by paying in advance.

In _Beaufort_ (Boundary St.), there are seven city courts used by local leagues and schools where play is free, no reservations required.

Three city parks in _Savannah_ have courts: _Bacon Park_ (Skidaway Rd.), _Daffin Park_ (1500 E. Victory Dr.), and _Forsyth Park_ (Gaston & Whitaker).

Some Lowcountry resorts also offer playing time for non-resort guests. (For Hilton Head tennis information, see that chapter). Fees are variable depending on season and time of day. Reservations are required. Inquire about tennis packages. They are _Kiawah Island_ (803-768-2121); _Shadowmoss Plantation_ (803-571-2914); _Wild Dunes_ (803-886-6000, Isle of Palms); and _Fairfield Ocean Ridge_ (803-723-0325).

WINDSURFING

A lthough the currents and tides make for tricky windsurfing conditions, the Lowcountry's warm water temperature and wide open spaces have attracted windsurfers for years. It is very important to check the local forecasts and tides before you go, and to surf in well-known areas. Even experienced windsurfers have found themselves thrust well beyond the confines of, say, Charleston Harbor, by the outgoing tide, only to find they have to wait until it turns to paddle or sail in.

Many resorts have windsurfers to rent, or provide instruction first on land, then in sheltered creeks or on a quiet stretch of beach. If you're staying in town, inquire at sporting goods shops (see listing earlier in this chapter) or call some of the following rental/instruction agencies:

> **Sailsports Sailboards** (803-884-1508; Mt. Pleasant).
> **Timeout** (803-577-5979; downtown Charleston).
> **Coastal Sailing School** (803-588-9277; Folly Beach).
> **McKevlin's Surf Shop** (803-886-8912; Isle of Palms).
> **Windsurfing Hilton Head** (803-671-2643; South Beach).

The Intracoastal Waterway near Hilton Head Island is a main path for pleasure and transit and sheer beauty.

Wade Spees

CHAPTER SEVEN

The Old World and the New World
SHOPPING

Wade Spees

Waiting for customers on the side of the road.

The time has long passed since ports in Lowcountry cities operated on a scale small enough to afford their residents the incidental pleasures of observing ships at the wharf, wondering what lay in their hold, watching as they were emptied and filled again. Yet such pastimes of commercial life were once commonplace. For many people, life was measured by the anticipation of an import — teas or seeds, books, furniture, food, or mail — and the reciprocal, satisfactory delivery of an export. If the export represented the summing up of what plantation culture and slavery had been designed to produce, the import confirmed the Lowcountry's view of itself as a tasteful, cultivated, wealthy society. It was as if the sight of bustling, wharfside activity enhanced — gave value to — the rather ordinary impulse to consume.

Today, the thrill is not gone; it's just been moved. The fun of shopping still emerges from its setting. In a big metropolitan area, it may come from a lavish and quirky department-store display or a manic, no-holds-barred holiday sale. In the Lowcountry, it happens more often in smallish places, in boutiques, in shops in old houses, in commercial buildings on ballast-stone alleys, under market sheds, or out in the open air of a busy corner.

Some of these places are run by partnerships of family members, or have been passed down — tin ceilings and all — to their present owners. Others are new but plan to be around a long time. However they came to exist, today they seem solid, inhabited, folded into the fabric of the past, not merely its echo chamber.

The antiques stores of the region might be considered a speciality. There is the world of artists and artisans, whose numbers — especially in Savannah

Getting ready for business on Beaufort's Bay St.

Wade Spees

among those associated with the Savannah College of Art and Design — are growing rapidly, as are the outlets for their work. There are unusual clothing stores, book dealers, and galleries. On weekend evenings, tourists and students crowd the shops of Charleston's old Market Area and Savannah's City Market and River Street waterfront, bringing a hum and buzz to otherwise quiet downtowns. Beaufort is getting a reputation for its hip stores, and Hilton Head has become a mecca for outlet malls, as listed at the end of this chapter. (For other specialty shops on Hilton Head, see Chapter Eight.)

Because of the region's temperate, multicrop climate, you can buy batches of lettuce, collards, potatoes, tomatoes, watermelon, and peaches off a truck during most of the year. The man with the bags of boiled peanuts may knock at your door only in summer, but most everyone else can, and does, peddle their goods year round.

There are, too, right in the city and certainly out in the country, stores that are old and vibrant centers of community life, places with shelves that bear small quantities of many things — places with dangling flypaper, squirrel-nut candies, pickled eggs, moon pies, single beers, and slushies. The modest mien of these stores guarantees that they'll never achieve National-Register status; they'll never be etherized, either. Drop in for a local newspaper and a "Co' Cola." Local favorites are *Charlie's*, 175 King St. in Charleston; *Wood Brothers*, on Hwy. 17 in Green Pond; and *Koth's*, 1601 North St. in Beaufort.

ANTEBELLUM ARTIFACTS

Charleston

Antiquities Historical Galleries of Charleston (803-720-8771; Shops at Charleston Place, in the Omni) Documents, autographs, maps, and prints from the 18th and 19th centuries.

Charleston Shoreline (803-723-6213; 40 N. Market St.) Civil War prints, engravings, stamps, artifacts, and documents.

Galleries of the South (803-723-3126; 364 King St.) A vast mix of media and periods, including Civil War and wildlife prints and African-American art.

Beaufort

Eastward-Ho (803-522-0261; Hwy. 21, Lady's Island) Antique and contemporary prints, framing.

Savannah

Claire West Antiques (912-236-8163; 413 Whitaker St.) Prints of antebellum life as well as old linens, furnishings, and accessories.

Pinch of the Past (912-232-5563; 232 E. Broughton St.) Architectural pieces of the past, including doorframes, columns, mantels, and hardware.

ANTIQUES

The period of poverty that engulfed the Lowcountry after the Civil War called for living by austere means and resourcefulness. It was not a time when renovating and redecorating were considered remotely possible.

Some residents count this as a blessing. For one thing, a lot of old houses were spared the wrecker's ball. For another, the English and American antiques and accessories of an earlier day, purchased during the boom years, remained in people's homes; their placement, scale, and restrained style harmonized with the rooms they were intended to adorn — however shabby or in need of paint those rooms had become.

Not all the high-ceilinged parlors in Charleston's Adam-style mansions or Savannah's Regency townhouses emerged intact; but enough of them endured so that their legacy of style remained influential. In the 1920s, they caught the eye of Northern decorators and curators, who either imitated their look or purchased them, literally lock, stock, barrel, and window sash. Later, when the families who had lived in the old houses produced a generation with the means to redecorate them, the urge to adorn them in the old style prevailed. Today, antiques stores throughout the Lowcountry retail this classic look, both in original pieces and in excellent reproductions.

While taste, or a good eye, is hard to define, it seems clear that the very experience of living in the Lowcountry has produced antiques dealers who have absorbed the region's lessons of enduring beauty. These dealers always seem to know what fits — whether it's a pair of simple sterling candlesticks or a stunning chest-on-chest. Even in the field of "what-nots" — objects plucked from their real-life context and given cultish status by the glossy "shelter magazines" — the Lowcountry shows a surfeit of whimsy and pleasure.

A short list of some of the more distinctive antiques shops follows. If you are poking around for something in particular, or a type of thing, ask for it. It's a small world, and dealers should be able to direct you elsewhere.

Charleston Area

Amelia Louise (803-723-3175; 192 King St.) This place is so small you can see everything by spinning around on one heel. The two women who run it seem to be able to find the gold thread, the verdigris, or the mahogany burnish shining through in every unusual piece of fabric, furniture, or decoration.

A'Riga IV Antiques (803-577-3075; 216 King St.) An impressive collection of old scientific instruments and medical kits, some of which can be quite oddly beautiful as art objects, as well as apothecary jars and ceramic containers that were put to domestic use years ago.

George C. Birlant & Co. (803-722-3842; 191 King St.) In business for over 60 years, selling brass, silver, crystal, and small and large English antiques, which they import directly. Big old-fashioned picture windows open onto the street; inside there's lots of room to walk around. Sometimes auctions take place here. Reproductions of Charleston's own cypress-and-iron "Battery Bench" available.

Century House Antiques (803-722-6248; 85 Church St.) There's a fineness about this shop that may have to do with the nature of its stock — English and Chinese export porcelain — or the feeling you get from being in the presence of an eye that has appreciated beauty for a long time. Botanicals and bird prints, too.

Estate Antiques (803-723-2362; 155 King St.) A superb collection of American antiques, Oriental rugs, and accessories. Jim and Harriet Pratt know their merchandise from the inside out, and they willingly share their knowledge with even the most committed browsers. The pieces here have good bones.

Grey Goose Antiques Mall and Auction Gallery (803-763-9131; 1011 St. Andrews Blvd.) A big, upscale antique house with everything from old and new Southwestern jewelry to Depression-glass.

Historic Charleston Reproductions (803-723-8292; 105 Broad St.) Adaptations and reproductions of 18th- and 19th-century furniture, lamps, fabric, brass,

Fine antique reproductions can convey as much charm as the real thing.

Wade Spees

wall coverings, and accessories that once graced Charleston homes. High-quality workmanship by companies like Baker Furniture, Scalamandre, and Mottahedeh.

Livingston and Sons Antiques (803-556-6162; 2137 Savannah Hwy.) A big warehouse (30,000 sq. feet) with lots of stuff. Bring a measuring tape: a sense of scale is elusive.

Period Antiques (803-723-2724; 194 King St.) Several different stylistic rhythms carry on here: there are 20th-century decorative art and furniture, country-style pine pieces, mirrors, antiques of one sort or another, and funky things that could brighten a corner.

Shalimar Antiques (803-766-1529; 2418 Savannah Hwy.) A totally unprepossessing place from the outside — it looks like an old motel and probably was — but inside, the top-quality collection of grandfather clocks, pine tables and beds, primitives, and trunks is lovely indeed. Local people, particularly people who live in old houses in the country, favor this store.

Vendue House Antiques (803-577-5462; 9 Queen St.) Classic English and continental antiques from the 18th and 19th centuries, with some smaller objects like boxes, fenders, and lap desks. Decorative collectibles.

Verdi (803-723-3953; 196 King St.) Selections of furniture and small things in the Empire and Biedermeier style.

Beaufort Area

Collector's Antique Mall and Craft Shops (803-522-8228; 208 Carteret St.) A little bit of everything, from old posters to salt-and-pepper sets and quilts.

Chitty & Co. (803-524-7889; 812 Port Republic) Fine European, American, and Oriental antiques, silver, porcelain, vintage lamps, chandeliers, sconces; lamp repair.

Den of Antiquity (803-524-6996; Hwy. 170) All sorts of furniture and collectibles spread through several rooms. Frequent new shipments from estate sales and auctions.

MacPherson's Antiques (803-524-4678; 1106 Carteret St.) The big house on the big bend as you approach downtown Beaufort. Country-style antiques, jewelry, glass, pictures, old tools.

Port Royal Antiques (803-524-6357; 913 Bay St.) Quilts, tea sets, silver and silver plate, Victorian-era lace and prints. There's a quaint kitchen area and a Christmas shop.

Southern Antiques (803-524-8554; 807 Bay St.) A mixture of country-style antiques, used furniture, and collectibles.

Stock Farm Antiques (803-757-2511; Hwy. 46, Bluffton) Paintings, prints, porcelain, rugs, and furniture, chosen with a sense of what fits in the big new houses at the resorts as well as the real old ones.

Antique prints of native birds and plants are widely available and very popular.

Wade Spees

Savannah Area

Alex Raskin Antiques (912-232-8205; 441 Bull St.) English and American furniture, as varied in scale and size as mirrors that would suit a ballroom to small painted primitives. The layout is informal — pieces in several rooms, sometimes piled up — and accommodates the odd, unassimilated gem. A local favorite.

Many Charleston and Savannah antiques stores are as small as one room, but they overflow with a sense of taste and style.

Wade Spees

Arthur Smith Antiques (912-236-9701; 1 W. Jones St.) Lots and lots of good antiques, overwhelmingly so. It will help if you know what you want.

Francis McNairy Antiques (912-232-6411; 411 Abercorn St.) Fine antiques, many of Southern origin; American folk art; and a wonderful collection of watercolors, drawings, and paintings. Even if you don't buy one piece, you can educate yourself to a sense of style here.

Savannah Galleries (912-232-1234; 7 W. Liberty St.) Another store with a huge inventory: rugs, porcelain, jewelry, paintings, silver.

BOOKS

The personal style of book-selling, in which a store's proprietor knows the taste of his customers and alerts them to new volumes, is still prominent in the Lowcountry. People who live at some distance from the main cities of Charleston and Savannah — whether they have come recently to live in the resorts or live in a small town — rely on a couple of book shops to mail books out regularly. Thus a healthy literary culture has come into being, one based on a strong, loyal web of readers. The advantage for the visitor is that shoppeople really know their stock, are full of suggestions, and are usually able to recommend an offbeat favorite, which they will order for you even if it's out of print, or not in stock.

The general prosperity and attraction to tourists of the region has also led to new bookstores that may be a part of a national chain but strive to accommodate titles relating to local topics in history, gardening, culture, and photography. There are also shops that carry used books, which — if a person could track them the way the wildlife experts track fish — would be seen migrating from one home library to another. Of course, one of the luxuries of the Low-country is that there is usually space enough to have, to keep, and to acquire more books.

Charleston Area

Armchair Sailor (803-577-0254; 3 Lockwood Dr.) The place for charts from the National Oceanic and Atmospheric Administration, as well as nautical titles and books on marine-science topics.

Atlantic Books (803-723-4751 at 363 King St.; 803-723-7654 at 191 East Bay St.) Thousands of used books in many subjects. Very strong in local history and memoirs, military titles, fiction, Civil War, Southern authors.

Audubon Shop and Gallery (803-723-6171; 227 Meeting St.) Field guides galore.

B. Dalton Bookseller (803-766-8339; Citadel Mall) The best-sellers of the Low-country (Pat Conroy, Eugenia Price, Alexandra Ripley, Josephine Humphreys) as well as a nice collection of photography books with regional focus.

Book Bag (803-723-8232; 379 King St.) Strong paperback selection for a small store. Adult fiction and nonfiction.

Book Exchange (803-556-5051; 1219 Savannah Hwy.) New and used books and collectible comics.

You could easily spend a quiet hour browsing at Charleston's Chapter Two — and you're more than welcome to do so.

Wade Spees

Chapter Two (803-722-4238; 199 East Bay St.) The best in Charleston, consistently rated among the best in the region. Superb history and art sections, fine magazines. Open late for browsers on Thursdays and Fridays. Frequent book-signings held here.

Doubleday Book Shops (803-723-6186; in the Omni at Market St.) Good children's section, best-sellers and nonfiction.

Edisto Bookstore (803-869-1885; 546 Hwy. 174, Edisto) The place to visit when you're out on Edisto Island and want a good read. Beach books, and also more solid fare.

Historic Charleston Foundation (803-724-8484; 108 Meeting St.) If you want to know more about regional history and the decorative arts, preservation efforts, architecture and related topics, stop in here. Also many volumes about historic properties here and elsewhere.

Hoppin' John's (803-577-6404; 30 Pinckney St.) A two-room shop that is nothing more or less than an institution. Cookbook author, food historian, raconteur John Taylor has assembled an impressive collection of cookbooks — and he's probably read every one.

Huguley's (803-724-8300; 269 King St.) A big card and stationery store with a good selection of Lowcountry and South Carolina books.

Noble Dragon (803-577-9334; 218 King St.) Old, new, and rare books amidst a little cafe with excellent cookies, beer, wine, and light snacks. A great late-afternoon stop.

Petterson Antiques (803-723-5714; 201 King St.) If the old books and magazines that sit on carts outside the store don't attract your eye, duck in and cast your gaze to the shelves and cases within. It may take time to find a treasure, but after all, you can never get enough of the atmosphere, which is free.

Preservation Society of Charleston (803-723-4381; 147 King St.) The headquarters of the Preservation Society has an unhurried, old-world feeling and many books on Charleston history, art, architecture, and culture.

St. Paul Book & Media Center (803-577-0175; 243 King St.) A religious bookstore with Bibles and a nice selection for younger readers.

Waldenbooks (803-766-5879; Citadel Mall) Best-sellers, good history and military section.

Beaufort Area

Bay St. Trading Co. (803-524-2000; 808 Bay St.) Best-sellers, books-on-tape, excellent children's section, comprehensive local and regional history, including many fine photography books. A good place to browse downtown.

Beaufort Bookstore (803-525-1066; Jean Ribaut Sq.) A large selection and wide variety of books from best-selling fiction and nonfiction to military and Lowcountry favorites.

Savannah Area

The Book Lady (912-233-3628; 17 W. York St.) Rare and out-of-print books; a nice place to drift through rows of shelves.

Dreamweaver (912-236-9003; 306 W. St. Julian St.) An offbeat selection of new-age books and tapes.

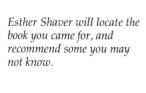

Esther Shaver will locate the book you came for, and recommend some you may not know.

Wade Spees

E. Shaver Booksellers (912-234-7257; 326 Bull St.) Right downtown and great for browsing. If some topic of Lowcountry history has captured your interest, you'll find it explicated here. Room after room of new and rare books, history, fiction, children's section, excellent art books. Best in Savannah.

Printed Page (912-234-5612; 211 W. Jones St.) A selection of rare and scarce books for bibliophiles and booklovers looking for a special title. By appointment.

Waldenbooks (912-352-2750; Oglethorpe Mall) Good selection of popular titles and books of regional interest. Nice children's and nature-oriented titles.

CLOTHING

In the Lowcountry, people still wear hats. Not just baseball caps or fedoras, either — hats with attitude and purposeful brims — but straw hats, garden-party hats, fishing caps, and velvet berets. They also dress their children, boys and girls, in smockery and suits. Yet among a population that tends to sartorial conservatism, there is usually a fillip of embellishment to be found, accompanied by the natural confidence to pull it off.

There are probably more choices for those inclined to fashion in Charleston than in any other Lowcountry city — some regular out-of-state visitors do all their serious shopping here — but Beaufort and Savannah have their own gems. The Hilton Head area has become a mecca for outlet stores, some of which carry clothes.

The following suggestions do not list clothing stores that are part of a national chain, although those to be found in the Lowcountry include Polo, Laura Ashley, Banana Republic, Gap, Express, The Limited, Benetton, and Talbot's.

For athletic clothes geared to specific sports, see the section "Sporting Goods and Clothing" in Chapter Six, *Recreation*.

Charleston Area

A.J. Davis & Co. (803-577-3088; 296 King St.) Men's clothes, plain and cheerfully sporty, and accessories.

Berlin's (803-722-1665; 114 King St.) Men's and women's clothes in traditional styles and top-quality brands. Since 1883.

Bits of Lace (803-577-0999; 212 King St.) Fine lingerie and other little fancy things for women.

Bob Ellis Shoes (803-722-2605; 332 King St.) Vast selection of fine footwear for men and women and a sales staff that keeps bringing out the boxes.

Christian Michi is an updated, old-fashioned emporium for scents, soaps, high-style home accessories, and designer clothes.

Wade Spees

Christian Michi (803-723-0575; 220 King St.) For women, high-fashion and sporty lines from top European and American designers. It's as if a small section of a hip New York department store left the city for life in the provinces.

Cousins (803-723-2643; 150 King St.) Simple, elegant, understated clothes with classic lines, for women. There's a quiet, relaxed atmosphere of real attention to your own style here.

Eighty-Two Church (803-723-7511; 82 Church St.) If this store were anywhere but in Charleston's Historic "South of Broad" district, it would probably be a museum by now. A lovely selection of hand-smocked dresses for girls to size 14, bonnets, clothes for newborns, christening outfits, sweaters, cotton rompers, and seersucker playsuits. Boy's clothing to size 6. Very nice baby gifts, too.

A new generation ready to be outfitted at Eighty-Two Church Street.

Wade Spees

Granny's Goodies (803-577-6200; 332 East Bay St.) Antique and vintage clothes for men, women, and children: poodle skirts, Hawaiian shirts, gloves and gauze, fur-trimmed opera capes, boas. Great selection and guaranteed laughs.

L'Unique, Ltd. (803-577-8860; 185 King St.) Evening wear for women with a flair for the decorative and unusual.

M. Dumas & Sons (803-723-8603; 294 King St.) Even the wallpaper here is riding to hounds. The old original source for what has become an "American Country" look.

The Oops Co.! (803-722-7768; 66 State St.) A basic preppy look made affordable because the stock comprises irregulars, seconds, or discontinued runs from top-quality catalogs.

RTW (803-577-9748; 186 King St.) A boutique for women who delight in gorgeous fabrics, sweaters that tumble with color, one-of-a-kind shirts, hats, shoes, and accessories, and who like to dress with a sense of fun and beauty. A rare find in any city.

Achieving the "right look" at RTW takes some time.

Wade Spees

Three Nineteen King (803-577-2699; 319 King St.) Chic fashions for men and women with attitude.

Beaufort Area

Charpentier Clothiers (803-522-4030; 926 Bay St.) A store for men and women with high-end classics for sale in a quiet, rather formal atmosphere — it's located in a terrifically restored, early 20th-century bank building. If people of the 90s are interested in less-but-better, they'll shop here.

Deal's (803-524-4993; 724 Bay St.) Sweaters, wool and cotton, denims, khakis, shirts in natural fibers, all at discounted prices. Irish imported apparel, too.

Jasmine (803-524-6660; 919 Bay St.) A women's boutique.

Lipsitz Department Store (803-524-2330; 825 Bay St.) A family-owned and family-run business for nearly 100 years. Everyday wear and shoes in all sizes, superior friendly service.

There's something for every member of the family at Lipsitz: what stores were like before they became boutiques.

Wade Spees

Plumage (803-522-8807; 104 West St.) Evening clothes and accessories.

Sea Island Lady (803-522-0143; Sea Island Parkway) Lingerie, lace, silk and cotton fancies.

Savannah Area

Gaucho (912-232-7414; 250 Bull St.) Jewelry, leather, and clothing for women with a rustic, dude-ranch feeling.

Jezebel (912-236-4333; 25 E. River St.) Light-hearted and good-looking dresses, casual wear for women.

John B. Rourke (912-355-1211; 7135 Hodgson Memorial Dr.) Classic men's suits, accessories, hats, and sportswear.

Yesterday's (912-236-2611; 106 E. Liberty St.) Vintage clothing and accessories.

CRAFTS

The Lowcountry's *sea grass baskets* are a regional specialty, and if you're interested in them, you won't have far to look while you're in <u>*Charleston.*</u> The basket weavers are out every day along **Broad and Church streets** and in the **Market Area**. (For a more complete description of the Market Area, see below under "Shopping Streets, Mews and Malls.") Prices vary for items as small as keepsake decorations or as large as fanner baskets and hampers. You're welcome to watch the process, which incorporates palmetto strips and pine straw with the pale grass. Other weavers sell their work at stands located north of Charleston on **Highway 17**.

Coiled sea grass baskets laid out on street corners attract viewers and buyers.

Wade Spees

If you're nearer to <u>*Beaufort*</u>, you'll find basket weavers' stands on **Highway 21** east of town.

Other crafts abound in shops throughout the Lowcountry. Here is a sampling:

<u>Charleston Area</u>

American Originals (803-853-5034; 153 East Bay St.) Crafts by local and national artists: pictures, baskets, rugs, pottery.

Charleston Collections (803-722-7267; 142 East Bay St.) One-of-a-kind drawings, prints, Charleston collectibles, local artists' crafts.

Charleston Crafts (803-723-2938; 38 Queen St.) Crafts and exhibits by members of this local co-op, who are considered superior in their fields, be they weavers, soapmakers, or photographers.

East Bay Gallery (803-723-5567; 264 King St.) Ironwork tables, pottery lamps, wooden inlaid boxes, colorful blown stemware.

Beaufort Area

The Craftseller (803-525-6104; 216 West St.) Local and regional artists' work including jewelry, benches made of old wood from local buildings, fabric art, handmade paper, wind-chimes.

Keepers of the Culture (803-522-9390; 305 West St.) Arts and crafts with an African-American theme; herbs, folk remedies.

Savannah Area

Bull St. Station (912-236-4344; 151 Bull St.) Model railroad supplies and other accessories for hobbyists of all kinds.

City Market Art Center (912-234-2327; 219 W. Bryan St.) Local artists, craftsmen working in studios; several galleries for local works.

The Crimson Monkey (912-786-6409; 1511 1/2 Butler Ave., Tybee Island) A showcase for Savannah artists in a variety of media, from watercolors to sculpture.

Gallery 209 (912-236-4583; 209 E. River St.) A co-op gallery with works of batik, fiber, glass, pottery, and more.

River Works Craft Gallery (912-236-2012; 105 E. River St.) American crafts featuring pottery and jewelry.

GALLERIES

Charleston

African American Gallery (803-722-8224; 43 John St.) Handmade batiks and African prints for men and women; African and African-American art, including sculpture, prints, and paintings.

Birds I View Gallery (803-723-1276; 119-A Church St.) Realistic paintings and prints — her birds and rabbits are drawn from those she's cared for — by longtime Charleston artist Anne Worsham Richardson.

Carolina Prints (803-723-2266; 188 King St.) Antique prints by masters such as Audubon, Catesby, and Schwert; pre-1945 American art and lots of Southern

Wade Spees

In the balmy spring, Lowcountry sidewalks become outdoor art galleries.

scenes, such as sporting activity and wildlife. Contemporary realistic art by local artists.

Gallery East (803-722-2858; 15 Mid Atlantic Wharf) Local artwork, jewelry, and sculpture, limited edition prints and posters, located in an old cotton warehouse.

Gallery 12 (803-723-0311; 290 King St.) A co-op gallery of 12 local artists working in diverse media, influenced by the light, air, and form of the Lowcountry environment.

Gallery West Indies (803-720-8876; 73 Broad St.) Sculptures from Haiti, West Africa, and Guatemala; Santos from Central America; colorful, vivid folk-art paintings.

Gordon Wheeler Gallery (803-722-2546; 182 East Bay St.) The realistic paintings of the artist, mostly watercolor, many in print editions, of the Lowcountry, including vistas and sporting scenes.

Lowcountry Artists, Ltd. (803-577-9295; 87 Hasell St.) A small, intimate gallery devoted to the work of nine artists who express themselves in ways as diverse as woodcuts to pencil drawings.

Marty Whaley Adams (803-722-7543; 2 Queen St.) Watercolors and portraits in a fluid, impressionistic hand.

Nina Liu and Friends (803-722-2724; 24 State St.) Wonderful contemporary art in media such as fabric, collage, ceramic, paper, and glass — works that can be startling, magical, and strong. The owner is herself an artist with a fine eye.

Southeastern Wildlife Exposition Gallery (803-723-1757; 211 Meeting St.) Experience the feeling of the exposition even if you didn't attend: wildlife art, sculpture, posters, carvings.

The Colony House (803-723-3424; 35 Prioleau St.) The second floor of this old Charleston restaurant has been given over to Lowcountry artists who exhibit their work several times each year.

Virginia Fouche Bolton (803-577-9351; 127 Meeting St.) Classic scenes of Charleston, its houses and people, including miniatures reproduced from original watercolors that make nice keepsakes.

West Fraser (803-577-6039; 17-B Broad St., by appointment) Landscapes, cityscapes, and maritime watercolors; prints and oil paintings of the Lowcountry and the Eastern seaboard. This acclaimed artist's unique way of making pictures out in the field — in a late 19th-century manner called *plein air* ("open light") — conveys his commitment to capturing the most evanescent qualities of the marine environment.

Beaufort

Art Images (803-524-2877; 103 Charles St.) Work by eight local artists, including collage, stained glass, prints, note cards, acrylics, and wearable art.

Gallery One (803-524-7967; 824 Bay St.) Original watercolors of the Lowcountry — old houses, shrimp boats, vistas, wildlife — by the gallery's owners and about three dozen additional artists. A friendly, welcoming place full of nice work.

Garden Studio Gallery (803-522-8911; 1908 Lenora Dr., by appointment) Watercolors by Sandra Baggette of brightly rendered Lowcountry scenes and gardens.

Indigo Gallery (803-524-1036; 809 Bay St.) Limited and open editions of many of the best-known Lowcountry artists, as well as serigraphs, original art, and framing.

Longo Gallery (803-522-8933; 407 Carteret St.) Clay and concrete sculpture, paintings, and found-object constructions by Suzanne and Eric Longo, exhibited in their home studio.

Nancy Forrester (803-524-4224; 315 West St.) Antique prints and an especially fine collection of botanicals.

Rhett Gallery (803-524-3339; 901 Bay St.) Prints and watercolors of the Lowcountry by Nancy Ricker Rhett — works that seem to get their light just right — as well as antique first-edition prints and maps, Civil War and nautical materials, and hand-colored engravings. Custom framing and shipping available.

Sonshine Studio (803-522-1222; 719 Bay St.) Art supplies, frames, and original art.

The Red Piano Too (803-838-2241; 751 Sea Island Parkway — Hwy. 21) — St. Helena Island) A superior collection of folk art by various artists — including St. Helena native Sam Doyle — sea grass baskets, quilts, beads, African objects, and prints (framing available on site). The collection is continually expanding in breadth and variety. Not to be missed.

Thum'prints Gallery (803-524-1211; Old Bay Marketplace) Posters, original art, and framing.

W. Jackson Causey (803-524-2595; 805 Craven St.) A front room of the artist's 19th-century house provides sunny studio and gallery space for his watercolors and pen-and-ink portrayals of Lowcountry scenes.

Savannah

City Market Art Center (912-234-2327; 219 W. Bryan St.) Working studios of 35 artists spread through several buildings make this Savannah's art colony.

Compass Prints, Inc. (912-234-3537; 205 W. Congress St.) Paintings and prints of golf and traditional maritime scenes by Ray Ellis, perhaps the best-known of Lowcountry artists. Also, books of his work and notecards.

Gallery 307 (912-234-5157; 307 Bull St.) This is the place for up-and-coming artists to exhibit.

S. Morris Gallery (912-233-7712; 137 Bull St.) A unique sensibility brings to this gallery both contemporary artwork and conceptual art and art of the Civil War.

Silver House Studio (912-233-3372; 108 E. Bay St.) Specializing in photography and video work, by students at the Savannah College of Art and Design and others.

The Crimson Monkey (912-786-6409; 1511 1/2 Butler Ave., Tybee Island) Work by Savannah-area artists including jewelry, sculpture, paintings.

Tybee Island Arts Association and Gallery (912-786-5920; 30 Meddin Dr., Tybee Island) Tybee-area artists display their work in a building on the grounds of the Tybee Island Lighthouse.

V. & J. Duncan (912-232-0338; 12 E. Taylor St.) You could browse for hours here through the files and piles of prints, maps, old advertising art, and illustrations here. A comprehensive, well-organized collection.

Victoria House Gallery (912-786-4495; 1801 Butler Ave., Tybee Island) An assortment of fine arts, crafts, ink drawings, and photography.

GIFTS

Charleston Area

Birds & Ivy (803-853-8534; 235 King St.) Accessories for your garden and even the coffee beans to brew while you're sitting in it.

Cabbage Row Shoppe (803-722-1528; 110 Church St.) Needlework, cards, and pretty keepsakes for your bureau at home.

Charleston Catalog Company (803-722-6121; 139 Market St.) Take home a piece of the Lowcountry, an original miniature, a botanical, or a taste of it.

The Climbing Bear (803-853-7066; 40 N. Market St.) Toys for children made the old-fashioned way. Wooden train sets and brightly painted things for little ones to pull behind them.

Indigo (803-853-9206; 189 East Bay St.) A changing mixture of antiques, old fishing rods and creels, handsome leather luggage that has seen the world, folk art, pottery.

J. Davenport (803-722-3212; 100 Church St.) Decorative accessories for home and garden in the city's soft urban style.

Kites Fly N Hi (803-577-3529; 40 N. Market St.) These kites, wind socks, and flags look good standing still; imagine how fine they'd be in a breeze back home.

Porgy & Bess (803-723-1887; 91 Church St.) What's here in the way of clothing and accessories is likely to be bright in color and long on puckishness, as in paper goods that read "This napkin has no cholesterol."

The Smoking Lamp (803-577-7339; 197 East Bay St.) Everything for the smoker, that most maligned modern species.

Stoll's Alley Shop (803-722-8585; 10 Stoll's Alley) Tucked away, in place and in time. Lovely linens, shams, blanket covers (just the right weight for the Lowcountry and still widely used), bed and bath accessories.

Beaufort Area

Basquettes (803-686-9722; 903 Bay St.) Fragrant soaps and specialty jellies, little treasures that fill up baskets — or Christmas stockings.

Beaufort Emporium (803-524-3726; 723 Bay St.) The shadow of the former hardware store this was remains in the breadth of its stock: models, cookware, birdfeeders, garden ornaments.

Boombears (803-524-2525; 501 Carteret St.) You may as well just dare yourself not to enjoy the toys, books, dolls, games, tin soldiers, stuffed animals, and stickers here. Unaccompanied adults welcome, too! A vibrant place, equal to the best you've seen.

Finder's Keepers (803-525-9200; 920 Bay St.) If you didn't make it to the beach, get your seashells here.

Fine Jewelry of Bluffton (803-757-3722; Hwy. 46, Bluffton) Barbara and Stephen Bush have a good selection of diamond, gemstones, and gold; if you don't see exactly what you want, they can probably order it for you or have it made up.

Fordham Hardware (803-524-3161; 701 Bay St.) Everything from hammocks to waste baskets, fireplace tools to floor wax. A Beaufort institution.

The Garden Party (803-522-8634; 102 West St.) Arrangements, gardening gadgets, outdoor art for gardeners who wish they could dig in the dirt all year long — just as they do in the Lowcountry.

House and Garden Gift Shop (803-522-0406; Sea Island Parkway) Cards, candles, vases, glassware, notepads for bridge and shopping, windsocks. Presents for your hostess and special keepsakes.

If you can't buy it at Fordham Hardware, you'll probably have to make it yourself.

Wade Spees

Precious Cargo (803-525-1075; 904 Bay St.) Needlework pillows with saucy sayings, folk art, accessories for the bar, collectibles from around the world.

Thorndike Williams Interior Design (803-524-7688; 308 Scott St.) In a little cottage that looks nearly tropical: fine reproduction furniture, prints, lamps, china, brass, fabrics, and antiques.

Savannah Area

Corrigan's (912-232-0300; 213 W. St. Julian St.) A great selection of stationery, candles, and cards; small crystal and brass items.

The Cotton Patch (912-234-7188; 48 E. Broad St.) Folk art and dried wreaths, dolls, and collectibles.

The Cottage Shop (912-233-3820; 2422 Abercorn St.) Linens for bed and table, stationery, lamps, crystal.

Davenport House Museum Shop (912-236-8097; 324 E. State St.) Gifts with a Savannah theme and a Lowcountry flavor in the first house restored by the Historic Savannah Foundation.

Japonica (912-236-1613; 13 W. Charlton St.) Small antiques for desktops and bedrooms, jewelry, cachepots.

The Little House (912-232-1551; 107 E. Gordon St.) In business 70 years, this is a charming shop of the sort that has nearly disappeared. Gifts for children, for weddings, for a special nook at home.

HOME FURNISHINGS/KITCHENWARE

Charleston Area

fred (803-723-5699; 237 King St.) Clean, spare design in black and white and stainless steel: kitchen basics, cutlery, towels and racks, mechanical wonders. A local favorite.

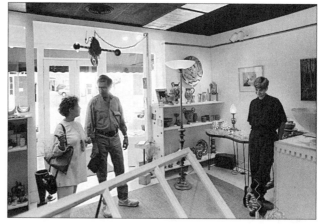

Several home furnishings shops offer goods as whimsical, elegant, and stylish as those you'd find for sale in Manhattan's trendy SoHo.

Wade Spees

Gibraltar (803-723-9394; 154 King St.) Kim Hay, who grew up here, has put together an exquisite collection of fabrics, furnishings, glassware, lovely jewelry, and ceramics of contemporary design by fine young artists and designers. Not to be missed.

Home (803-723-9063; 268 King St.) Cookbooks, gifts, ceramics, table settings that bring Provence or Tuscany to your sunny rooms.

K Sabatier Cutlery (803-577-4117; 217-A Meeting St.) Fine French knives for carving, paring, and cleaving, at outlet prices.

Le Creuset (803-722-8318; 221 Meeting St.) Famous French enameled cookware at factory prices. (The factory, and another store, are located off I-95 at Yemassee, if you're heading south.)

Marc Howard (803-722-2762; 314 King St.) Lush, multicolored leather pillows, museum-store desk accessories, modern clocks, high-tech floor lamps.

Beaufort Area

The Checkered Moon (803-522-3466; 208 West St.) Whimsical wall pieces, painted objects, garden accessories.

The Garden Gate (803-524-0767; 1001 Charles St.) The old iron gates and fretted, grill-work balconies of the Lowcountry are the centerpieces of strong, simple coffee tables. The rescued, weathered iron seems haunting even under glass. By appointment only.

Savannah Area

Bob Christian Decorative Art (912-234-6866; 12 W. Harris) Specialists in faux finishes of an astonishing variety. Special orders taken.

The Gypsy Moth (912-232-6800; City Market) Folk art, birdhouses, funky wooden medallions and sculpture, day of the dead mementos, wooden animals, rugs.

The Mulberry Tree (912-236-4656; 17 W. Charlton St.) Quilts, replicas of old toys, baskets, and small art objects.

Portico & Co. (912-231-9001; 31 Barnard St.) Country artifacts like tablecloths, twig furniture, pottery and baskets for city homes and gardens.

Small Pleasures (912-236-0111; 15 E. Harris St.) Hand-painted furniture, decorative accessories.

SHOPPING STREETS, MEWS, AND MALLS

In addition to the specific shops mentioned above, there are sections in Lowcountry cities that are jam-packed with stores, some of them super-speciality shops — for chocolate, perfume, wooden boxes, or tee-shirts — some of them little cluster malls where tiny shops take root.

In *Charleston*, there's the *Market Area*, where a long strip of old open-air sheds runs down the center of the street — which is, in turn, bisected at several points by lateral shopping streets. You could enjoy a nice after-dinner walk here, or have coffee and dessert at a sidewalk cafe and watch the Citadel cadets with their dates, the tourists, the families who have drifted down on a warm night. The range of what you can buy is enormous, from a Civil War lithograph to a hand puppet to a turnip.

Shops along Factors Walk in Savannah sell everything from conventional greeting cards to life-size posters.

Wade Spees

In <u>**Savannah**</u>, the places are **River Street**, where the old warehouses have been divided into layers of shops, bars, and restaurants, and the **City Market**, with its shops and restaurants.

All these areas run on their own clock: there's a lot happening long after dark.

<u>**Hilton Head**</u> draws the crowds and the outlet malls. There are three in the area, two on the island, one on the way there. In each, there are several varieties of stores and ample parking; store to store, the selection is usually very good, it turns over quickly, and the prices represent significant savings. There are fast-food style places to eat within the malls and play areas for children. Some of the better-known, name-brand factory outlet stores are listed below. (Specialty shops elsewhere on Hilton Head are listed in Chapter Eight.)

<u>***Low Country Factory Outlet Village***</u> (Hwy. 278 about four miles from the Hilton Head bridge) includes sportswear retailers: ***J. Crew*** (803-837-5335), ***Reebok*** (803-837-4930), ***Eddie Bauer*** (803-837-6188), ***Danskin*** (803-837-4990). For kids, try ***Bugle Boy*** (803-837-6079), ***Baby Guess*** (803-837-7393), ***Toy Liquidators*** (803-837-5210). For high fashion, ***Geoffrey Beene*** (803-837-6613). For kitchenware, ***Corning/Revere*** (803-837-6262).

<u>***Pineland Mill Shops***</u> (Mid-island, Hilton Head) includes clothing: ***Tanner*** (803-689-6494), ***Cape Isle Knitters*** (803-681-4150), ***Barbizon Lingerie*** (803-681-4344), ***Hilton Head Shirt Shop*** (803-681-9526), ***Bass Shoes*** (803-681-4164). For housewares, there's ***Royal Doulton*** (803-681-2192) and ***International Silver*** (803-689-2948).

Connecting breezeways and broad sidewalks make a sprawling outlet mall feel more like a village.

Wade Spees

<u>**Shoppes on the Parkway**</u> (Mid-island, Hilton Head, south of Palmetto Dunes) has good sportswear at **Royal Robbins** (803-785-3808), **Duck Head** (803-842-7686), **Players World of Golf** (803-785-4653). For high fashion, try **Anne Klein II** (803-842-9290). **Gorham** (803-686-6637) has cutlery, and for bedding there's **Palmetto Linen Outlet** (803-785-2515).

CHAPTER EIGHT
Courts, Courses, Sails, and Sand
HILTON HEAD

The Hilton Head Island that a visitor sees today is a far different place from what it was even 30 years ago. To longtime Lowcountry residents, it seems to have sprung up practically overnight. It represents a startling change — in landscape, population, commerce, even traffic — to those who, in the past, were accustomed to seeing growth in their region come slowly — if it came at all. It is the Lowcountry's boom town, envied for its economic and recre-

Wade Spees

The Harbour Town lighthouse and marina at Sea Pines are the symbols of the widely copied "resort-plantation" culture of Hilton Head Island.

ational resources, and its business opportunities, scrutinized as a example of the delicate balance between thoughtful planning and runaway success.

Unlike the rest of the Lowcountry, Hilton Head is a place of condensed pleasure: in one day, a visitor can enjoy a range of activities — being on the beach or water, playing golf, shopping, dining out — that might have taken a week's vacation to savor in the past, had even the possibilities existed. Its resort areas are groomed and glossy, offering premium service; its residential neighborhoods and streetscapes designed to harmonize with the natural landscape. It offers many attractions for families. Add to these reasons the wonderfully mild climate and location amid ocean and river, and it's easy to understand why more than 1.5 million visitors come every year.

Until about 1960, soon after a bridge linked Hilton Head to the mainland, the island's history mirrored that of other Sea Islands. First settled by planters with slaves who raised rice, indigo, and cotton on about 16 plantations, later occupied during the Civil War by Federal troops, and faced with hard times and isolation after that, the island remained as rural and poor as any place

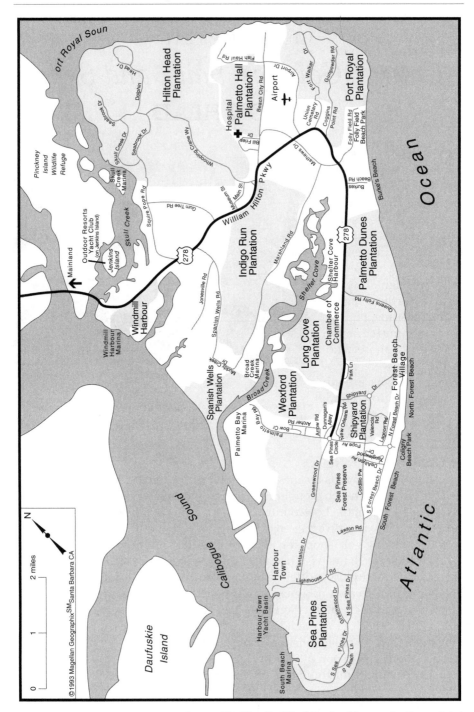

Courtesy of The Hilton Head Island Chamber of Commerce (used by permission)

HILTON HEAD ISLAND

was. The African-American families who made up most of the island's population farmed and fished; the visitors who came were gentleman hunters.
Transportation was supplied by small packet steamers, sailboats, and barges.
Eventually time and lush vegetation covered what traces remained of antebellum plantation life and the bustling wartime encampments.

The resort and residential development that began in earnest in the early
1960s led to the "plantation" layout that orders the island's geography today.
The ones where most tourist activities are based and which might be called
semiprivate are Hilton Head Plantation, Sea Pines Plantation, Shipyard Plantation, Palmetto Dunes, and Port Royal Plantation. Others include Spanish
Wells Plantation, Indigo Run, Palmetto Hall, Windmill Harbour, Long Cove,
and Wexford. Within and around them are the dozens of golf courses, tennis
courts, and marinas that define island recreation. Shops and restaurants are
usually gathered in malls and shopping centers; many smaller residential
areas lie scattered across the island.

Even as the geography has changed (much of it literally sculpted into golf
courses), so have the island's residents. Today the population by race is nearly
90 percent white, by age nearly 28 percent over 60 years old. There are established schools and churches that didn't exist 30 years ago, and an excellent
daily newspaper, *The Island Packet*. Development and a changing cast of visitors give Hilton Head the sense of a new place; for a contrasting sense of
island timelessness, you must seek out its authentic Lowcountry character: its
vistas of marsh and ocean, the flocks of pelicans that dive for fish, the loggerhead turtles that lay their eggs in the dark, the whistling songbirds, and the
groves of live oak and pine that shelter deer and dove.

THE WAY THIS CHAPTER WORKS

Unlike other places covered in this guide, Hilton Head stands alone. For
many visitors, it is the first and only stop in the Lowcountry. Suggestions
for lodging, recreation, culture, restaurants, nightlife, and shopping are presented with introductions. At the end of the chapter are listings of basic information, which you may find useful before you visit or once you're there, as
well as a calendar of major seasonal events.

As you plan, you might want to decide what, if any, particular quality
you'd like your trip to have. If you think you just want to play golf or tennis,
you might look into options in the "Lodging" section for "stay-and-play"
packages. If you're traveling with friends or family, you may want to rent a
house. If you decide upon a resort, you may well not need a car — most resort
amenities are within walking or biking distance.

The high season starts with the big tennis and golf tournaments hosted at
Sea Pines Plantation in March and April. May and early June can be a quiet
time before the crowds of summer; the fall, right up to Thanksgiving, is

thought by many to be a quiet, lovely time of year. When the island is crowded, you can expect traffic tie-ups, and you may want to make reservations well in advance for tee times and dining. In general, there are so many options to choose from that you are not likely to be at all disappointed.

LODGING

One by-product of the development boom on Hilton Head Island is the proliferation and variety of places to stay. Whatever your budget or the number of people traveling, you will find a place that suits. The accommodations industry is resourceful — it services approximately 1.5 million visitors each year.

There are more than 3,000 hotel and motel rooms and 6,000 rental units including cottages, houses, and fully furnished condominiums (known as villas) scattered across the island, from sites on or near the beach to those around golf courses, marinas, or lagoons, in residential subdivisions or low-rise housing complexes, or even on the main highway. Your accommodations may be elegant or simple; offer as much or as little privacy as you wish; come with or without kitchens; lie within walking distance, or not, from the beach and recreational amenities.

Rates vary from as little as $40 per night for an economy motel room to as much as $5,000 per week for a luxurious oceanfront home with a swimming pool. The range reflects differences in size and location — oceanfront is premium; resort privileges add to the price — and also the time of year: summer is the most expensive season, followed by spring (especially April, the time of the Family Circle Tennis Tournament and the MCI Heritage Golf Classic). The

Oceanfront hotels dominate some sections of the beach: the convenience, view, and cool breezes can't be beat.

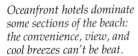

Wade Spees

fall brings ideal golfing conditions, so prices can stay high through September. In the winter months, rates can be half what they are in high season. Like many resort areas, Hilton Head adds an accommodations tax to lodging bills, and some establishments place a surcharge on credit-card payments. It's wise, when planning, to ask for an estimate of your overall bill.

Whatever accommodation you choose, be sure to ask about special rate packages or coupons they might offer for restaurants, health clubs, or shops. Many hotels have discounts for golf and tennis; some have family plans, including activities for kids. In larger hotels, children often stay free. Lodgings that are not located in private resorts often have arrangements to allow you access to some of their recreational facilities.

The easiest way to make reservations in a hotel or motel is to call directly. To inquire about home and villa rentals, call a property management company. Central reservation agencies can give you a sense of the whole picture, and they may be especially helpful in designing a package tailored to your specific interests. If you're interested in camping, look into the two recreational vehicle parks listed under "Recreation," later in this chapter. If you're staying on a boat, see the section on Marinas in the Recreation listings.

The following rates are for one night's stay, per person, double occupancy. They do not include taxes, surcharges, or any special recreation/entertainment discounts. Prices quoted are for high-season accommodations.

Rates	Inexpensive	Up to $55
	Moderate	$55 to $75
	Expensive	$75 to $150
	Very Expensive	$150 and up

Credit Cards	AE — American Express
	CB — Carte Blanche
	D — Discover Card
	DC — Diner's Club
	MC — MasterCard
	V — Visa

LUXURY OCEANFRONT HOTELS

HILTON RESORT
803-842-8000/1-800-845-8001.
In Palmetto Dunes.
Price: Very Expensive.
Credit Cards: All major cards.
Handicap Access: Yes.

A luxury hotel that claims the largest rooms on the island — 560 sq. ft. each — with private balconies and kitchenettes. At the oceanfront setting, there's an adults-only pool and a family pool, whirlpools, and a health club. Restaurants and nightclubs within the complex.

HYATT REGENCY
803-785-1234/1-800-233-1234.
In Palmetto Dunes.
Price: Very Expensive.
Credit Cards: AE, DC, MC, V.
Handicap Access: Yes.

The largest hotel on the island, with 505 rooms, indoor pool, Olympic-sized outdoor pool, and children's pool. Health club available to guests, as are tennis and golf privileges and sailboat and bicycle rental. Several restaurants offer both formal and casual poolside dining.

MARRIOTT'S HILTON HEAD RESORT
803-842-2400/1-800-334-1881.
In Shipyard Plantation.
Very Expensive.
Credit Cards: AE, DC, MC, V.
Handicap Access: Yes.

A 313-room oceanfront luxury hotel with special trimmings such as in-house barber and beauty salon, gift shop, and popular lounge for evening entertainment. Pools, golf course and putting green, tennis courts, health center, sailing, and water sports all on site.

WESTIN RESORT
803-681-4000/1-800-933-3102.
At Port Royal Plantation.
Price: Very Expensive.
Credit Cards: AE, DC, MC, V.
Handicap Access: Yes.

Often considered the most luxurious of the island's resort hotels, praised for its Sunday brunch as well as its elegant decor. Five-diamond rating by AAA. Each guest room has a private balcony, and many of the small villas have their own Jacuzzis. If outdoor dining and health clubs and all the recreational amenities are not your style, you can sip tea by the fireplace. Cocktails and dancing in the Gazebo Lounge.

SMALLER HOTELS

BEST WESTERN OCEAN WALK SUITES
803-842-3100/1-800-528-1234.
36 S. Forest Beach Dr.
Price: Moderate
Credit Cards: All major cards.
Handicap Access: Yes.

A 142-room hotel featuring rooms with kitchenettes, mini-refrigerators, and cable television. Complimentary Continental breakfast, family-oriented dining, three tennis courts, pool. Adjacent to public beach access.

DAYS INN RESORT AND CONFERENCE CENTER
803-842-6662/1-800-325-2525.
Tanglewood Dr.
Price: Moderate.
Credit Cards: All major cards.

Located at South Forest Beach, next door to miniature golf and waterslide park; pools; full-service restaurant.

HAMPTON INN
803-681-7900/1-800-426-7866.
1 Airport Rd.
Price: Moderate.
Credit Cards: All major cards.

Most convenient motel to the airport; shopping nearby at Port Royal Plaza. Swimming pool, complimentary breakfast.

RADISSON SUITE RESORT
803-686-5700/1-800-852-0886.
12 Park Ln., in Central Park.
Price: Expensive.
Credit Cards: All major cards.
Handicap Facilities: Yes.

Each of the 156 suites features a fully equipped kitchen, and some suites have wood-burning fireplaces. Complimentary Continental breakfast buffet. A recreation area includes basketball, volleyball and tennis courts, pool, jogging trails, and a playground. Free shuttle to the beach four times daily.

HOLIDAY INN OCEAN-FRONT
803-785-5126/1-800-465-4329.
Forest Beach Dr. at Coligny Circle.
Price: Expensive.
Credit Cards: All major cards.
Handicap Facilities: Yes

The island's most popular public-access beach is at your doorstep, and there's plenty of people-watching at the Tiki Hut, a beachside snack bar. Outdoor pool and rock music during the summer months.

PLAYERS CLUB RESORT
803-785-8000/1-800-497-7529.
DeAllyon Rd.
Price: Moderate.
Credit Cards: AE, MC, V.

If you've come for a tennis vacation, Players Club offers tennis discounts and an unbeatable location next to the Van der Meer Tennis Center, a professional teaching complex. Outdoor pool; indoor lap pool and health club.

SEA CREST MOTEL
803-785-2121/1-800-845-7014.
4 N. Forest Beach Dr.
Price: Moderate.
Credit Cards: MC, V.

An old (and for a long time the only) motel on Hilton Head. One-bedroom efficiencies and two-bedroom apartments, cable television, oceanside pool and deck; close to shopping and restaurants.

**SOUTH BEACH
MARINA INN**
803-671-6498/1-800-367-
3909.
In Sea Pines Plantation.
Price: Expensive.
Credit Cards: AE, MC, V;
5% surcharge on credit
card charges.

Located in a New England–style marina village in Sea Pines Plantation, this 17-room inn sits above waterfront shops and restaurants. The rooms are condominium suites with living and dining rooms and kitchenettes, overlooking the courtyard or marina. The inn has a Cape Cod feeling: throw rugs, brass beds, and hardwood floors. Tennis, water sports, restaurants, and the beach are close by.

BUDGET CHOICES

Each of these national-chain motels of approximately 100 rooms has a swimming pool and is close to inexpensive restaurants or shopping areas.

FAIRFIELD INN (803-842-4800/1-800-228-2800; 9 Marina Side Dr. at William Hilton Pkwy. south of Palmetto Dunes Resort).

HOLIDAY INN EXPRESS (803-842-8888/1-800-800-8000; Pope Ave. near Coligny Plaza).

MOTEL 6 (803-785-2700; William Hilton Pkwy.).

RED ROOF INN (803-686-6808; 5 Regency Pkwy.).

SHONEY'S INN (803-681-3655/1-800-222-2222; 200 Museum St. near Main St. Village).

VACATION PROPERTY RENTALS

Most vacation rental properties are concentrated on the south end of the island in Sea Pines Plantation, Shipyard Plantation, South Forest Beach, and Palmetto Dunes Resort. Several villa rental complexes are located mid-island on or near Folly Field Beach. The northern half of the island is geared mainly to permanent residents; the island's other private communities do not permit short-term rental programs.

Villas and homes generally rent by the week, but nightly rates are available. The least expensive summer rates are about $500 per week, which can buy you a small villa outside a plantation more than one-half mile from the beach. For $2,500 per week in the summer, you could secure an oceanfront home with pool. In the winter, rates drop substantially.

Most rental companies manage properties in a variety of sizes, shapes, and locations. A good vacation rental should offer free swimming, free or discounted tennis, and discounts on golf; it should also be within walking distance of the beach. Some offer dining and shopping discounts, too. Before you make your final decision, you might consider where you want to be and what it is you wish to do. You need not pay premium oceanfront prices if you're going to be on the links all day.

Before you sign a rental agreement, make sure you understand policies regarding deposits, refunds in the event of cancellation, times of arrival and departure, and charges, if any, for cleaning services. If you have special needs — handicap-accessible or nonsmoking rooms, cots or cribs for children — alert the agent. Of the agencies listed below, and they are just some of many, the two largest are affiliated with resorts — Sea Pines Resort (Sea Pines Plantation) and Sand Dollar Management (Palmetto Dunes Resort).

Hilton Head Beach and Tennis Resort (803-842-4402/1-800-777-1700) Located at Folly Field, a 200-unit oceanfront villa complex with 10 tennis courts, two pools, restaurant, and pool bar.

Island Getaway Rentals (803-842-4664/1-800-476-4885) Beachfront and ocean-oriented homes and villas in Port Royal Plantation, Sea Pines, and Palmetto Dunes. Golf packages for more than 20 courses.

Lancaster Resort Rentals and Sales (803-686-6008/1-800-845-7017) This established independent management company has more than 200 rental properties from Sea Pines to mid-island. Fairway views in Sea Pines; oceanfront homes on residential North Forest Beach and in Palmetto Dunes.

Sand Dollar Management (803-785-1161/1-800-845-6130) Manages more than 500 properties in Palmetto Dunes Resort, which includes Shelter Cove Marina condominiums.

Sea Pines Resort (803-785-3333/1-800-845-6131) One- to five-bedroom properties in Sea Pines and Shipyard plantations, located anywhere from beach to woods to fairway to marsh. More than 500 listings.

Shoreline Rental Co. (803-842-3006/1-800-334-5012) More than 200 villas and homes, mostly ocean-oriented except for those at Sea Pines' Harbour Town.

Trident Rentals at Palmetto Dunes (803-785-3447/1-800-237-8306) One- to four-bedroom villas and four-bedroom oceanfront homes, plus fairway and harborfront villas, included among 150-plus listings.

Worthy Owner Rental Group (803-785-5577/1-800-476-9674) Longtime family-owned property management company with about 200 homes and villas listed in Sea Pines Plantation. Up to eight bedrooms.

RESERVATION SERVICES

The following services can assist you with making reservations in advance of your trip:

Condo Hotline (803-785-2939/1-800-258-5852).
Hilton Head Central Reservation (803-785-9050/1-800-845-7018).
Hilton Head Travel Directory (803-671-7262/1-800-521-7262).
Sea to Tee Reservations (803-842-5759/1-800-465-3461).
Vacations on Hilton Head (803-681-9272/1-800-232-2463).

RECREATIONAL VEHICLE PARKS

Outdoor Resorts RV Resort and Yacht Club (803-681-3256; Jenkins Island, north end of Hilton Head) Full hookups, 200 RV sites, bath houses, two pools, three tennis courts, laundry, exercise room, sauna and whirlpool.

Outdoor Resorts Motor Coach Resort (803-785-7699; 19 Arrow Rd.) Full hookups, 401 sites, six tennis courts, pool, man-made lake, shuffleboard, horseshoes, basketball, playground, laundry, bathrooms with tubs and saunas.

RECREATION

In the last 10 years, Hilton Head has come into its own as a town that services full-time residents, but there's no doubt its identity still rests on its reputation as a place where visitors come to pursue golf, tennis, fishing, and water sports, and to enjoy the beach. The following listings offer some sense of the amazing range of what the island has to offer.

BEACH ACCESS

Twelve miles of gently sloping beaches define the island's ocean edge. They can be as wide as 600 feet at low tide. (For tidal information, tune into island cable television Channel 31 or check the local paper, *The Island Packet*.) Although many entry points to the beach are restricted — behind private resort plantation gates — there are several public beach access points. The most popular are *Coligny Beach Park* (located at the end of Pope Ave.) and *Folly Field Beach Park* (off Folly Field Rd.). Both have metered parking spaces, and Coligny has an additional lot where you can park all day for $4. *Burke's Beach*, on the north end of the island near Folly Field, has limited parking. Within the plantations, the beaches are accessible by marked footpaths.

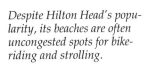

Despite Hilton Head's popularity, its beaches are often uncongested spots for bike-riding and strolling.

Wade Spees

Dogs are not permitted on the beach from 9 a.m. to 6 p.m. from the beginning of Memorial Day weekend through Labor Day weekend. Motor vehicles and glass containers are not allowed. Fishing and boating is prohibited in designated swimming areas; alcohol is banned. The beaches are patrolled by sheriff's deputies in jeeps.

BEACH ACTIVITIES: DOING THE DUNES

There's more to do on the beach than lie in the sun. *Shore Enterprises* (803-785-3494) rents a variety of beach and water-oriented vehicles, including bicycles, giant four-wheeled "aquacycles" that resemble floating tractors, catamaran sailboats, floats, boogie boards, and beach umbrellas and chairs. Outlets are located near the beach.

The Museum of Hilton Head Island (803-842-9197) offers guided walks several days per week on the island's beaches. Each tour lasts about two hours and explains the island's ecology, flora, and fauna. Children will like learning about shells and hunting hermit crabs. In 1992, the prices were $5 adults, $3 children. Call in advance to purchase tickets.

BICYCLING

You can rent bikes of all varieties in many locations, and most outlets offer island-wide pickup and delivery. If you're traveling with youngsters, you'll be able to obtain baby-carriers, helmets, bikes with training wheels, baby "trailers" that hook on the back of bikes, and jogging strollers. Some places rent in-line skates, too.

Miles of bike paths and scores of bikes to rent provide hours of exploring fun for people of all ages.

Wade Spees

Public bike paths extend from the tip of North Forest Beach to the end of South Forest Beach, along Pope Ave., up William Hilton Pkwy. to Folly Field Rd. Bike paths also thread through the plantations. If it's not too windy, riding on a hard-packed beach is an exceptional pleasure.

Rates vary by the hour, full day, or week. You can expect to pay about $5–$6 per hour, on the average; daily rates run about $8–$10, and a typical weekly rate is $25. For information, check the following outlets:

> **Alligator Beach Bike Rentals** (803-785-4346).
> **Beach Factory Ltd.** (803-686-6565).
> **Bikes Plus** (803-671-5588).
> **Bike Rack** (803-787-8777).
> **Cycle Center Rentals** (803-686-2288).
> **Harbour Town Bicycle** (803-785-3546).
> **Peddling Pelican Bike Rentals** (803-785-5470).
> **Sea Pines Bicycle Rentals** (803-842-1996).
> **South Beach Cycles** (803-785-2161).

BILLIARDS

Try your hand on the green felt at these island parlors: *Nicholas' Golden Cue* (803-842-9119; Northridge Plaza); *Callahan's Sports Bar* (803-686-7665; 49 New Orleans Rd.); *Frank's Oasis Restaurant* (803-686-3388; 27 Archer Rd.).

BIRD-WATCHING

Hilton Head still has some very quiet places for birds to nest and feed. You can visit them during daylight hours at the following sites:

Sea Pines Forest Preserve (entrances at Greenwood Dr. and Lawton Dr. in Sea Pines Plantation; $3 admission per car to enter Sea Pines Plantation) This 400-acre site offers a self-guided walking tour, which takes 1–2 hours. There are also picnic areas with grills.

Newhall Audubon Preserve (Palmetto Bay Rd.).

Whooping Crane Conservatory (Hilton Head Plantation) Features a board-walk and self-guided nature trail.

For nearby off-island sites, see the section "Nature Preserves" in Chapter Six, *Recreation*. If you find an injured bird, don't feed it or handle it, but instead call the *Bird Hospital* (803-689-3598).

BOATING AND WATER SPORTS

For sailboat charters and bare-boat rentals, contact the companies listed below and also check the "Marina" section in this chapter. If you want to nurture a wilder streak, look into renting a jet ski, floating with a parasail, riding a wave-runner, or "sledding" on a rubber tube. Some companies have special lessons for kids, so ask.

Breakwater Adventures (803-689-6800; Hudson's Landing, Squire Pope Rd.) Runabouts, pontoon boats, and cruisers equipped with appropriate fishing gear and safety equipment. Licensed guides available. Waterski and tube rentals; parasailing.

Commander Zodiac (803-671-3344; South Beach Marina) Sunfish, Hobie Cat, and Prindle sailboats for rent, private lessons and rides. Sailing school for youngsters to age 16. Visit the dolphins in engine-powered rubber rafts.

Island Watersports (803-671-7007; South Beach Marina) Power and sail boats for as many as 14 passengers, by the hour, half day, or day. Guided private cruises; sunset sails, wave-runners, and skis for rent.

Outside Hilton Head (803-671-2643; South Beach Marina) Learn to windsurf with confidence in three to six hour courses ($45 to $75) or private lessons ($35 per hour) and apply the cost to a new board. Board rentals available by the hour ($15) to a six-day week ($150).

Palmetto Bay Marina (803-785-7131; off Palmetto Bay Rd.) Ride into the sunset aboard the island's biggest and fastest charter boats ($15 adults); sailing lessons and smaller boats available.

Para-Sail Hilton Head (803-363-2628; Harbour Town) Go like the wind in a Sea Rocket powerboat, certified to carry up to 12 passengers. Parasailing and boat rental; catamaran rides for up to six people; sailing lessons.

BOWLING

Main Street Lanes (803-681-7750; Main St. Village).

CANOEING AND KAYAKING

Explore miles of Lowcountry waterways in a canoe or kayak, on your own or with a guided tour. Hourly kayak lessons in 1992 ran about $25; rentals by the day about $55. *Adventure Kayak Company* (803-842-8378; 8 Archer Rd.); *Breakwater Adventures* (803-689-6800; Hudson's Landing, Squire Pope Rd.); *Calibogue Kayak Company* (803-384-8125; 803-671-7486; Shelter Cove Marina); and *Outside Hilton Head* (803-686-6996; Shelter Cove; 803-671-2643; South Beach Marina Village) offer tours lasting several hours (prices ranging from $12.50 to $50 per person), in which paddlers receive some instruction and then venture out to a sandbar or into the web of coastal marshlands. It's a nice way to leave the world behind and observe marine life up close. *Fish Creek Landing* (803-785-2021; Palmetto Dunes) also rents canoes and paddle boats by the hour for lagoon trips.

CRUISES

Adventure Cruises (803-785-4558; Shelter Cove Harbor) has several outings, including trips to Daufuskie Island and sunset cruises, but among its most popular is its Murder Mystery Theater Cruise, during which passengers mingle with professional actors to solve a "crime." The cruise runs Tues. and Thurs. at 9 p.m. Prices: Adults $25; teens $20; children 12 and under $15.

Sport Crabbing and Dolphin Watch (803-785-2919; Shelter Cove Marina) Take a two-hour trip and cast for crabs off a comfortable, covered boat. Prices: Adults $12.50; children $9.50.

The Gypsy (803-363-2900; South Beach Marina) Sunset cruises; a morning kid's cruise in which children throw a cast net for shrimp, pull crab pots, and spot dolphins; and a fully narrated dolphin watch cruise. Trips last approximately two hours. Prices in 1992: Adults $10; children $5.

Vagabond Cruises (803-842-4155; Harbour Town Marina) Dolphin-watch, sightseeing, and sunset cruises; also Daufuskie tours. Prices: Adults $12–$15; children $5–$8.

FAMILY AMUSEMENTS

If you're coming with your children to Hilton Head, a place richly endowed with simple pleasures, activities like beachcombing, bike-riding, flying a kite, or taking a walk after supper may fully satisfy your idea of a great family vacation. Here are some ways to have even more fun together. Check newspaper listings to confirm schedules or find special family-oriented events.

Coastal Zone Education Center (803-837-4848; Sawmill Creek Rd., Bluffton) Call ahead for information about scheduled beach and marsh walks, and mini-classes in nature and ecology studies

Fun Factory (803-686-5386; 12 Arrow Rd.) It's all here, including batting cages, skee ball, air hockey, pool tables, foosball, bumper cars, and roller skating. You'll probably spend two hours trying everything out, then another hour getting everyone to leave.

Island Recreation Center (803-681-7273; 20 Wilborn Rd.) A year-round activity center with camps, clinics, and sports programs organized by the day, week, and month for children, teens, and adults. Check to see if events like bike races, fishing tournaments, rollerblading races, water carnivals, or craft classes (among others) might coincide with your visit. Call ahead: registration may be required.

Kreation Station (803-842-5738; 106 Cordillo Pkwy.) Summer art classes and camps for kids.

Summer Concerts: In the evening, family entertainers gather large audiences for free concerts and shows. Check the local paper for listings and plan to arrive early to secure parking. In *Sea Pines Plantation* (under the Liberty Oak at Harbour Town), singer and guitarist Gregg Russell performs nightly from 8 to 10 except Sunday. The audience sits on benches, and kids are encouraged to participate. Family sing-a-longs also take place on at Shelter Cove Harbour, and once a week, usually Tuesday, there are fireworks. Various performers also turn up at *Coligny Plaza* (off Pope Ave.) each night to entertain families. At *South Beach Marina* (Sea Pines Plantation), you can enjoy music while the sun sets over the docks.

Waterfun Park & Mini Golf (803-842-8108; 6 Tanglewood Dr.) Putt-putt golf courses and waterslides.

FISHING

For general information about prices and the kinds of experiences you can expect to have when fishing from a charter boat, refer to the "Fishing" entry in Chapter Six, *Recreation*. The same conditions apply on Hilton Head: there are several options as to size of boat, length of day, number of anglers aboard, and the type of catch you wish to pursue.

Boats are fully equipped with tackle, etc., and depart from several marinas for inshore waters, artificial reefs, and the Gulf Stream. In 1992, prices for four to six passengers for a half day of fishing ran from about $245 to $305. Here are some suggestions.

A Fishin' Mission (803-785-9177; 145 Squire Pope Rd.) Join Captain Charles Getsinger aboard a 34-foot Sportfish to catch amberjack, barracuda, king mackerel, and other species.

Atlantic Fishing Charters (803-671-4534; Harbour Town Yacht Basin) Five large boats rigged with fish-finding equipment; you can fish at night for shark.

Blue Water Charters (803-671-3060; South Beach Marina) Trophy fishing and taxidermy services; fishing aboard three boats, offshore or inshore.

Captain Fuzzy Davis (803-689-5873; 145 Squire Pope Rd.) A well-known island fisherman and angling authority takes you on inshore and tarpon-catching charters.

Drifter (803-671-3060 days; 803-842-9320 nights; South Beach Marina) Four- and five-hour trips from $27 per person; $5 discount for children under 12. Shorter evening shark-fishing trips. The boat carries 67 people; families welcome.

Gullah Gal and **Runaway** (803-842-7001 days; 803-726-4736 evenings; Shelter Cove Marina) Small parties ride aboard 34- and 35-foot customized sport fishing boats. Bottom fishing a speciality.

Tammy Jane (803-689-5873; Schilling Boathouse) Trawl for shrimp with 40-foot nets and share the catch (boat carries 21 passengers). Trips last about 4 hours; kids welcome. Adults $25; children under age 6, $20.

FITNESS CENTERS

For the fitness-minded who don't want to skip a beat with their regular exercise — or for those who are minded to start a new program — here are centers available on Hilton Head:

Downtown Athletic Club (803-785-7596; 22 Arrow Rd.).
Hilton Head Health Institute (803-785-7292; 14 Valencia Rd.).

Island Nautilus Center (803-681-5321; 400 Pineland Mall).
Ladies Workout Express (803-686-4930; New Orleans Rd.).

GOLF

There are more than 30 courses in the Hilton Head area; of these, 24 are on the island itself. Most of the area's courses are open to the public. However, except for a handful of courses off the island, they are not public in the traditional sense of the word. They are located within private communities — like Sea Pines, Shipyard Plantations, Palmetto Dunes Resort, and Port Royal Plantation — but are open to nonresident players. Neighboring Daufuskie Island has three golf courses, only one of which is available for public play. For courses in and around Beaufort — all of them less than an hour's drive from Hilton Head — check the courses listed under "Golf" in Chapter Six, *Recreation.*

Reservations to secure tee times are recommended as far in advance of your stay as possible. Unless noted, all the courses are 18 holes.

Price Codes

Prices include greens and cart fee unless mentioned otherwise. The rates noted are high-season rates — spring and fall. Summer is known as mid-season, and rates can drop by 20 percent. By the low season — winter months — prices can drop by 40 percent. Rates are lower for afternoon or twilight play.

Inexpensive	Up to $50
Moderate	$51 to $64
Expensive	$65 to $75
Very Expensive	Over $75

Daufuskie Island

Bloody Point Club (803-686-7000; accessible by ferry from Salty Fare Marina, Hilton Head) Par 72. Range of tees: 5,220-yard ladies course to 6,900-yard champion course. Pro: Todd Killian. Price: Very Expensive; includes round-trip ferry.

Hilton Head Plantation

Country Club of Hilton Head (803-681-4653) Par 72. Range: 5,373-yard ladies course to 6,919-yard champion course. Pro: Bob Thomas. Price: Expensive.

Indigo Run

Golden Bear Golf Course (803-689-2200) At the time of this writing, an 18-hole, par-72 course was scheduled to open. Range: 4,980-yard ladies course to 6,980-yard championship course. Price: Moderate.

Palmetto Dunes Resort

Arthur Hills Course (Pro shop: 803-785-1140; advance reservations: 803-785-1138) Par 72. Range: 4,999-yard ladies course to 6,651-yard champion course. Pro: Bob Faulkner. Price: Very Expensive.

George Fazio Course (803-785-1130) Named in top 50 of *Golf Digest*'s resort course listings. Par 70. Range: 5,273-yard ladies course to 6,873-yard champion course. Pro: Bob Faulkner. Price: Expensive.

Robert Trent Jones (803-785-1136) The lagoon system is a factor is 11 of the 18 holes here. Par 72. Range: 5,425-yard ladies course to 6,710-yard champion course. Pro: Clark Sinclair. Price: Expensive.

Palmetto Hall Plantation

Arthur Hills Course (Pro shop: 803-689-411; advance reservations 803-785-1138) A new course acclaimed by *Golf Magazine*. Par 72. Range: 4,956-yard ladies course to 6,918 champion course. Pro: Bill Layman. Price: Expensive.

Port Royal Plantation

Barony Course (803-686-8801/1-800-925-3508) Par 72. Range: 5,253-yard ladies course to 6,530-yard champion course. Pro: Gary Duren. Price: Moderate.

Planter's Row Course (803-686-8801/1-800-925-3508) Par 72. Range: 5,126-yard ladies course to 6,520-yard champion course. Pro: Gary Duren. Price: Expensive.

Robber's Row Course (803-686-8801/1-800-925-3508) A George Cobb/Willard Byrd course near what was Fort Walker, a Civil War camp. Par 72. Range: 5,299-yard ladies course to 6,711-yard champion course. Pro: Gary Duren. Price: Moderate.

Sea Pines Plantation

Harbour Town Golf Links (803-842-8484/1-800-845-6131) The Heritage Golf Classic is played on this course, designed by Jack Nicklaus and Pete Dye, rated among the top 25 in the world. Par 71. Range: 5,019-yard ladies course to 6,912-yard "Heritage" course. Pro: John Farrell. Price: Very Expensive.

Ocean Course (803-842-8484/1-800-845-6131) First course on the island, with a memorable beachfront 15th hole. George Cobb design. Par 72. Range 5,284-

yard ladies course to 6,614-yard champion course. Pro: John Richardson. Price: Expensive.

Sea Marsh Course (803-842-8484/1-800-845-6131) Par 72. Range: 5,527-yard ladies course to 6,615-yard champion course. Pro: John Richardson. Price: Expensive.

Shipyard Plantation

Shipyard Golf Club (803-686-8802/1-800-925-3508) Twenty-seven holes; par 72 (for 18). A favorite of the senior PGA Tour. Range: 5,391-yard ladies course to 6,830 champion course. Pro: Peter Rouillard. Price: Expensive.

Off-Island

Executive Golf Club (803-837-6400; Hwy. 278, Bluffton, at entrance to Hilton Head National) Nine holes, par 30, lit for night play. Range: 1,452-yard "grey" course and 1,656-yard "maroon" course. Price: Inexpensive.

Hilton Head National (803-842-5900; Hwy. 278, Bluffton) Par-72, Gary Player–designed course. Range: 4,649-yard ladies course to 6,761-yard champion course. Director of Golf: Bobby Mendenhall. Price: Moderate.

Island West Golf Club (803-689-6660; 803-757-6660; Hwy. 278, Bluffton) Par 72. Range: 4,948-yard ladies course to 6,803-yard champion course. Pro: Eddie Brown. Price: Moderate.

Old South Golf Links (803-785-5353; Hwy. 278, Bluffton) Par 72. Range: 4,947-yard ladies course to 6,772-yard champion course. Pro: Brady Boyd. Price: Moderate.

Rose Hill Country Club (803-842-3740; Rose Hill Plantation, Hwy. 278, Bluffton) Par 72. Range: 5,276-yard ladies course to 6,818-yard champion course. Pro: Brian Quigley. Price: Inexpensive.

HORSEBACK RIDING

Lawton Fields Stables (803-671-2586; 190 Greenwood Dr., Sea Pines) Rides for adults and children. Call ahead. An especially nice ride is through the Sea Pines Forest Preserve along marked trails.

Waterside Rides (803-689-3423; Jonesville Rd., off Spanish Wells) Tours along the edge of the marsh and woods.

MARINAS

The Hilton Head area has 10 marinas that offer numerous boat rental facilities, fishing charters, and other services such as dry-dock storage, launching ramps, fuel, showering facilities, ship's stores, and repair shops. Charter fishing boats, small powerboats, sailboats, and yachts over 140 feet are berthed side by side, offering a striking example of the myriad ways residents and visitors choose to enjoy the water.

Broad Creek Marina (803-681-7335; Marshland Rd.) 100 slips accommodating boats up to 33 feet. Ship's store with boat cleaning supplies and equipment. Open daily 8 to 5. Daufuskie Island ferry service provided twice daily by Broad Creek Transportation (803-681-7925).

Freeport Marina (803-785-8242/1-800-398-7687; Cooper River Landing, Daufuskie Island) The gateway to Daufuskie Island and island touring headquarters. Golf-cart rental for transportation, restaurant, gift shop, marina store.

Harbour Town Yacht Basin (803-671-2704; 803-671-4534; Sea Pines Plantation) 85 slips accommodating boats up to 130 feet. Marina store, various types of boat for rent; tours, instruction and cruises available. Near shops and restaurants in Harbour Town. Open 7 a.m. to 7:30 p.m. in summer, to 5:30 in winter.

Outdoor Resorts Yacht Basin (803-681-3256; Jenkins Island at northern tip of Hilton Head) 101 slips, maximum length of boat 70 feet. Amenities of Outdoor Resorts RV Park (see "Lodging" listing in this chapter) as well as charters, waterski rentals and instruction, ship's store. Open 8 to 6.

Palmetto Bay Marina (803-785-3910/1-800-448-3875; 164 Palmetto Bay Rd.) 125 slips, maximum length accommodated 85 feet. Marina store, fishing and sailing charters, and youth sailing program. Open 8:30 to 6:30 in summer, to 5:30 in winter.

Schilling Boathouse (803-681-2628; 145 Squire Pope Rd.) Dry stack only; maximum 33 feet. Ship's store; near restaurants.

Shelter Cove Harbour (803-842-7001; Palmetto Dunes Resort) 170 slips, maximum length accommodated 155 feet. Fish and tackle store, charters, cruises, rentals; rod and reel rental. In villagelike area of shops and restaurants. Open 7:30 a.m. to 8 p.m. in summer, to 6 p.m. in winter.

Skull Creek Marina (803-681-8436/1-800-237-4096; Hilton Head Plantation) 151 slips, maximum length 200 feet. Sailing charters and night fishing, restaurant and lounge, courtesy bike and van transportation. Open 9 to 6 summer, to 5 in winter.

South Beach Marina (803-671-3577; Sea Pines Plantation) 100 wet slips, 20 dry slips, maximum length 40 feet. Tackle and bait shop, boat and motor repair, rentals, cruises, instruction, junior sailing school. Restaurants and shops at the marina village. Open 7:30 to 6:30 summer, 8:30 to 6:30 in winter.

Windmill Harbour (803-681-9235; 161 Harbour Passage just south of bridge to mainland) Located within a private residential community; 261 slips, maximum length 70 feet. Harbor is tide-free, controlled by locks. Marina store, yacht club.

MINIATURE GOLF

There are more than a half-dozen miniature courses (par 40 to par 65) featuring water hazards, doglegs, and sand traps, laid out in realistic settings. A great way to spend two hours. Most are lighted for night play.

Island Putt & Drive (803-842-9990; William Hilton Pkwy. at Folly Field Rd.).

Legendary Golf (Two locations: 803-686-3399 at 900 William Hilton Pkwy; 803-785-9214 at 80 Pope Ave.)

Pirate's Island Adventure Golf (803-686-4001; William Hilton Pkwy. and Marina Side Dr.).

Waterfun Park and Mini Golf (803-842-8108; 6 Tanglewood Dr.).

TENNIS

There are more than 300 tennis courts — hard, clay, and even grass surfaces — available for public play, located within resort communities and outside them. Call ahead for reservations — the staff may even be able to set you up with a game. Pros on site offer lessons and clinics year round, and fully stocked shops provide stringing services and sales of equipment, clothing, and accessories. Court rental fees in 1992 ranged from $15 to $22 per hour. Many places offer reduced walk-on rates for midday play (12 to 4).

Hilton Head Island Beach and Tennis Resort (803-785-7566; 40 Folly Field Rd.) 10 hard, lighted courts.

Palmetto Dunes Tennis Center (803-785-1152; Palmetto Dunes Resort) 19 clay, 2 hard, 4 artificial grass courts. Some lighted for night play. Discounted rates for resort guests.

Tennis is a year-round sport at Hilton Head, where resorts feature clinics, national tournaments, and top-ranked professionals.

Wade Spees

Port Royal Racquet Club (803 686-8803; Port Royal Plantation) 10 clay, 4 hard, 2 natural grass courts. Night play available. Reduced rates for Westin Hotel guests and villa renters within the plantation.

Sea Pines Racquet Club (803-671-2494; Sea Pines Plantation) 25 clay, 5 hard courts. Hard courts are lighted for night play. Exhibition matches are frequently held during the season, and the Family Circle Magazine women's tournament is held here.

South Beach Racquet Club (803-671-2215; Sea Pines Plantation) 11 clay courts, 2 lighted.

Van der Meer Shipyard Racquet Club (803-686-8804; Shipyard Plantation) 14 clay, 6 Laykold courts. Night play available.

Van der Meer Tennis Center (803-785-8388; tennis clinic: 1-800-845-6138; DeAllyon Rd.) 24 courts: 17 hard, 3 clay, 4 indoors. Eight lighted for night play. The center is nationally known for its rigorous teaching programs for youngsters and pros, as well as players who simply wish to improve. Numerous clinics, camps, and private lesson options.

TOURING

If you're interested in exploring more of Hilton Head and the surrounding area, here are some suggestions. The towns of *Bluffton* and *Beaufort* are easy day trips. Each has a historic area of old houses, as well as shops and restaurants. *Savannah* is about an hour away, and in a day you could tour the historic district, shop, have at least one meal, and be back in time for sunset over the marsh. A trip to *Charleston* requires a bit more time and planning, including approximately four hours by car round trip.

For Bluffton information, see the entry below. For Beaufort, Savannah, and Charleston, see the listings in Chapter Four, *Culture*; Chapter Five, *Restaurants and Food Purveyors*; and Chapter Seven, *Shopping*.

Executive Air Ltd. (803-689-5300) can make arrangements for private flights over the area for up to five passengers. Price: $1.70 per statute mile.

Camelot Limousine and Tours (803-842-7777) On and off-island transportation, personalized tours, maximum of six people per vehicle.

Carriage Tours (803-363-2232; 190 Greenwood Drive) A horse-drawn carriage will take you through the 600-acre Sea Pines Forest Preserve.

Hilton Head's neighbor, Daufuskie, still bears witness to the way Sea Island life used to be before the resorts.

Wade Spees

Daufuskie Seafari (803-785-5654) Round-trip ferry to Daufuskie Island and tours of island sites such as the school house that figured in Pat Conroy's book *The Water is Wide*.

Discover Hilton Head (803-842-9217) Daily tours of the island by car.

Low Country Adventures (803-681-8212/1-800-845-5582) Island and off-island tours by van, including day trips with a tour guide to the historic areas of Charleston, Savannah, and Beaufort.

Visiting Bluffton

From Hilton Head, cross the bridge on Hwy. 278. Turn left on Hwy. 46 and follow it to Calhoun St. It is worth the trip alone to see the ***Church of the Cross*** on Calhoun St., an unpainted wooden church (circa 1857) with beautiful interior detailing, original pews, and Gothic-style windows.

Bluffton was a summer community of island planters, and in 1863 it was nearly burned to the ground by Union troops. Ten antebellum buildings remain; another 16 or so were built after the Civil War. Taken together, they give a view of classic Lowcountry village life. Far from extravagant, they are nonetheless suffused with a sense of form appropriate both to both the landscape and to their function as seasonal dwellings owned by families who had most likely seen better days.

A complete, self-guided walking tour takes about two hours — houses are marked by plaques, but not all are visible from the street. One book will help you appreciate them: *A Longer Short History of Bluffton, South Carolina and its Environs*, produced by the Bluffton Historical Preservation Society (803-757-3650; P.O. Box 742, Bluffton, SC 29910), price $9.95. This publication includes historic essays and descriptions of homes, a map, and wonderful photographs.

Other sites of interest in Bluffton are the working studio of potter *Jacob Preston* (803-757-3084; Church Rd.; by appointment); *Laura Barrett Antiques* (803-757-6630; Heyward St.); *Joe Bowler Collection* (803-757-6711; Calhoun St., prints and original art); *The Store* (803-757-3855; Calhoun St., a wonderful emporium — local institution). Locals eat at the *Squat & Gobble* (803-757-4242; Hwy. 46), which provides plain, good grub.

CULTURE

As Hilton Head has grown, so has its arts community. It is infused with energy from new, young residents and attentively cultivated by the many retired people hoping to recreate in their adopted home the range of cultural activities that interested them in the cities and towns they left behind. You don't need to cross the bridge to the mainland to participate in the arts anymore — one look at the weekly listings in the Arts & Entertainment section of *The Island Packet* proves that.

As of this writing, a top-notch visual and performing arts facility is being planned for the island under the direction of the Cultural Council of Hilton Head. Its theater, gallery space, classrooms, and offices promise to gather under one roof the diverse elements of the arts community, for the benefit of residents and visitors alike. In addition, the recently organized Museum of Hilton Head Island is contributing through its programs and guided walks an understanding of the island's complex evolution, both in its natural ecology and its human habitation.

ART

Hilton Head Art League (803-671-9009; Sea Pines Center) A gallery with regularly scheduled shows of work by members and others.

CINEMA

Island Theatre (803-785-4468; Coligny Plaza) One screen.
Main Street Cinemas (803-681-8778; Main St.) Three-screen complex.
Park Plaza Cinemas (803-785-5001; Park Plaza) Five-screen complex.

DANCE

Apogee Dance Company (803-686-4445; Dunnagan's Alley) Contemporary, innovative troupe that gives two major dance presentations each year at the Hilton Head Playhouse.

Hilton Head Dance Theater (803-785-5477; 24 Palmetto Business Park Rd.) Talented students from local schools and visiting companies perform on the Hilton Head Playhouse stage.

HISTORIC SITES

Several sites dating as far back as the time of Native American settlements and covering the period of the Civil War are accessible to visitors. For more information and location maps, contact the Museum of Hilton Head Island (803-842-9197).

Baynard Ruins (Sea Pines Plantation) The remains of a plantation house and outbuildings first constructed circa 1800 can be seen on a short, self-guided walk. A well-written brochure available on site gives a fine introduction to its history and construction, and to cotton cultivation. The ruins are made of tabby, a popular homemade Lowcountry building material that resulted from the burning of oyster shells (to make lime), whole shells, sand, and water. This is one of few sites where you can still see it.

Fish Haul Plantation (off Beach City Rd., near the county baseball complex) Only the chimneys of slave dwellings remain of what was once a thriving Sea Island cotton plantation. Federal troops camped here from the time of Union occupation in 1861.

Fort Howell (Beach City Rd.) A large earthwork built by the Union troops in 1864 to strengthen the defense of Mitchelville.

Fort Mitchel (Hilton Head Plantation) An earthwork fortification circa 1862, constructed as part of the island's defense system.

Indian Shell Ring (Sea Pines Forest Preserve) Native Americans occupied Hilton Head, as they did other Sea Islands, and left their mark in huge rings and shell middens. It is thought that this site represents the refuse of oyster shells piled behind each of many huts that stood in a small circle.

Zion Chapel of Ease (William Hilton Pkwy. at Mathews Dr.) A small chapel, built circa 1786 for the convenience of worshipers who lived too far from the Episcopal church at Beaufort, once occupied this site. The **Baynard Mausoleum**, circa 1846, within its cemetery, is the largest antebellum structure extant on the island.

MUSEUM

The Museum of Hilton Head (803-842-9197; 800 Plantation Center) As of this writing, a permanent museum dedicated to the island's ecology and history is being developed. The museum has undertaken archaeological digs and has gathered a collection of more than 75,000 artifacts relating to the island's history and culture. Gifts, books, and pamphlets about the area are offered for sale. Activities include seasonal nature walks around the island (call ahead for tickets) and on its own wetland boardwalk; a loggerhead turtle monitoring/protection program (May–August); lectures, and an oral history project. Hours are 10 to 4, Monday through Friday.

MUSIC

Hilton Head Orchestra (803-842-2055; 207 Marriott Center) Seasonal performances, including a spring Pops concert, usually in May.

Hilton Head Jazz Society (803-842-4457) The group sponsors formal and informal performances at various island sites, usually the first Sunday of the month.

THEATER

Hilton Head Playhouse (803-785-4878; Dunnagan's Alley at Arrow Rd.) Originally a community theater, the Playhouse has expanded to showcase local as well as out-of-town performers in popular musical and dramatic productions, about eight per year. The **Studio Theater**, located nearby in the Park Plaza Center, recently opened as the Playhouse's second stage.

RESTAURANTS AND NIGHTLIFE

The restaurants and nightspots included in the listing below are just some of the hundreds of places to eat or relax and listen to music. They are grouped by price and further described in abbreviated reviews. All major credit cards are accepted unless otherwise noted. Where you go may well depend on whether you're traveling with children, whether you like rock, acoustic guitar, jazz or dance music, where on the island you are staying, and your budget. Fast-food and moderately priced national chain eateries are well represented on Hilton Head, too.

The price categories are the same described elsewhere in the guide, and represent per-person expenses estimated without tax, tip, or bar beverages. In general, dining out tends to be slightly more expensive on Hilton Head than in similar restaurants elsewhere. For your planning, the groupings tend to reflect the higher end of what a meal may cost.

Inexpensive	Up to $10
Moderate	$10 to $20
Expensive	$20 to $30
Very Expensive	Over $30

INEXPENSIVE

Bess' Inc. (803-785-5504; Fountain Center) A deli with plain and gourmet selections, super desserts, and salads. Catering available.

Giuseppi's (803-785-4144; Shelter Cove) Pizza to eat in or delivered around the island. Two other locations: Sea Pines Center (803-671-5133) and Main St. Village (803-671-7850).

Market Street (803-686-4976; Coligny Plaza) Greek pizza loaded with feta cheese and vegetables or souvlaki. Serving three meals a day, seven days a week.

Melvin's Barbecue (803-842-6358; 2 Marina Side Dr., near Red Roof Inn) Best place for barbecue; locally owned, fast service.

P.J.'s New York Deli (803-842-2550; Mall at Shelter Cove) Breakfast, hefty lunch sandwiches, and deli specials to tide you over until late-night supper. Kosher selections available, also imported beers. A good stop while shopping. Also at Shelter Cove Marina.

MODERATE

Crazy Crab (803-363-2722; Harbour Town) Good family restaurant, wonderful location, decorated in a nautical/old ship style. Lunch, dinner, and take-out daily to 10 p.m.

Flamingo's (803-686-5212; Park Plaza) A little piece of Art Deco–style Miami Beach, with neon lighting, pink flamingos, and sleek furniture. Unique on the island, great for dessert and coffee. Dinner 5 p.m.–midnight, Mon.–Sat.

Hudson's Seafood (803-681-2772; Squire Pope Rd.) Large 25-year-old family restaurant with children's menu, located on the docks at Skull Creek. Oyster bar, blackened and stuffed seafood entrees, even some "drydock" specials. Lunch and dinner daily.

Old Oyster Factory (803-681-6040; Marshland Rd.) One of the best locations for a restaurant on Hilton Head, overlooking Broad Creek and extensive marshes. Come here for happy hour, when there are specials on oysters and crab legs. Large bar area and a very relaxed, seaside feel.

San Miguel's (803-842-4555; Shelter Cove Marina) Mexican cuisine. Outdoor cafe especially family-friendly. Superb place to watch the sunset and sip margaritas. Extremely popular — orders can get backed up at dinner so you may be in for a wait.

Stellini (803-785-7006; 15 Pope Ave.) Of the handful of Italian restaurants on the island, this is a local favorite. Not a place to wear jeans to, but freshly prepared food in a casual place with an authentic "Little Italy" feel. Dinner except Sunday, reservations recommended.

Truffles Cafe (803-671-6136; Sea Pines Center) Long an island favorite. Casual atmosphere, homemade soups, huge salads, great French-bread sandwiches, fresh vegetables, and grilled entrees. Continuous serving, lunch through dinner.

Wild Wings (803-785-9464; Coligny Plaza) Rock music over loudspeakers, televisions in the corner, big platters of wings (17 kinds) and burgers, plus lots of beer and margaritas. Popular with the college crowd and with families, because it's noisy and casual by nature. Lunch and dinner to 2 a.m.

EXPENSIVE

High Z's Creative Cuisine (803-785-3434; New Orleans Rd.) Small formal restaurant with a mellow European atmosphere, beautifully presented meals, and the best pâtés on the island.

Julep's (803-842-5857; Gallery of Shops, near Sea Pines Circle) Upscale Southern cuisine, New South/Atlanta style. Young lawyers and local professionals flock here. Dinner daily. Reservations recommended.

Le Bistro (803-681-8425; Pineland Mall) Mediterranean and Moroccan cuisine, including Greek specials, spicy stews, and lamb dishes. White tablecloths don't mean dressy, just old-world chic. Lunch and dinner; closed Sunday.

Longhorn Steaks (803-686-4056; South Island Square) A steak-and-potatoes saloon with lively atmosphere and hearty meals. Lunch and dinner.

South Seaport Cafe (803-671-7327; South Beach Marina) Eat dinner with a view of the marina village, afterwards hear live music upstairs. Reservations recommended.

Stripes (803-686-4747; Marriott Center) This is the top choice of many island residents. The setting is nothing spectacular, but the food is inventive — black bean cakes, mahi-mahi with almonds, carmelized onion sauces — and the portions are never skimpy or over-stylized. Lunch and dinner.

VERY EXPENSIVE

Many Hilton Head restaurants capitalize on a sublime view and local, catch-of-the-day cuisine.

Wade Spees

Cafe Europa (803-671-3399; Harbour Town) Located at the Harbour Town Lighthouse, a longtime island restaurant in the island's classiest setting. The menu reflects high-style continental cuisine: veal, duckling, beef, and seafood. Brunch starts at 10 a.m.; lunch, featuring great crepes, is especially nice outside in the marina setting; dinner to 10 p.m. Reservations recommended.

Carolina Cafe (803-681-4000; Westin Resort) There's no better Sunday brunch on Hilton Head. It just goes on forever. In a luxurious hotel with all the trimmings, a real treat for your last day.

Charlie's L'Etoile Verte (803-785-9277; 1000 Plantation Center) Charlie Golson, a Savannah native, never went to cooking school, spent vacations in quiet Bluffton, and lives next door to the house he grew up in; but his years abroad amidst chef-friends seem to have fed his talent. His 10-year old restaurant is often called the best on Hilton Head, and Lea Sanin one of its top chefs. Dinner features a dozen fish dishes (the pompano is a usual sell-out) as well as a beef and veal choice; soup stocks are made up from scratch; the country bread is baked on bricks every day in the open kitchen; most of the wine list is French. Service is attentive and knowledgeable. The two connecting dining rooms can be noisy when full. Share the Cobb Salad at lunch, and don't pass up homemade desserts. Reservations highly recommended. Serving Tues.–Sat.

Primo (803-785-2343; Orleans Plaza) A top-quality Italian restaurant with an updated, contemporary twist on the standards. Full menu featuring pastas with wonderful variety of sauces, grilled seafood, veal and beef. It's formal but not stuffy. Go with a big appetite and plan to spend a while savoring everything from antipasti to espresso. Dinner from 6 p.m. Reservations recommended.

NIGHTLIFE

The beat goes on and on at Hilton Head, and especially in summer, the crowds jam the dance floor. Some places that offer live entertainment have cover charges or drink minimums — call ahead for prices and information, or check newspaper entertainment listings. Those that serve food are noted. The legal drinking age is 21; bars close at midnight Saturday unless special liquor licenses are in hand. The style is supremely casual.

Big Rocco's (803-785-9000; Central Park) A huge place: deli in one section, lounge in another huge restaurant. Turquoise walls give it a glamorous, big-city, feel. Large dance floor and great bands, including jazz; stick to the late-night bar food.

Callahan's (803-686-7665; New Orleans Rd.) Late-night pool/billiards/darts bar and sports lounge, popular with locals. Live music and dance floor.

Casablanca (803-686-5120; Hilton Head Plaza) Piano bar, fireplace, and an intimate feeling, in which patrons can take turns in the spotlight. Organized audience participation some nights with karaoke — take the microphone, read the monitor, and go for it.

Club Indigo (803-785-1234; Hyatt Regency) Caters to upscale, over-30 crowd. Beach music and pop for dancing.

Coconuts Comedy Club (803-686-6887; Heritage Square) The nation's best comedians perform here. Four to eight shows weekly starting at 9:30 p.m. After the acts, there's often a blues or jazz session, too. Cover charge.

Mockingbird Lounge (803-842-2400; in the Marriott) Ritzy lounge, blues, jazz and rhythm-and-blues bands; dancing.

Old Post Office Emporium (803-785-3933; 12 Pope Ave.) Large nightclub with stage and dance floor, books out-of-town acts and hometown favorites such as the Truly Dangerous Swamp Band and the Mundahs. Reggae and rock are standard. Action generally starts around 10:30 p.m.

Quarterdeck (803-671-2222; Harbour Town) Laid-back waterfront lounge open from noon to 2 a.m. Peak periods include late afternoon, suppertime (kids welcome), and late night. Outdoor rocking chairs make sunset viewing a treat. Upstairs and downstairs bars; great nightly dancing to beach music and contemporary hits.

Reilly's (803-842-4414; Gallery of Shops) Irish pub in feel, sports-talk in the air. Very popular Friday happy hour for weary locals. Friendly, neighborhood-bar atmosphere.

Remy's (803-842-3800; 28 Arrow Rd.) Late-night bar with raucous live music in a rustic setting. Munchies like buckets of oysters, fries, and shrimp served late.

Salty Dog (803-671-2233; South Beach Marina) Used to be a local secret, known as the best low-key place to just hang out under the sycamores and sip a frozen drink. Great outdoor grill/buffet, excellent choice for families with small children. Short walk from the beach — no need to dress up. The music is Jimmy Buffet and soft guitar.

Wingo's (803-686-3545; Park Plaza) Big, popular dance club with a disc jockey seven nights a week pumping up the volume with rock-and-roll favorites.

SHOPPING

As Hilton Head has grown, it has tried to minimize both the visual and physical impact of strip development along its major thoroughfare, Hwy. 278 — the William Hilton Parkway. (You have to look hard to spot the fast-food outlets, for though they exist, their signs are required to be more tasteful here than elsewhere.) As a result of this wish to maintain some degree of natural landscape, the small shopping centers and larger, well-designed malls that have sprung up to serve 1.5 million visitors per year are self-enclosed destinations. They have their own plentiful parking, and a mix of tenants that includes restaurants, pizza and ice-cream counters, supermarkets, and boutiques. Here are some highlights.

Harbour Town, in Sea Pines Plantation, remains the only shopping area with a unique village character — in its case, rather Mediterranean in feel, located around the harbor basin, clustered near the lighthouse. It is worth paying the $3-per-car entrance fee to Sea Pines to wander and browse, if not buy.

The *Mall at Shelter Cove* is a more conventional shopping center, anchored by big department stores like Belk and JCPenney. National chains like Banana Republic, the Gap, Ann Taylor, the Limited, and Polo/Ralph Lauren are represented. There is a food court, and the mall is enclosed, making it a good rainy-day outing.

Main Street Village, the *Village at Wexford, Sea Pines Center*, and *Shelter Cove Harbour* are smaller areas you might explore if you are staying in accommodations nearby. *South Beach Marina Village* and *Coligny Plaza* are especially good spots for finding beach-related souvenirs and inexpensive resort-wear.

In addition — as noted at the end of the Shopping chapter — there are three outlet malls: *Shoppes on the Parkway* and *Pineland Mill Shops* are on Hilton Head; just off the island is the *Low Country Factory Outlet Village*. Stores here offer bargains in every category, including housewares, toys, shoes, high fashion, and sportswear. Their inventories are large and well organized.

The tourist-based economy has also allowed many smaller speciality shops to flourish as they might not otherwise do, in a place where the permanent population numbers under 25,000. As a result, shopping trips can yield both the obvious and the offbeat: golf clubs and gifts, as well as original art and collectibles. Here are some ideas.

ART AND ANTIQUES

Antiques and Oddities (803-785-2560; 17-A Archer Rd.) Antique jewelry.

Decorator's Wholesale Antiques (803-681-7463; 1 Cardinal Rd.) Stripped pine furniture from the British Isles favored by the "shelter" magazines for beach houses. Also antiques with polished metal details.

Harbour Art Gallery (803-785-2787; Shelter Cove Harbour) Familiar Low-country scenes in various media; golf prints.

Harbour Town Antiques Ltd. (803-671-5999; 149-C Lighthouse Rd.) Furniture, prints, nice small collectibles.

Island Ideas Gallery (803-842-6261; 1200 Plantation Center) Commissioned portraits, landscapes, floral paintings, posters, and prints.

Joe Pinckney Art Enterprises Ltd. (803-681-5661; 15-I Airport Rd.) Original portraits and wildlife art.

John Stobart Gallery (803-671-2739; Harbour Town) Limited-edition maritime prints; original oils and watercolors.

Joy's Corner (803-689-6699; Main St. Village) Antiques, Irish crystal.

Moonshell Gallery and Artist Studio (803-671-2262; 224 S. Sea Pines Dr.).

Palmer Sculpture Studio (803-837-3677; by appointment) Work by Walter Palmer.

Red Piano Art Gallery (803-785-2318; 220 Cordillo Pkwy.) Lowcountry landscapes, sculpture, fine art, and artifacts.

Swan House Antiques (803-785-7926; 7 Bow Circle) Quality rugs, china, silver, and furniture on consignment .

Thum'prints Gallery (803-681-7863; 3 Northridge Plaza) Original art by local artists in diverse media.

BOOKS AND MUSIC

Audubon Nature Store (803-785-4311; Village at Wexford) Field guides, children's guides on local flora and fauna.

You can shop on Hilton Head for an abundance of things to play with in the outdoors, and the right outfit to wear while doing so.

Wade Spees

Book Warehouse of Georgia (803-837-5181; Low Country Factory Outlet Village) Remainders in all categories.

Christian Book Store (803-681-3868; 119-A Mathews Drive) Religious and inspirational literature.

Disc Jockey (803-842-2844; Mall at Shelter Cove) Music in all formats; music videos, movies, and accessories.

Island Bookseller (803-671-3773; Sea Pines Center) Adult and children's titles, local authors.

Port Royal Bookstore (803-689-9996; Port Royal Plaza) Big selection of books, tapes, CDs, magazines.

Shepherd's Staff (803-689-3777; 1519 Main St. Village) Books, videos, music, and toys with a Christian theme.

Waldenbooks (803-785-4301; Mall at Shelter Cove) Books for beach reading, children's section, history, cooking, coffee-table books.

CLOTHING

A Shore Thing (803-686-2330; South Beach Marina) Silk-screened tee-shirts, and resort wear.

Camp Hilton Head (803-842-3666; Shelter Cove) Fun, casual beachwear embossed with unique logo of Camp Hilton Head. Locations at Harbour Town and Coligny Plaza, too.

Carriage House (803-689-6200; 1405 Main St. Village) Traditional women's clothing, dresses, and swimwear.

Kid's Express (803-686-5790; Mall at Shelter Cove) Wide selection of fun and back-to-school clothes for youngsters.

Out Island Trader (803-842-8988; Village at Wexford) Sandals, jewelry, tropical print fabrics, and sportswear with a chic Caribbean feel.

Peepers (803-785-4464; Coligny Plaza) Sunglasses by the dozens — you may need more than one pair.

Porcupine (803-785-2779; The Gallery of Shops, near Sea Pines Circle) Designer sportswear for women, lingerie, excellent shoe selection, swimwear.

Porcupine for Kids (803-785-8151; Shelter Cove Harbour) High-end fashions for kids.

Trader Joe's Outfitters (803-671-2264; Sea Pines Center) Outdoor gear with a fashion twist.

Outside Hilton Head (803-686-6996; Plaza at Shelter Cove) Top-of-the-line durable sports clothing (Patagonia, Woolrich, Teva), footwear, and accessories. Also at South Beach Marina.

CRAFTS

Harbour Town Crafts (803-671-3643; Harbour Town) Quality American handcrafts, large and small, whimsical and functional.

Smith Galleries of Fine Crafts (803-842-2280; Village at Wexford) Over 200 American artisans are represented in media such as glass, wood, metal, clay, and textiles.

Unique Lines' Rocker Gallery (803-842-5614; 32 Palmetto Bay Rd.) Contemporary crafts and handmade jewelry.

GIFTS

Fun & Bradstreet (803-785-2132; Shelter Cove Harbour) Clever toys, kites, and windsocks; fun things for the beach.

Gullah Market (803-681-7374; 103 William Hilton Pkwy.) Crafts by African-American artisans, fresh vegetables, flea-market bargains, and more.

Sweetgrass baskets woven by native islanders and for sale at the Gullah Market are trademarks of old Sea Island culture.

Wade Spees

Goldsmith Shop (803-785-2538; 3 Lagoon Rd.) Handmade settings, pendants, and Hilton Head charms.

Golf Classics and Collectibles (803-686-3100; Village at Wexford) Everything for the golfer.

Island Child (803-686-5437; Village at Wexford) Educational toys, clothing, activities, and games for kids.

Hammock Company (803-686-3636; Coligny Plaza) Limited-edition wildlife and duck stamp prints; Pawley's Island hammocks; bird feeders; gifts with a nature theme.

Magic Puppet (803-785-3280; Coligny Plaza) Toys, puppets, magic tricks, playmobil sets, books.

Mole Hole (803-785-8090; Coligny Plaza) Figurines and china collectibles; cards and oil lamps. Also at the Mall at Shelter Cove.

Nell's Harbour Shop (803-671-2133; Harbour Town) An island original filled with china, glass, papers, and collectibles.

Ship's Store (803-842-7001; Shelter Cove Harbour) Everything for the sailor, including charts, boat shoes, and nautical accessories.

Sign of the Mermaid (803-681-2231; Main St. Village) In business 20 years selling paper goods, accessories, linens, and whimsical housewares.

South Beach General Store (803-671-6784; South Beach Marina) An old-fashioned emporium.

Stardust (803-842-7346; 10 Park Plaza) Cards, tee-shirts with witty sayings, calendars, gifts for people who love cats.

Uniquely Hilton Head (803-785-3250; at Hall's Nursery, 852 William Hilton Pkwy.) Small and large gifts for the garden, including statues, furniture, and plants.

GOURMET FOOD

Chocolate Canopy (803-842-4567; Crossroads Center, Palmetto Bay Rd.) Homemade chocolates galore.

Cinnamon Bear Country Store (803-661-5558; Main St. Village) Gourmet coffee, candies, and gifts.

Healthy Days Natural Food Store (803-785-7297; Coligny Plaza) Flours, herbal teas, sugar-free items.

Kitchens of Daufuskie (803-785-6541; 7 Bow Circle) Lowcountry delicacies to take home and savor.

Signe's Heaven Bound Bakery (803-785-9118; 2 Bow Circle) Fresh baked breads, pastries, sandwiches; also eat-in.

Susie Q's Teas and Gifts (803-686-2136; 32 Palmetto Bay Rd.) Coffees and teas, desserts to go.

Heavenly Ham (803-785-4267; Plaza at Shelter Cove) Smoked meats, honey-glazed hams, ribs.

SPORTSWEAR AND SPORTS EQUIPMENT

Adventure Kayak Co. (803-842-8378; 8 Archer Rd.) Ocean kayaks, Folbots, canoeing equipment.

Nevada Bob's Golf Shop (803-686-4653; 1016 William Hilton Pkwy.) All you need for the links, with many discounted prices.

Outside Hilton Head (803-671-2643; South Beach Marina) Equipment for windsurfing, canoeing, kayaking, and camping.

Player's World (803-842-5100; Market Place at Sea Pines Circle) Island's largest sporting-goods store.

Sportline (803-686-8855; Mall at Shelter Cove) Tennis racquets and same-day stringing; runner's accessories.

HILTON HEAD INFORMATION

The *Hilton Head Island Chamber of Commerce* (803-785-3673; P.O. Box 5647, Hilton Head Island, SC 29938), located mid-island, is a logical source of general information. Information on specific items follows.

ACCESS

By Plane

Hilton Head is served daily by *USAir* (via Charlotte) and *American Eagle* (via Raleigh/Durham). The closest international airport is at *Savannah*, about

45 miles away, served by *American Airlines, Delta, United,* and *USAir.* Most resorts have courtesy van service to and from Savannah. A typical taxi fare is $55 for one or two people, $25 per person for three people or more.

By Car

From I-95 southbound: take Exit 28 (Coosawhatchie, Hwys. 462/278); follow 462 to U.S. 278, the access road to Hilton Head. *From I-95 northbound:* take Exit 5 (Hardeeville, Hwys. 170/46); proceed via 46 and 170 to U.S. 278 and Hilton Head.

By Taxi

These companies serve the island. Some offer limousine service as well as cabs. All offer transportation to and from Hilton Head Airport and service to Savannah International as well.

> **Carlin Cab Co.** (803-785-4854.)
> **Checker Cab** (803-842-8294).
> **Ferguson Transportation** (803-842-5883).
> **Hilton Head Taxi and Limousine** (803-785-8294).
> **Lowcountry Taxi and Limousine** (803-681-8294).
> **Yellow Cab Co.** (803-686-6666).

BANKING: AUTOMATIC TELLER MACHINES

Anchor Bank (Pope Ave. and Northridge Plaza): Avail, Honor, Relay.

First Union (Sea Pines Circle, Main St., Northridge Plaza): Cirrus, Honor, Plus, Relay.

NationsBank (Pope Ave., William Hilton Pkwy., Shelter Cove Mall, Pineland Mall): Avail, Cirrus, Honor Plus, Relay.

South Carolina National (Sea Pines Circle, Pineland Mill Shops at Mathews Drive): Avail, Cirrus, Honor, MC, Plus, Relay, Visa.

CHILD CARE

There are several child-care services that will care for visitors' children in a day-care facility and/or will send baby-sitters to their hotel room or villa. In addition, check with the front desk at your own hotel for their services.

Companions, Nurses and Nannies (803-785-3600) Listing and referral service.

Cradle 'N All (803-686-5055; 18 Bow Circle) Child-care facility.

Island Children (803-842-2611; 6 Phoenix Center) Drop-in and home-sitting services.

EMERGENCY NUMBERS

The following apply to Hilton Head; for emergency services elsewhere in the Lowcountry, see the listings in Chapter Nine, *Information*.

> **Beaufort County Sheriff's Dept.** (803-785-3618).
> **Fire, Ambulance, Police** (911).
> **State Highway Patrol** (803-524-0163; after midnight 803-524-4696).

KENNELS

These kennels offer boarding for pets, as well as pet grooming, supplies, and other services:

> **Evergreen Pet Lodge** (803-681-8354; 105 Airport Rd.).
> **Low Country Kennels** (803-681-3991; 10 Fish Haul Rd.).

MEDICAL FACILITIES

Family Medical Center (803-842-2900; South Island Square, Hwy 278).
Hilton Head Hospital (803-681-6122; Bill Fries Dr.) Full-service hospital with 24-hour emergency room.
Hilton Head Rescue Squad (911).
Urgent Care Center (803-785-9400; 10 Pope Ave.) Open daily 9 to 7 for minor medical emergencies.

YEARLY EVENTS

The following list is meant to provide some idea of seasonal activities that take place on Hilton Head. Before you make your plans, or for more information regarding exact dates, contact the *Hilton Head Island Chamber of Commerce* (803-785-3673; P.O. Box 5647, Hilton Head Island, SC 29938).

MARCH

SpringFest (803-686-4944) Activities include performances of a musical at the Hilton Head Playhouse; college tennis championships and exhibition play; festivals of food, wine, and chocolate.

Family Circle Magazine Cup Women's Tennis Tournament (803-363-4502; Sea Pines Plantation).

APRIL

Easter Celebrations: Egg hunts, sunrise services, Easter dinners, and more. Contact the Chamber of Commerce for dates and locations.

MCI Heritage Classic Golf Tournament (803-671-2448; Sea Pines Plantation).

St. Luke's Tour of Homes (803-785-4099; St. Luke's Episcopal Church).

MAY

The world's pro golfers play the course at Sea Pines during the MCI Heritage Golf Tournament every spring.

Wade Spees

Croquet Southern Regionals (803-689-5600; Port Royal Croquet Club, Port Royal Plantation).

Sea Pines Senior Clay Court Championships (803-363-2052; Sea Pines Plantation).

Tour of Island Gardens (803-681-8333; All Saints Episcopal Church).

JUNE

HarbourFest (Shelter Cove Harbour) Weekly evening activities, entertainment, fireworks, and shag-dancing lessons, through Labor Day.

Harbour Town Family Singalongs (Sea Pines Plantation) Family entertainment every evening except Sunday, through Labor Day.

King Mackerel/Cobia Fishing Tournament (803-842-7001; Shelter Cove Marina).

Van der Meer Tennis Classic (803-785-8388; Van der Meer Tennis Center, DeAllyon Rd.).

JULY

Island Fireworks at Harbour Town, Shelter Cove, and Hudson's Landing.

Del Monte Banana Open Doubles (803-785-1152; Palmetto Dunes Resort).

Junior Clay Court Championships (803-785-1152; Palmetto Dunes Resort).

AUGUST

King Mackerel Fishing Tournament (803-842-7001; Shelter Cove).

Rod Laver Mixed Doubles Tennis Tournament (803-686-8803; Port Royal Racquet Club).

SEPTEMBER

Celebrity Golf Tournament (803-671-2448; various island locations).

National Seniors Windsurfing Championships (803-686-6996; Hilton Resort).

Festa Italiana (Shelter Cove) Bocci tournaments, Italian food, opera.

OCTOBER

Junior Davis Wightman Cup (803-785-1152; Palmetto Dunes Resort).

USPTR International Tennis Championships (803-785-9602; Van der Meer Tennis Center).

Head of the Broad Regatta (803-681-4207; Palmetto Rowing Club) Regatta starts at Broad Creek Marina.

CHAPTER NINE
Practical Matters
INFORMATION

By the middle of the 18th century, a dependable postal service and reliable roads linked Charleston to the outlying plantations.

Wade Spees

What follows is information to make your visit to the Lowcountry run more smoothly. It's a modest compendium of essentials — what's there and how it works — intended to make planning your trip easier and enjoying your stay simpler. The chapter covers the following topics:

AMBULANCE, FIRE, POLICE

The general emergency number in the Lowcountry is **911**, whether you're in Charleston, Beaufort, Hilton Head, or Savannah. Outside the cities, most of the counties either have the basic 911 service or have plans to acquire it. In *Colleton County*, the following numbers will serve until the system is fully in place:

Walterboro City Police	803-549-1811
Walterboro City Fire Dept.	803-549-2222
Rural Ambulance/Fire/Sheriff	803-549-1911
S.C. Highway Patrol	803-538-2111

Naturally, in an emergency, you can always dial "0" for the Operator's assistance in reaching the right agency.

A selected roster of other numbers, for emergencies or other business, follows:

Poison Control:

South Carolina	1-800-922-1117 (from within S.C. only)
Georgia	1-800-282-5846 (from within Ga. only)

Rape Crisis Hotline:

Charleston	803-722-7273
Beaufort/Hilton Head	1-800-637-7273; 803-525-6699
Savannah	912-232-3383

Disaster/Hurricane Emergency Preparedness:

Charleston County	803-554-5951
Beaufort County	803-525-7353
Colleton County	803-549-5632
Hampton County	803-943-7518
Jasper County	803-726-7706
Chatham County	912-652-7600

State Police:

S.C. Highway Patrol, Charleston Area	1-800-768-1506
Ga. State Patrol, Chatham County	1-912-651-3000

Police:

City of Charleston	803-577-7434 (non-emergency)
Town of Edisto Beach	803-869-2440
City of Beaufort	803-525-7580
Town of Port Royal	803-524-5123
Town of Hilton Head	803-785-3618 (sheriff)
Town of Bluffton	803-757-2263; (sheriff: 803-757-3499)
Town of Hardeeville	803-784-2233 (emergency)
City of Savannah	912-232-4141; 912-651-6675

AREA CODES/TOWN GOVERNMENT & ZIP CODES

AREA CODES

The area code for all of South Carolina is **803**. The area code for Savannah, Georgia, and its metropolitan region is **912**.

TOWN HALLS

The cities of Charleston, Beaufort, Hilton Head, and Savannah are governed by a mayor and city council. This form of government has been in place for some time, except at Hilton Head, where a desire on the part of residents to have some autonomy from the county — specifically to control the island's tremendous growth — spurred action several years ago to form a "limited service" town government, as oxymoronic as that may sound in these bureaucratic days. Now the trend is toward consolidation of services whereby the cities and the counties they are part of share in their cost and delivery.

Charleston, Beaufort, Walterboro, Ridgeland, Hampton, and *Savannah* are the region's county seats. For general information call:

Charleston County	803-723-6762
Beaufort County	803-525-7100
Colleton County	803-549-5791
Jasper County	803-726-7703
Hampton County	803-943-7500
Chatham County	912-652-7175

There are also smaller, scattered municipalities governed by smaller councils.

For general information, contact the following town hall offices:

Town	Address	Telephone
Beaufort	302 Carteret St, 29902	803-525-7000
Bluffton	Hwy. 46; P.O. Box 386, 29910	803-757-2642
Charleston	80 Broad St.; P.O. Box 304, 29402	803-577-6970
Edisto Island	2414 Murray St., 29438	803-869-2505
Folly Beach	21 Center St., 29439	803-588-2447

Hampton	608 First St. West, 29924	803-943-2951
Hilton Head	1 Town Center Court, 29928	803-842-8900
Isle of Palms	1303 Palm Blvd., 29451	803-886-6428
Port Royal	1406 Paris Ave., 29935	803-524-5125
Ridgeland	108 E. Wilson; P.O. Drawer B, 29936	803-726-3351
Savannah	Bay St. at Bull; P.O. Box 1027, 31402	912-651-6790
Thunderbolt	2702 Mechanics Ave., 31404	912-354-5533

If you spend most of your time on the water, why not lash your mailbox to the dock?

Wade Spees

| Tybee Island | Butler Ave.; P.O. Box 128, 31328 | 912-786-4573 |
| Walterboro | 242 Hampton St; P.O. Box 709, 29488 | 803-549-2545 |

BANKS

South Carolina and Georgia banks are linked electronically to banking systems throughout the United States. Money can be wired from your home bank or funds can be withdrawn from automatic teller machines provided your ATM card corresponds with the networks serving the area. The following list provides information on several banks throughout the Lowcountry.

Bank Addres	Phone	Instant Teller Networks
Charleston		
First Federal of Charleston 34 Broad St.	803-724-0800	Relay, Honor, Avail Cirrus
Nationsbank 322 Broad St.	803-724-3920	Honor, Plus
First Union Bank 177 Meeting St.	803-727-1000	Relay, Plus
South Carolina National 170 Calhoun St.	803-723-8311	Relay, Cirrus
Beaufort		
Nationsbank 500 Carteret St.	803-521-6000	Honor, Plus
South Carolina National 1011 Bay St.	803-522-2227	Relay, Cirrus
Hilton Head		
The Anchor Bank Pope Ave. at New Orleans	803-785-4848	Relay, Honor, Avail
First Union Sea Pines Circle	803-842-4200	Honor, Cirrus, Plus Relay
Savannah		
The Savannah Bank 25 Bull St.	912-651-8200	Avail, Honor, Plus Cirrus (No ATM; bank issues cards to customers)
First Union 2 E. Bryan St.	912-944-2041; 1-800-733-4008	Honor, Cirrus, Plus, Relay
Nationsbank 300 Bull St.	912-944-3000	Honor, Plus

BIBLIOGRAPHY

L owcountry life, past and present, is well documented, and its bookstores have ever-growing "local interest" sections to prove it. Here is a suggested reading list of some classics, the books you're likely to find in residents' libraries. The asterisk indicates the title is out of print but it is likely to be found in the the local-history section of used-book stores in the area.

You may want to pick up a few books before you go; certainly do so when you're there. And, since the best part of a trip is often reliving it at home, check your local bookstore upon returning for further reading. The list is by no means complete: think of it as a mere guide to the shelves.

ART & ARCHITECTURE

Cole, Cynthia, ed. *Historic Resources of the Lowcountry.* Yemassee, SC: Lowcountry Council of Governments, 1979, second ed. 1990. 202 pp., index, illus., photos, $29.95. The definitive four-county survey of historic houses and sites with fine historical and architectural explanation.

Lane, Mills. *Architecture of the Old South: South Carolina.* Savannah, GA: Beehive Press, 1984. 258 pp., photos, $75. Exquisite, large format, black and white photos.
———. *Architecture of the Old South: Georgia.* Savannah, GA: Beehive Press, 1986, 252 pp., photos, $75.

Ravenel, Beatrice St. Julian. *Architects of Charleston.* Columbia, SC: University of South Carolina Press, 1992. 338 pp., photos, index, bibliog., $19.95. First published in 1945, a detailed examination of the lives and works of the city's builders, engineers, and architects.

Rosengarten, Dale. *Row Upon Row: Sea Grass Baskets of the South Carolina Lowcountry.* Columbia, SC: McKissick Museum, 1986. 64 pp., photos, $10. A thorough and lovingly documented catalogue of a vibrant Sea Island art.

Severens, Kenneth. *Charleston Antebellum Architecture & Civic Destiny.* Knoxville, TN: University of Tennessee Press, 1988. 330 pp., photos, index., $49.95. A specialized topic explained in clear prose for the interested amateur or professional architect.

Severens, Martha R. *Charles Fraser of Charleston.* Charles L. Wyrick, Jr., ed. Charleston, SC: Carolina Art Assoc., 1983. 176 pp., illus., $14.95. The subject was a miniaturist of the 19th century whose portraits of local gentry, in the collection of the Gibbes Art Gallery, are exquisite and whimsical.

AUTOBIOGRAPHY, BIOGRAPHY, DIARIES & LETTERS

Bartram, William. *Travels through North & South Carolina, Georgia, East & West Florida*. New York: Viking Penguin, 1988. 452 pp., $7.95. The account of an 18th-century trip through the Lowcountry by the famous botanist.

Chesnut, Mary Boykin. *A Diary From Dixie*. Cambridge, MA: Harvard University Press, 1980. 608 pp., $12.95. A classic account, good on Charleston society.

Daise, Ronald. *Reminiscences of a Sea Island Heritage*. Columbia, SC: Sandlapper, 1986. unpaged, photos, $18.95. Archival black-and-white photos accompanied by text and stories of Sea Island Gullah culture.

Forten, Charlotte L. *The Journal of a Free Negro in the Slave Era*. New York: Norton, 1981. 286 pp., index, $8.95. The vivid impressions of a Northern teacher who came to the Sea Islands to educate the newly freed slaves.

Georgia Writers' Project, ed. *Drums and Shadows*. Athens, GA: University of Georgia Press, 1986., $11.95. The collection of oral histories first published under the WPA program in 1940. Invaluable as it allows you to really hear the voices of the coast.

Higginson, Thomas Wentworth. *Army Life in a Black Regiment*. New York: Norton, 1984. 279 pp., appendix, index., $6.95. Higginson was the white commander of the First South Carolina Volunteers, headquartered in Beaufort, S.C. during the Civil War. Its honest, self-effacing narrative of camp life, countrysides and skirimshes is invaluable.

Kemble, Frances Anne. *Journal of Residence on a Georgia Plantation in 1838-1839*. Athens, GA: University of Georgia Press, 1984. 488 pp., $11.95. Although the setting is the coastal Georgia plantation of the author's husband, Pierce Butler, her insights into plantation life and the culture of black female slaves make this perhaps the best account of that time.

*McTeer, J.E. *High Sheriff of the Lowcountry*. Colorful recollections of the author's days as a Lowcountry lawman.

Olmsted, F.L. *A Journey in the Seaboard Slave States*. Westport, CT: Negro Universities Press of Greenwood Pub., 1969. Illus., index, $35.00. A reprint of the 1856 edition in which the author acutely observes the coastal region and standards of living there.

Pearson, Elizabeth Ware, ed. *Letters From Port Royal 1862-1868*. New York: Arno Press, 1969. $14.00. In 1862, dozens of Northern abolitionists flocked to the Federally occupied area around Beaufort, S.C. to educate the newly freed slaves and manage the abandoned cotton plantations. This collection of letters by the Boston contingent is as pungent and moving a commentary on race relations and liberal expectations as exists.

*Pennington, Patience. *A Woman Rice Planter*. Cambridge, MA: Belknap Press of Harvard University Press, 1961. The author was a Lowcountry native who managed her father's rice plantations after the Civil War and wrote about the experience for New York newspapers. The illustrations are by Alice Ravenel Huger Smith, a lyrical interpreter of the rural Lowcountry.

Towne, Laura. *Letters and Diary Written from the Sea Islands of South Carolina, 1862-1884*. New York: American Bio. Series, 1991. 310 pp., $79. Another wonderful journal of a teacher; she established Penn School, the first school for free slaves in the United States.

Verner, Elizabeth O. *Mellowed By Time*. Charleston: Tradd St. Press, 1978. $15.00. Sketches and memories of old Charleston by a distinguished artist whose favored media were etching, pastel, and pencil drawing.

CULTURAL STUDIES

Bluffton Historical Preservation Society. No. II *A Longer Short History of Bluffton, South Carolina and its Environs*. Bluffton, SC: Bluffton Historical Preservation Society, 1988. 49 pp., photos, $9.95. An excellent local history with photographs of classic Lowcountry cottages.

Carawan, Guy & Candy, eds. *Ain't You Got a Right to the Tree of Life? The People of John's Island, South Carolina — Their Faces, Their Words & Their Songs*. Athens, GA: University of Georgia Press, 1989. 256 pp., photos, $29.95.

Johnson, Guion G. *A Social History of the Sea Islands*. Westport, CT: Greenwood Press, 1969. 185 pp., index, bibliog., $38.50. A reprint of the 1930 edition of a series in which scholars from the University of North Carolina examined the lives, speech, culture, and folkways of Sea Island natives. Others include *Folk Culture on St. Helena Island* by Guy B. Johnson and *Black Yeomanry* by T.J. Woofter, which, if you can find it, has stirring documentary photographs.

Jones-Jackson, Patricia. *When Roots Die: Endangered Traditions on the Sea Islands*. Athens, GA: University of Georgia Press, 1987. 189 pp., photos, bibliog. $19.95.

Taylor, John Martin. *Hoppin' John's Lowcountry Cooking*. New York: Bantam, 1990. 345 pp., illus., $24.00

FICTION

Conroy, Pat. *The Water is Wide*. New York: Bantam, 1972. 320 pp., $4.95. Novelist Pat Conroy's first book was an autobiographical account of his experiences as a Beaufort County schoolteacher on isolated Daufuskie Island. His novels, including *The Great Santini* and *The Prince of Tides*, have Beaufort as their setting (even in the movie version).

Griswold, Francis. *Sea Island Lady*. Beaufort, SC: Beaufort Book Co., reprint of the 1939 original. 964 pp., $19.95. A big, fat Southern novel set in Beaufort.

Hewyard, Du Bose. *Porgy*. Charleston, SC: Tradd St. Press, 1985. 130 pp., illus., $20. A reprinting of the great tale, set in and around Charleston.

Humphreys, Josephine. *Rich in Love*. New York: Viking Penguin, 1987. 262 pp., $8.95. Set in Mount Pleasant, near Charleston, this novel (basis of the 1993 movie) captures the world view of a precocious 17-year-old girl. The author's other novels, *Dreams of Sleep* (1984) and *The Fireman's Fair* (1991), also have the Charleston area as their setting.

Naylor, Gloria R. *Mama Day*. New York: Random House, 1989. 312 pp., $9.95. A magical story set in a mythical place that nearly mirrors the Georgia/South Carolina Sea Islands.

Peterkin, Julia. *Scarlet Sister Mary*. Marietta, GA: Cherokee Press, 1991. 352 pp., $18.95. A reprint of the 1928 edition.

Powell, Padgett. *Edisto*. New York: Farrar, Straus & Giroux, 1984. 192 pp., $11.95. A boy's coming-of-age on a Sea Island.

Sayers, Valerie. *Due East*. New York: Doubleday, 1987. 264 pp., $15.95. The first novel in a group that chronicles life in a town like Beaufort, S.C., where the author grew up. Others include *How I Got Him Back* (1989) and *Who Do You Love* (1991).

HISTORY

Bridenbaugh, Carl. *Myths and Realities: Societies of the Colonial South*. New York: Atheneum, 1963. 208 pp. Index, bibliog., $1.25

Dollard, John. *Caste and Class in a Southern Town*. Madison, WI: University of Wisconsin Press, 1989. 466 pp., index, $14.50. A reissue of the 1937 work which, while not specifically about the Lowcountry, has everything to say about race relations in small towns throughout the region.

Lowcountry pleasures can be as simple as finding a sand dollar.

Wade Spees

*Jacoway, Elizabeth. *Yankee Missionaries in the South: The Penn School Experiment*. Baton Rouge, LA: LSU Press, 1980. 301 pp., index, bibliog.

*Jones, Katharine M. *Port Royal Under Six Flags*. Indianapolis, IN: Bobbs-Merrill, 1960. 368 pp., illus., bibliog. A good general introduction to the area, with long passages quoting original documents.

Rogers, George. *Charleston in the Age of the Pinckneys*. Columbia, SC: University of South Carolina Press, 1984. 198 pp., index, $9.95. If there is one book you should read about Charleston's heyday, this is it.

Rose, Willie Lee. *Rehearsal For Reconstruction: The Port Royal Experiment*. New York: Oxford University Press, 1976. 450 pp., index, bibliog., $13.95. A beautifully written and thoroughly researched account of the Northern abolitionists who went to the Sea Islands of Beaufort at the time of the Civil War. If you have a serious interest in the subject, the bibliography of this book is where you should start.

Rosen, Robert. *A Short History of Charleston*. San Francisco, CA: Lexikos, 1982. 160 pp., illus., photos, bibliog., $8.95. A good introduction to explaining Charleston by a native son.

Rosengarten, Theodore. *Tombee: Portrait of A Cotton Planter*. New York: McGraw, 1988. 752 pp., index, $12.95. This prize-winning book reproduces the diaries of an antebellum St. Helena Islander, Thomas B. Chaplin, and creates a context of explanation for them. This is the story — not the myth

— of life on a cotton plantation, handled in vivid prose by the region's best contemporary historian.

Stampp, Kenneth. *The Peculiar Institution: Slavery in the Ante-Bellum South*. New York: Vintage, 1989. Index, $10.00. A classic study, first published in 1956.

Wise, Stephen R. *Lifeline of the Confederacy: Blockade Running During the Civil War*. Columbia, SC: University of South Carolina Press, 1988. 403 pp., illus., index, $16.95.

Wood, Peter. *Black Majority: Negroes in Colonial South Carolina from 1670 through the Stono Rebellion*. New York: Norton, 1975. 384 pp., index, $9.95.

PHOTOGRAPHIC STUDIES

Blagden, Tom. *The Lowcountry*. Greensboro, NC: Legacy Publications, 1988. 104 pp., photos, $49.95. Views of the coastal world by an immensely talented photographer. His words of introduction, of praise for the region's natural beauty, resonate with visitors and locals alike. Look also for his book on the ACE (Ashepoo-Combahee-Edisto) River Basin: *South Carolina's Wetland Wilderness: The ACE Basin*. Englewood, CO: Westcliffe Publishers, Inc. 1992. 112 pp.

*Dabbs, Edith, ed. *Face of An Island*. An album of the early 20th century photographs taken on St. Helena Island by Leigh Richmond Miner and reproduced from the glass plates. A treasure.

Ellis, Ray. *South by Southeast*. Birmingham, AL: Oxmoor House, 1983. 122 pp., $50. Watercolors of the coastal region by noted painter and Hilton Head resident.

Isley, Jane; Baldwin, Agnes; Baldwin, William P. *Plantations of the Lowcountry*. Greensboro, NC: Legacy Pub., 1987. 151 pp., $19.95. Color photographs and meticulously researched histories of historic homes.

McLaren, Lynn. *Ebb-Tide, Flood-Tide*. Columbia, SC: University of South Carolina Press, 1991. 105 pp., $40. Color photographs of favorite Lowcountry places.

Schultz, Constance, ed. *A South Carolina Album 1936-1948*. Columbia, SC: University of South Carolina Press, 1992. 143 pp. A collection of the photographs taken under the auspices of the Farm Security Administration, and later under the direction of its chief, Roy Stryker.

RECREATION/TRAVEL

Ballantine, Todd. *Tideland Treasures*. Columbia, SC: University of South Carolina Press, 1991. 218 pp., $14.95.

Federal Writers' Project Staff. *The WPA Guide to the Palmetto State*. Walter B. Edgar, ed. Columbia, SC: The University of South Carolina Press, 1988. 514 pp., photos, index, $16.95. A reprint of the superb guide.

Georgia Conservancy. *A Guide to the Georgia Coast*. Savannah, GA: The Georgia Conservancy, 1989. 199 pp., index, illus.

Moeller, Jan and Bill. *The Intracosatal Waterway*. Camden, ME: Seven Seas Press, 1979 (updated 1991). 149 pp., $16.95.

Trask, Fred. A *Guide to Historic Beaufort*. Beaufort, SC: Historic Beaufort Foundation, 1970. 125 pp., maps, illus, photos. The definitive guide, especially good in describing walking and driving tours.

Trask, George. *Beautiful Beaufort By the Sea*. Beaufort, SC: Coastal Villages Press, 1992. 48 pp., maps, illus., $4.95. A breezy, informal roundup of local points of interest and things to do.

Wright, Cantey Holmes. *The Edisto Book*. Columbia, SC: Mac Kohn Printing, 1988. 109 pp., map, illus. Good local history.

Wyrick & Co. *The Charleston Guide*. Charleston, SC: Wyrick & Co. 1987. 30 pp., $3.50.

CLIMATE, WEATHER & WHAT TO WEAR

Before there were house tours in Charleston and St. Patrick's Day in Savannah, there was the spring season for tourists who came to see the blossoms. And they weren't disappointed — azaleas bursting into bloom all over downtown, jasmine flowering on fence posts, dogwood and magnolia peeping out from under the shadows of live oaks in the woods.

In fact, there is something in bloom year-round in the Lowcountry, from late-summer mums to camellias to paper-white narcissus which scent the air at Christmas. This long season comes as a result of the semitropical to subtropical climate and the ever-present breezes that characterize the coastal region. Rarely do days pass in succession without sunshine. The annual rainfall for the region is about 51 inches.

The winters are generally mild — maybe 10 days of frost, and a half-dozen hard freezes. Spring comes early. Farmers generally break ground on February 1. In the old days, the cotton crop was finished by "lay-by time" in late August, when slaves, temporarily released from heavy field work, would tend to their cemeteries and families.

Endless Summer

"From this early spring-time onward, there seemed no great difference in atmospheric sensations, and only a succession of bloom. After two months one's notions of the season grew bewildered, just as very early rising bewilders the day. In the army one is perhaps roused after a bivouac, marches before daybreak, halts, fights, somebody is killed, a long day's life has been lived, and after all it is not seven o'clock, and breakfast is not ready. So when we had lived in summer so long as hardly to remember winter, it suddenly occurred to us that it was not yet June. One escapes at the South that mixture of hunger and avarice which is felt in the Northern summer, counting each hour's joy with the sad consciousness that an hour is gone."

— From *Army Life in a Black Regiment*, 1869
by Thomas Wentworth Higginson

By May 1, it's hot, and that heat will penetrate every living thing through the end of September. They say the mean (and it sure is) summer temperature in the Lowcountry runs between 70 degrees and 88 degrees. Now that we've given a name — the Heat Index — to what it feels like when the 90 percent humidity is factored in, it's really probably near 95 degrees, or so it feels, for several months each year.

Water and warm air, an unbeatable Lowcountry combination.

Wade Spees

If you arrive in summer, be prepared to move slowly, wear hats, slather on the sunscreen, and drink plenty of liquids. Even on a hazy day, the sun will burn you. Take extra precautions, too, if you're planning athletic pursuits: the tennis court is no place to be at midday.

The wild cloudbursts that drench the region in summer, and the often-spectacular thunder and lightening shows that accompany them, may cool things off a bit. More likely, they'll just bring mosquitos.

Then there are the gnats. Just when you're enjoying a creamy autumn day in the 70s, they find you. Avon's Skin So Soft has proved an effective repellent, as does staying out of the shade or standing in a breeze.

The seasons each bring their color, their migratory birds, their harvest of fish or shellfish or duck or deer. And twice a year, it seems as if a whole new shipment of air is carted in, too — in late October, when the marsh has turned golden and the clouds pull themselves into exquisitely defined cumuli; and again in late February, when the prevailing northeast winds of winter start to shift south and southwest.

But perhaps the best quality of Lowcountry weather is its subtlety and contradiction: the warm day in January that you were not expecting, the roaring fire in October that banishes the dampness and chill in the morning, but by late afternoon seems an inferno.

For clothing, always take more cotton shirts than you think you'll need: flowers should wilt, not people. Take comfortable shoes for touring (high-heeled shoes are often not allowed to cross the threshold of House Museums) and a light sweater or windbreaker. An overcoat or parka may be too much in winter; sweaters and shells work better.

Weather Information:

Charleston	803-744-3207
Beaufort	803-524-2999
Savannah	912-352-1111

HANDICAPPED SERVICES

Most of the region's accommodations, museums, restaurants, and touring services provide access and facilities for those with special physical needs. If you're planning a trip, it would be wise to call ahead to confirm details. Some problems remain in retrofitting the older historic buildings for complete handicapped access, but your guides or hosts or the Visitor Center's staff in each city will gladly assist you — several offer handicap-accessibility guides. See the section "Tourist Information" at the end of this chapter for addresses of city or county offices of tourism and travel.

HOSPITALS

Charleston

Baker Hospital 2750 Speissegger Dr.; 803-744-2110
Charter Hospital of Charleston 2777 Speissegger Dr.; 803-747-5830
Roper Hospital 316 Calhoun St.; 803-724-2000
Bon Secours St. Francis Xavier Hospital 135 Rutledge Ave.; 803-577-1001
Trident Regional Medical Center 9330 Medical Plaza Dr.; 803-797-8800

Beaufort

Beaufort Memorial Hospital 121 S. Ribaut Rd.; 803-522-5200
Beaufort Naval Hospital Ribaut Road; 803-525-5600

Hilton Head

Hilton Head Hospital Bill Fries Dr.; 803-681-6122

Savannah

Candler General 5353 Reynolds Ave.; 912-354-9211
Immediate Med 2014 E. Victory Dr.; 912-234-8466
Memorial Medical Center 4700 Waters Ave.; 912-350-8000
St. Joseph's Hospital 11705 Mercy Blvd.; 912-925-4100

LATE NIGHT FOOD AND FUEL

The metropolitan areas of Charleston and Savannah, and the resort centers of Hilton Head, stay lit and active well after midnight — especially during the spring and summer — so finding gas or even grits should not be a problem. However, if you're traveling at night, remember that the Lowcountry is largely rural, traversed by long stretches of quiet highway. Unless you plan to gig for flounder and fry them up by the side of the road, it's best to travel with snacks.

Charleston

International House of Pancakes (food) 1521 Savannah Highway. Open 24 hours Sunday through Thursday, to midnight Friday and Saturday.

Circle-K Convenience Store (grocery and fuel) 2284 Savannah Highway. Open 24 hours.

Beaufort

The Pantry (grocery and fuel) 2231 S. Ribaut Rd. Open 24 hours.

Island Plaza (grocery and fuel) Hwy. 21, Frogmore. Open 24 hours.

Huddle House (food) Ribaut Road at Allison. Open 24 hours.

Huddle House (food) Sea Island Parkway. Open 24 hours.

Bi-Lo Supermarket (food) Jean Ribaut Square. Open 24 hours.

Hilton Head

Huddle House (food) Northridge Drive. Open 24 hours.

The Pantry (grocery and fuel) Hwy. 278 and Arrow Road. Open 24 hours.

Savannah

Daybreak Restaurant at Days Inn (food) 201 W. Bay St. Open 24 hours.

International House of Pancakes (food) 110 Mall Blvd. Open 24 hours on weekends.

Kettle Restaurant (food) 6801 Abercorn. Open 24 hours. Wheelchair accessible.

BP Gas (grocery and fuel) 7203 Abercorn. Open 24 hours.

MEDIA

Charleston

NEWSPAPERS AND MAGAZINES

The Post & Courier (803-577-7111; 134 Columbus St., Charleston 29403-4800) The daily paper of Charleston.

Omnibus (803-722-6771; P.O. Box 69, Charleston 29402) Charleston's "Picture Paper for People Who Can Read," a solid monthly publication, featuring fine record reviews (jazz and blues), cooking columns, fiction and thoughtful editorials.

The Upwith Herald (803-577-5304; 334 East Bay St., Charleston 29401) Irreverent, silly, goofy, lots of space for windy writers, distributed free.

Charleston Magazine (803-722-8018; 635 East Bay St., Charleston 29403) A glossy monthly with features about Charleston and the Lowcountry. Super graphics.

RADIO

WAVF-FM 96.0; Rock.
WSCI-FM 89.3; S.C. Educational Radio.
WTMA-AM 1250; Talk radio.
WYBB-FM 98.0; Classic rock.

TELEVISION

WCBD-TV Channel 2, ABC.
WCIV-TV Channel 4, NBC.
WCSC-TV Channel 5, CBS.
WITV-TV Channel 7, PBS.
WTAT-TV Channel 24, Fox.

Beaufort and Hilton Head

NEWSPAPERS AND MAGAZINES

The Beaufort Gazette (803-524-3183; 1556 Salem Rd., Beaufort 29902) Daily except Saturday. Local coverage, wire-service features and columns.

The Island Packet (803-785-4293; Pope Ave. Mall, Hilton Head Island, 29928) A solid, hard-hitting paper that has grown as the island has. Excellent local political coverage, a wide variety of local columnists and wire stories. Daily and Sunday.

The Hilton Head News (803-785-5255; P.O. Box 5446, Hilton Head Island 29938) Weekly.

Beaufort Magazine (803-525-0066; 305 Carteret St. Beaufort 29902) A new glossy quarterly with profiles, features, facts, and great design.

RADIO

WJWJ-FM 89.9; S.C. Educational Radio.
WBEU-FM 98.7; Rock, contemporary hits.
WOLW-FM 92.1; Classic oldies.
WHHR-AM 1130; All news.
WFOX-FM 106.1; Rock.
WIJY-FM 108; Easy-listening music from the 60s–90s.
WHTK-FM 99.7; Rock.
WLOW-FM 106.9; Big band.

TELEVISION

WJWJ-TV Channel 16, S.C. Educational Television.
WTGS-TV Channel 28, Fox.

Savannah

NEWSPAPERS AND MAGAZINES

Savannah News-Press and the Savannah Morning News (912-236-9511; 111 W. Bay St., Savannah 31401) Daily and Sunday.

Savannah Tribune (912-233-6128; 916 W. Montgomery St., Savannah 31401) Weekly featuring news of the African-American community.

The Herald (912-232-4505; 1803 Barnard St., Savannah 31401) Weekly featuring news of the African-American community.

The Guardian (912-238-2434; P.O. 8548, Savannah 31412-8548) Weekly newspaper published by the Savannah College of Art and Design.

Savannah Magazine (912-236-9511; 111 W. Bay St., Savannah 31401) Monthly published by the *Savannah News-Press.*

Contents (912-232-9889; P.O. Box 8879, Savannah 31412) Monthly magazine of literature, music, art, and design, distributed free.

RADIO

WGCO-FM 98.3; Oldies.
WIZA-AM 1450; Gospel.
WJCL-FM 96.5; Country.
WLOW-FM 106.9; Easy-listening, big band.

TELEVISION

WTOC-TV Channel 2, CBS.
WSAV-TV Channel 3, NBC.
WJCL-TV Channel 22, ABC.
WVAN-TV Channel 9, PBS.

REAL ESTATE

If you came to the Lowcountry and couldn't bear to leave it behind without owning a piece, take your place in line. Practically every new resident who has settled here recently was once in your position. Even the ones who thought the Lowcountry would be their "retirement home" have quit fighting the urge and moved in early.

There are hundreds of real estate agents, many independent, some affiliated with large national brokerage agencies. One of them might be the proprietor of your bed and breakfast, and if not, he or she will probably have a suggestion. For starters, you should pick up the free, widely available, real estate magazines that are published weekly throughout the Lowcountry. These will give you a general idea of what's out there and how much it costs. Once you're ready to look, select an agent in the place you like best. Walk-ins are welcome, and if you can't find what you're looking for, ask for referrals in other towns, too.

ROAD SERVICE

Here is a list of some emergency road services in the Lowcountry:

Charleston

AAA Carolina Motor Club (803-766-2394).
Bouchillion Automotive Center (803-744-6539) 24-hour towing.

Beaufort

Napa Auto Care (803-525-6272) 24-hour towing.
Low Country Muffler and Auto Repair (803-525-0897) 24-hour towing.

Hilton Head

Coastal Towing (803-689-3869) 24-hour towing.
Mid Island Garage (803-681-4636) 24-hour towing.

Savannah

Jackson Bros. Car Care Center (912-236-0631) 24-hour towing, especially if you're stuck on I-95 or I-16.
Yarbrough Wrecker Service (912-354-8141) 24-hour towing.

TOURIST INFORMATION

A number of organizations in the Lowcountry cater to visitors' needs. You may benefit from them during your stay; or you may simply want to have their addresses in case you wish to follow up on a yearly event or request further information.

FISHING AND HUNTING REGULATIONS

S.C. Department of Wildlife and Marine Resources P.O.Box 167, Columbia 29202; 803-734-3888

Game and Fish Division, Ga. Dept. of Natural Resources (912-651-2221; Rte. 2, Box 219-R, Richmond Hill, GA 31324).

VISITOR INFORMATION

S.C. Division of State Parks PRT, Edgar Brown Building, 1205 Pendleton St., Columbia 29201; 803-734-0156.

Lowcountry and Resort Islands Tourism Commission P.O. Box 366 Hampton, S.C. 29924; 803-943-9180.

Charleston Trident Convention & Visitors Bureau P.O. Box 975, Charleston 29402; 803-853-8000.

Edisto Island Chamber of Commerce P.O. Box 206, Edisto Island 29438; 803-869-3867.

Greater Beaufort Chamber of Commerce P.O. Box 910, Beaufort 29901-0910; 803-524-3163.

Hilton Head Island Chamber of Commerce P.O. Drawer 5647, Hilton Head 29938; 803-785-3673.

The Savannah Area Convention and Visitors Bureau P.O. Box 1628, Savannah 31402-1628; 912-944-0456.

Wade Spees

It's been called "The Slowcountry": maybe slowing down is the best way to appreciate it.

Index

Information pertaining to Hilton Head is generally listed in subentries.

LODGING BY PRICE

Price Codes

Inexpensive	Up to $50
Moderate	$50 to $110
Expensive	$110 to $180
Very Expensive	Over $180

Downtown Charleston
MODERATE
Brasington House
Capers Motte House
Coach House, The
1837 Tearoom and B&B
King Charles Inn
36 Meeting Street B&B

MODERATE–EXPENSIVE
Ansonborough Inn
Barksdale House
Elliott House Inn
Kitchen House, The
Planter's Inn
Two Meeting Street Inn

MODERATE–VERY EXPENSIVE
Maison DuPre
Vendue Inn and Vendue West

EXPENSIVE
Battery Carriage House Inn
Queen Victoria Inn

EXPENSIVE–VERY EXPENSIVE
Anchorage Inn, The
John Rutledge House Inn
Lodge Alley Inn
Mills House, The
Omni Hotel at Charleston Place

Charleston Environs
INEXPENSIVE–MODERATE
Holliday Inn of Folly Beach

MODERATE
Cassina Point Plantation B&B

MODERATE–EXPENSIVE
Holiday Inn
Sea Cabins

EXPENSIVE
Middleton Inn
Fairfield Ocean Ridge

EXPENSIVE–VERY EXPENSIVE
Kiawah Island Inn and Villas
Seabrook Island Resort
Wild Dunes Resort

Beaufort Area
INEXPENSIVE
Royal Frogmore Inn

MODERATE
Old Point Inn
Sea Island Inn
Twosuns Inn

MODERATE–EXPENSIVE
Bay Street Inn
Rhett House Inn

Hilton Head
See separate listings.

RESTAURANTS BY PRICE

RESTAURANTS BY CUISINE

Savannah

AMERICAN
Bistro Savannah
Chutzpah & Panache
City Market Cafe
Clary's Cafe
Crystal Beer Parlor
Elizabeth on 37th
John & Linda's
River House
Savannah River Queen
    Dinner Cruise

CONTINENTAL
45 South
Window's

ITALIAN
Garibaldi's
Vinnie Van GoGo's

MEXICAN
Nacho Mama's

SEAFOOD
Bowen's Island Restaurant
River House

SOUTHERN
Bistro Savannah
John & Linda's
Mrs. Wilkes' Boarding

House
Smitty's Dixie Chef

SOUTHERN GOURMET
Elizabeth on 37th
45 South

Savannah Area

SEAFOOD
Crab Shack at Chimney
    Creek

SOUTHERN
Breakfast Club, The

HILTON HEAD LODGING BY PRICE

Price Codes
Inexpensive	Up to $55
Moderate	$55 to $75
Expensive	$75 to $150
Very Expensive	$150 and up

Hilton Head

INEXPENSIVE
Fairfield Inn
Holiday Inn Express
Motel 6
Red Roof Inn

Shoney's Inn

MODERATE
Best Western Ocean Walk
    Suites
Days Inn Resort and Con-
    ference Center
Hampton Inn
Players Club Resort
Sea Crest Motel

EXPENSIVE
Radisson Suite Resort
Holiday Inn Oceanfront
South Beach Marina Inn

VERY EXPENSIVE
Hilton Resort
Hyatt Regency
Marriott's Hilton Head
    Resort
Westin Resort

HILTON HEAD RESTAURANTS BY PRICE

Price Codes
Inexpensive	Up to $10
Moderate	$10 to $20
Expensive	$20 to $30
Very Expensive	Over $30

INEXPENSIVE
Bess' Inc.
Giuseppi's
Market Street
Melvin's Barbecue
P.J.'s New York Deli

MODERATE
Crazy Crab
Flamingo's
Hudson's Seafood
Old Oyster Factory
San Miguel's
Stellini
Truffles Cafe
Wild Wings
EXPENSIVE
High Z's Creative Cuisine
Julep's

Le Bistro
Longhorn Steaks
South Seaport Cafe
Stripes

VERY EXPENSIVE
Cafe Europa
Carolina Cafe
Charlie's L'Etoile Verte
Primo

HILTON HEAD RESTAURANTS BY CUISINE

AMERICAN
Carolina Cafe
Crazy Crab
Flamingo's
Hudson's Seafood
Longhorn Steaks
Melvin's Barbecue
South Seaport
Stripes
Truffles Cafe
Wild Wings

BARBECUE
Melvin's Barbecue

CONTINENTAL
High Z's Creative Cuisine
Cafe Europa
Charlie's L'Etoile Verte

DELI
Bess' Inc.
P.J.'s New York Deli
Truffles Cafe

DESSERTS
Bess' Inc.
Flamingo's

FRENCH
Charlie's L'Etoile Verte

GREEK
Market Street
Le Bistro

ITALIAN
Primo
Stellini

MEDITERRANEAN
Le Bistro

MEXICAN
San Miguel's

PIZZA
Giuseppi's
Market Street

SEAFOOD
Crazy Crab
Hudson's Seafood
Old Oyster Factory

SOUTHERN
Melvin's Barbecue

SOUTHERN GOURMET
Julep's
Stripes

About the Author

Cecily McMillan moved to the Lowcountry of South Carolina in 1980, having graduated from Harvard University and worked as a journalist for *The Real Paper* in Cambridge, Mass., and the *Baltimore News-American*. In addition to freelance writing on southern topics, she handled public relations for the South Carolina Education Television Network station in Beaufort, South Carolina. She came to know the Lowcountry further during her terms on the local planning commission, as a board member of a rural health center, and as an officer of the Beaufort County Democratic Party.

Her writing on the South has frequently appeared in the *New York Times* Travel Section and the Sunday Style Section, and in magazines such as *Southern Changes* and *Southern Exposure*.

She is the mother of a son, aged 8.

Good fences as good neighbors, offering food for body and soul. Above: tomatoes ripening on the Isle of Hope near Savannah; below: flowering quince on Legare Street in Charleston.

Wade Spees